Also Available

A Companion to the New Testament: The Gospels and Acts
A Companion to the New Testament: The General Letters and Revelation

"Matthew Skinner's impressive new three-volume companion to the literature of the New Testament offers readers a welcome travel guide through the sometimes-rough terrain of the New Testament world. A respected scholar and seasoned teacher, Matthew Skinner has listened carefully to the questions and concerns raised by his students—online and in the classroom, in faith communities and in the public square. As a result, these volumes offer not only scholarly signposts for understanding the ancient world, but also sage advice for those roadblocks that often leave contemporary readers stranded. Reading the New Testament is an exciting adventure; you will want this companion by your side the entire way."

—MICHAL BETH DINKLER, Assistant Professor of New Testament,
Yale Divinity School

A Companion to the New Testament
Testament
Paul and the Pauline Letters

Matthew L. Skinner

BAYLOR UNIVERSITY PRESS

Unless otherwise stated, Scripture quotations are from the New Revised Standard Version Bible, copyright 1989, Division of Christian Education of the National Council of the Churches of Christ in the United States of America. Used by permission. All rights reserved.

Cover Design by Savanah Landerholm
Cover image: A fresco is pictured inside the catacomb of Priscilla in Rome, November 19, 2013. The catacomb, used for Christian burials from the late 2nd century through the 4th century, is now open to the public after years of restoration. Photograph © REUTERS/Max Rossi.

This book has been catalogued by the Library of Congress
with the ISBN 978-1-4813-0783-3.

Printed in the United States of America on acid-free paper with a minimum of 30 percent recycled content.

Dedicated with love and pride
to Miranda.

May you never stop learning.

Contents

Acknowledgments

Innumerable people helped me complete this three-volume companion, whether they knew they were doing so or not: encouraging friends, intelligent Bible scholars, patient family members, generous people who pored over and commented on drafts of chapters, my own teachers, and other authors whom I have never met in person. Likewise, untold experiences have prepared me to write these books, including the hours I have spent learning about the New Testament as a student in classrooms, as a reader in libraries and cafés, as a participant in scholarly research and discussions, and as a member of Christian worshiping communities.

While working on the project, however, I came to realize that the most valuable helpers have been the students I have been fortunate enough to teach over the last sixteen years. Students in classrooms, conferences, churches, and online settings have spurred me to learn about teaching the New Testament and about paying attention to how people respond to the challenges of interpreting biblical writings. As a result, I have come to a deeper appreciation of how the New Testament continues to function in people's lives—how people's ongoing efforts to engage the New Testament as a conversation partner shape their imagination about God, themselves, their neighbors, and their world. My students have influenced me through their earnest and sometimes insistent expectations that my teaching must help them wrestle intelligently with the New Testament. They want to read the New Testament well, not so they will earn academic credits or succeed in a pro forma academic requirement, but so they will be critically equipped in their quests to know what it means for them to be Christian. They expect my teaching to spark their insights about what it means for today's Christian communities to engage the Bible thoughtfully and with an eye toward articulating a contemporary faith—a generous faith that energizes their intelligence and fosters wonder while it retains lively yet adapting connections to ancient Christian communities.

Students like the ones I have described benefit from books that demonstrate the value of knowing the New Testament's contents, its history, its controversies, and its potential for contributing to theological discourse. Such books need to invite new students into the conversations and raging debates that the New Testament has provoked over the centuries. I have therefore designed these three volumes as traveling companions—resources that can assist readers in their own journeys into the New Testament. I trust the finished product exemplifies the kind of teaching that my students teach me to do.

I am grateful to belong to an academic community that takes pedagogy seriously and recognizes the value of faculty scholarship and publishing. Luther Seminary's willingness to grant me a sabbatical leave during the 2015–2016 academic year made this project possible. My gratitude extends to my faculty colleagues who took up the slack when I was away for a year.

A number of people lent their time and expertise by reading pieces of the project and helping me discover how I could make certain chapters clearer: Eric Barreto, Greg Carey, Karoline Lewis, Carey Newman, and four anonymous reviewers. Finally, without the assistance of Barbara Joyner and Betsey Skinner, I would not have been able to find the productive environments I needed to complete the work. The two of them have my deepest thanks and my love.

Introduction

The apostle Paul is one of the loudest and most influential voices in the New Testament. The loudness and influence derive from Paul's sheer prominence in the New Testament library. Paul authored more of the New Testament's twenty-seven writings than any other contributor. His voice therefore emerges emphatically and repeatedly in the literary conversations the New Testament initiates about Jesus Christ and his significance. Paul has also remained influential in Christian churches' ongoing efforts to speak and enact their theological commitments that derive from their sustained interactions with the Bible. With his own words and also through his more expansive legacy beyond his lifetime, Paul left a profound and enduring impression on the movement Jesus began.

Paul wrote letters to Christian communities, and he inspired others to write as well. He plays a major role in the narrative of Acts. Other New Testament writings, 2 Peter and James, mention him or teachings that resonated with his. To understand the scope and duration of Paul's impact on the development of Christian churches and their theology, one therefore needs to look at more than just the thirteen "Pauline Letters," the New Testament writings that attribute their existence to him. Yet those letters offer the best place to begin an exploration of Paul's particular contributions, for they ask readers to consider Paul himself, the life he lived, his activity as a tireless Christian evangelist, his insights into Jesus and the character of the Christian gospel, his perspectives on what authentic Christian living should look like, and how his ideas and character influenced other Christ-followers who sought to extend his influence and perpetuate his legacy. In one way or another, all thirteen letters direct attention toward Paul; together they stand as continuing testimonies to Paul's theological convictions, determined persistence, and lasting importance.

Yet Paul, if he could weigh in on the current discussion, would likely insist that the focus should not fall on his accomplishments and fame; perhaps he would point out that all of his efforts sought to establish the prominence of Jesus Christ and to declare Christ as the specific means by which "the power of God for salvation" (Rom 1:16) becomes manifest. Accordingly, the main focus of this companion falls on the messages of the Pauline Letters and how they have influenced ways of articulating Christian beliefs. At the same time, interpreters of the New Testament must consider Paul himself if they are to understand the Pauline Letters, their origins, their theological rhetoric, and their significance. Lingering for a while on Paul and the stories behind the Pauline Letters can make for fascinating work. Doing that work opens the letters up for closer investigation. The apostle and the writings that bear his name have a reputation for attracting great admiration, great revulsion, and even great indifference from various readers. Examining the letters together allows interpreters to travel deeper inside of Paul's patterns of thinking and his reputation so they can evaluate Paul for themselves and observe how he speaks about himself, his experiences, his insights, his values, and his ministry so that he might pursue his main objective: to express good news about Jesus Christ.

It is important to note at the outset that Jesus and Paul were hardly parallel figures. Although both were first-century Jews, they inhabited very different social worlds. As the Gospels describe it, Jesus stayed close to home in Galilee and appears to have avoided major population centers during the bulk of his public ministry. Paul's own letters refer to the apostle's extensive travels throughout the Roman Empire and his interactions with a wide variety of people. Paul also appears to have enjoyed many more advantages as a result of his superior social status, as far as that status was determined by his education, his occupation, his cultural facilities, and his family's status. Some of Paul's advantages appear starkly in the New Testament, such as the evidence that the conditions of his incarcerations were not always as severe as they could have been (e.g., Phil 1:12–13; 2:25; Phlm 13). Paul's ability to receive care and write letters while in custody strikes a memorable contrast to the Gospels' descriptions of Jesus' harsh treatment from the hands of the authorities. Social standing provided honor, honor had its benefits, and benefits afforded Paul opportunities. In addition, the Gospels describe Jesus starting a movement among Jews, even though he occasionally attracts interest from gentiles. As for Paul, in his letters he describes himself as "an apostle to the Gentiles" (e.g., Rom 11:13), someone determined to bring gentiles into the new community created through Christ's death and resurrection. Studying Paul requires interpreters to consider the people among whom he ministered and the distinctive kinds of social contexts he inhabited. Interpreters gain insight into those contexts through close scrutiny of his letters and through knowledge of ancient cultural realities. This companion instructs its readers accordingly.

It is worth emphasizing that Paul wrote letters to churches in different places, to churches shaped by different kinds of circumstances. Studying his letters provides a stark reminder that there was no such thing as *the* New Testament world. The world in which Paul preached the gospel, conducted his ministry, and wrote his letters was variegated. The letters require interpreters to pay attention to particular conditions in Christian communities in different locales. The letters also call attention to diversity in how Paul aimed for his correspondence to influence audiences. The tender tones of 1 Thessalonians and Philippians differ from the urgent scolding in Galatians and the occasional exasperation in 2 Corinthians. Likewise, letters such as 1 Timothy, 2 Timothy, and Titus raise important questions about how Christian communities adapted over time to negotiate specific kinds of cultural landscapes and to face new challenges or opportunities. Together, the thirteen letters call attention to the work Paul and others performed in helping Christian communities learn what it meant to live, believe, and hope in light of what God had done for them through Jesus Christ. As with the rest of the New Testament, the letters indicate that the early decades of the Christian churches were a lively time of growth, change, discovery, tension, and debate.

A Companion to Studying the New Testament as Christian Scripture

Along with the other two volumes in this series, this book offers itself as a companion to the New Testament, not a replacement or a necessary prerequisite for the New Testament. The book will be most helpful to readers who read it alongside the New Testament, for it will help them see more in the New Testament's pages, equipping them to observe and participate in the theological conversations that the biblical texts initiate. Each investigation of a given Pauline letter explores the letter's origins, its general contents and purposes, and a number of its more prominent or provocative theological themes. The companion aims especially to help seminarians, graduate students, and advanced undergraduates as they learn to approach the New Testament as a collection of books that emerged from particular times and places and that continue to prompt Christian communities to articulate and embody their theological convictions.

Reading the first volume of the companion prior to this one will prove helpful to some readers, although doing so is not essential. The main benefit for those who first read that volume, on the Gospels and Acts, is the very general familiarity the book provides about the world in which the New Testament writings arose—a description of the basic political, religious, and social aspects of life in Roman-controlled territories during the first century. That historical information is important, especially insofar as it directs attention to conspicuous characteristics of Roman society such as the prevalence of slavery, the role of honor and shame in social interactions, and the various connections between Roman civic life and religious observances. At the same time, even that general knowledge must not occlude the fact that the cultural landscapes in which Paul circulated were hardly uniform. Each investigation of the individual Pauline Letters in the current volume will therefore highlight specific details about a given letter's original context and explain how knowledge of that cultural context matters for interpreting the letter. Readers who desire additional information can find it in the materials listed in the bibliography of Recommended Resources for Ongoing Exploration of the New Testament, which appears in identical form at the end of each of the companion's three volumes.

Like the other parts of the companion, this volume occasionally focuses its discussion on five different interpretive foci, subjects that allow readers to venture deeper into the New Testament writings' rhetoric, messages, and social assumptions. Those foci, which are explained in greater detail in the introduction to the companion's volume on the Gospels and Acts, are the Old Testament, the Roman Empire, women in the early church's life and theology, apocalyptic theology, and the New

Testament's ongoing theological relevance. Although not each of the foci applies in equal measure to every New Testament writing, the five of them allow the companion to illuminate consistency and diversity in the New Testament's efforts to speak about God and the characteristics of Christian faith. Because the foci call attention to prominent social, theological, and moral assumptions woven through the New Testament, they allow the companion to reveal more of what there is to see in the New Testament.

Finally, this volume, like the two other parts of the companion, uses the terms *Christ-followers* and *believers* to refer to the people who belonged to Christian communities during the time the New Testament books were written. Although those terms do not align with the terminology used in all New Testament writings, using them consistently allows the companion to avoid the mostly anachronistic nouns *Christians* or *Christianity*. In doing so, the companion aims to avoid confusion about the fact that it took many generations before "Christianity" took shape as a distinctive religion and before those who expressed faith in Jesus Christ came to understand themselves as a group fully differentiated from Jews and from the Judaism out of which the Christian movement gradually and sometimes painfully emerged.

1

Who Was Paul?

W ith the obvious exception of Jesus Christ, no other human figure within the New Testament strikes as prominent or as weighty a presence as the apostle Paul. Paul's voice emerges boldly and frequently from the New Testament because he wrote multiple books, expressed brassy and sometimes divisive convictions about what the gospel is and what it entails, traveled extensively around eastern and northern regions of the Mediterranean world, and proved to have a significant and durable influence on Christian theology for centuries to come.

As Acts indicates, the influx of gentiles into the ranks of Christian communities made a considerable impact on early Christian theology and identity. Without jettisoning Jesus' Jewishness or the gospel's essential connections to the hopes, promises, and expectations expressed in Jewish Scriptures, Christ-followers in the mid-first century CE determined that gentiles were welcome in the church. Moreover, gentile believers could share fully in God's benefits through Christ without having to identify as Jews or observe the law of Moses. Along with Acts, Paul's letters give evidence of Paul's deep and lasting engagement in those developments as one who founded churches composed entirely or mostly of gentiles and who offered theological rationales for gentiles' full inclusion in the family of God alongside Jews without having to take up torah observance.

Paul was, therefore, situated within theological currents that dramatically influenced many early churches and their theological understanding, especially during the short span in which he wrote the letters that found their way into the New Testament, approximately 50–58 CE. Paul did not work alone and did not construct his theological perspectives without receiving input from others. Nor did he do so without enduring opposition, but the survival of several of the letters he wrote or cowrote has amplified his distinctive contributions over time, making him the person from those formative years of the church's history whose ideas have remained preeminent. Christian theology would undoubtedly look very different today were it not for Paul's influence.

Despite how consequential Paul's teachings have been, for many readers his letters remain hard to understand or difficult to connect to modern life. His moral assumptions, theological arguments, and religious experiences appear rather foreign. This is because they are indeed foreign, rooted in a very different cultural context with distinctive religious, political, ethical, and rhetorical presuppositions. Encountering Paul is very much a cross-cultural experience. To understand him and his ideas, as Paul presented them in his letters, it is valuable to survey what Paul's life was like prior to his encounter with the risen Christ, to review Paul's career as a proclaimer of the gospel and an occasional letter writer, to acknowledge his complex and controversial legacy, and to note some of the most prominent theological convictions that energize the letters he wrote to his fellow Christ-followers.

Where to Meet Paul

Paul speaks most clearly through his surviving letters. Anything Paul himself wrote provides primary source material for learning about him and his ideas, without other authors interpreting Paul on his behalf or otherwise serving as mediators. Although Paul clearly wrote additional letters that did not survive (see references to others in 1 Cor 5:9; 2 Cor 1:23–2:4; 7:8), the New Testament includes thirteen letters that claim to have been written or dictated by Paul. Not all of them may qualify as primary sources, however, for there are compelling reasons to question whether Paul actually wrote more than seven of them. The issue of how the other six letters might have originated will receive attention in due time. For now it is enough to note that some letters come from Paul's hand or were dictated from his mouth, while others may have been composed by followers who wrote in his name to extend his voice and influence. The present overview of Paul keeps its focus mainly on what primary sources reveal about Paul, explaining the basic insights those documents offer into what Paul himself expressed about his thoughts and experiences.

The most notable secondary source for learning about Paul—the Acts of the Apostles—devotes much attention to Paul, yet, as an exploration of Acts reveals, the differences between what Acts says about Paul and what Paul's own letters say about him are difficult to reconcile. Paul did not write Acts. The depiction of Paul that appears in Acts does not easily square with the portrait of Paul painted by his own writings. The issues shaping the debates about Acts and what it might reveal about Paul and his teachings are complex. By and large, firm answers remain elusive and debated. Paul's letters provide no way of thoroughly corroborating or contradicting the travel itinerary and the depiction of Paul's ministry that Acts puts forward. Because Paul's preaching in Acts does not correspond uniformly with his letters' ways of articulating key theological ideas, and because Acts presents Paul's ministry so as to make it resemble and parallel Peter's ministry, interpreters may have good reasons to avoid embracing Acts as a clear, undistorted lens into what Paul actually thought and taught. But maybe Acts does not mean to provide such a lens in the first place. Acts celebrates Paul and his legacy as a missionary; the book shows less interest in restating Paul's beliefs and deeds. Acts is not a comprehensive biography of Paul or a definitive account of his travels, and so it is fruitless to depreciate the book for not being one of those things. The point here is not to introduce the full extent of the debates or to resolve them but merely to note them.

Instead of trying to reconstruct what Paul really thought or exactly what his life was like, interpreters do best to begin by examining what the most direct sources about him can reveal. Reading Paul's letters demonstrates the importance of considering what they say about several prominent issues, such as what Paul believed about Jesus and the foundations of Christian identity and practice, the character of Paul's interactions with other Christ-followers who may or may not have agreed with his ideas, why Paul devoted so much energy and theological passion to the question of the gospel's significance for gentiles, whether Paul continued to practice or advocate certain Jewish observances after he began to follow Jesus, and the shape and purpose behind Paul's extensive travels through various regions of the Roman Empire.

At the end of the day, no matter how many of the New Testament writings Paul composed, and no matter how closely Acts does or does not align with Paul's letters, there are not many sources for learning about who Paul was and what he believed, and certainly no comprehensive sources. Without question, however, Paul's legacy continued in the church's memory even long after he was gone, as seen in some New Testament writings and in other documents produced by Christ-followers in the second and third centuries. Those literary works testify to Paul's longstanding influence in Christian churches as a leader, theological thinker, and role model. As prominent and colorful as Paul's legacy was in some quarters far beyond his death, learning about this complex person's origins—who he was and what he himself taught—offers the best foundation for understanding how Paul became so influential and controversial in the first place: through his ministry and teaching. His own letters provide the most extensive and direct insights. They serve as the best place to receive an introduction to Paul.

Paul's Background

Paul was a Jew. He traced his ancestry to the tribe of Benjamin and was educated within a Pharisaic tradition (Phil 3:4–6; 2 Cor 11:22). The specific contours of Pharisaic training in the mid-first century remain largely unknown, but they certainly included extensive instruction in torah and the traditions of legal interpretation, known as oral torah. That education must have impressed on Paul the value of living in conformity with torah. Most of his letters also evince his familiarity with numerous Jewish scriptural writings, not only the books of the law. He turns to Scripture and interprets specific passages in ways that endorse those texts' enduring importance as a source for understanding who God is.

When Paul cites Scripture, he cites material from the Septuagint, which could indicate Greek was his first or preferred language, suggesting he was raised and educated in the broader Jewish diaspora—outside of Palestine. Paul's writings show additional influence of Hellenistic customs and thinking as well. His use of language pertaining to citizenship and economics, imagery from the world of athletics, familiar philosophical tropes, and Hellenistic rhetorical conventions all demonstrate his familiarity with urban culture in the Greco-Roman world. Paul's ability to travel across the Roman Empire signals that he had the financial resources, benefactors, and skills necessary to sustain his ministry. His letters sometimes refer to his self-sufficiency (e.g., 1 Cor 9:3–15; 1 Thess 2:9; 4:9–12), and Acts identifies him as a man skilled in a particular trade, leatherworking (Acts 18:3). Indeed, the evidence suggests Paul's profession also provided him opportunities to circulate in a local setting and tell others about Jesus Christ during their casual interactions.

Paul's basic cultural competence benefited his traveling ministry, for he possessed an aptitude for fitting in with the dominant culture and speaking in understandable, persuasive ways. Although on several occasions Acts identifies Paul as "Roman" (Acts 16:37–38; 22:25–29; 23:27) and refers to his origins in the city of Tarsus of Cilicia (Acts 9:11, 21:29, 22:25), details that could conceivably place Paul within an elite social stratum, Paul's own letters never corroborate this information or comment about his legal citizenship. Paul could have navigated Roman cultural networks with skill even if he lacked the benefits of formal legal citizenship. That citizenship placed people in rarefied air within the social world of Paul's time, and it remains unclear whether Paul enjoyed such elite prerogatives. Paul's education, trade skills, and social standing appear to have made him relatively culturally sophisticated but not one of his society's nobility.

Prior to becoming a follower of Jesus, Paul persecuted Christ-followers (Gal 1:13–14, 23; 1 Cor 15:9; Phil 3:6). Beyond that generalization, he provides very few details. His letters do not mention his use of physical violence or judicial action, like Acts does (Acts 8:3; 9:1–2, 13–14; 22:4–5; 26:9–11). The vigor he mentions in Gal 1:13 concerning his former dedication to harassing believers might indicate zealous refutation and ceaseless verbal polemic, if not force. His specific motives for seeking to dismantle the fledgling Christian movement remain even less clear. Christian claims about Jesus as the Messiah would not necessarily equate to blasphemy or a denial of Jewish monotheism. More likely Paul found it repulsive when Christ-followers declared their allegiance to a *crucified* Messiah. He could very well have perceived dangerous consequences for all Jews if a growing subset of his fellow Jews continued to express loyalty to someone shamefully killed as an enemy of the Roman Empire. The Christian movement, in Paul's eyes, could have attracted unwelcome Roman scrutiny toward Jews throughout the empire or could have weakened a sense of collective Jewish identity and a hope for the nation's renewal, especially if quarrels over this disputed Messiah grew too disruptive in Jewish communities.

Sometime, probably between the years 31 and 35 CE, between one and four years after Jesus' crucifixion and when Paul was between fifteen and thirty years old, Paul changed. Although he never ceased to understand himself as a Jew, Paul's theological understanding shifted conspicuously when he became a follower of the risen Jesus Christ. While Acts describes Paul's experience of meeting Jesus as a onetime and rather dramatic event (Acts 9:1–9), Paul says simply in his own words that he received the good news of Jesus Christ "through a revelation of Jesus Christ" himself (Gal 1:12). In another letter Paul claims that he, like Jesus' original disciples, also saw the risen Christ (1 Cor 9:1, 15:8). His emphasis on direct encounter forms part of the basis for Paul's self-identification as an apostle, a person commissioned and sent directly by Jesus. Paul did not merely come to believe in the gospel message; he experienced Christ, crucified yet raised.

To say Paul changed does not imply Paul assumed a wholly new religious worldview as a result of embracing Jesus as God's Messiah. Paul's perspective on Jesus certainly changed, which also changed his understanding of how the God of Israel had kept promises and brings people into permanent membership in the family of God's people. Paul did not convert to a new religion or surrender a former identity as a Jew; rather, in his understanding, God called him to embrace a new understanding of Jesus as the Christ and therefore the means by which God accomplishes God's ultimate purposes on behalf of the people of Israel and the entire world. With that calling came an additional one: Paul understood himself as summoned to participate in making those salvific accomplishments of God known to all (e.g., Gal 1:16). He would be an evangelist, a proclaimer of God's good news.

Paul's description of his life-altering experience as "a revelation of Jesus Christ" provides one of many indications that themes from Jewish apocalyptic theology influenced his understanding of the Christian gospel. His choice of the word *revelation* (Greek, *apokalupsis*) on its own proves nothing in terms of a direct connection to specific Jewish writings known as "apocalypses" and to more widespread apocalyptic ideas, which will receive more attention and explanation shortly. Instead, the wider context of the term in the opening paragraphs of Galatians suggests a connection to apocalyptic themes. In that context, Paul implies that his new outlook expressed and even mirrored God's transformational and revelatory activity in Jesus Christ. In other words, Jesus intruded and reordered Paul's life and his theological vision just as God reorders the shape of the cosmos and the plight of humanity through Jesus Christ. The notion of such a dramatic divine incursion into the world's usual affairs resonates with Jewish theological assumptions that were nourished on apocalyptic motifs. Paul indicates that his unanticipated encounter with the risen Christ, like the salvation God accomplishes through Christ, manifests God's determination to act decisively on the world's stage to bring God's promises into their full realization. In Paul's view, God's work in Jesus signals nothing short of the dawning of a new era. Paul's experience of being unexpectedly and totally redirected from persecutor to proclaimer (Gal 1:23) reconfirms, likewise, that God will triumph over all opposition in the end.

Paul's Ministry

It is impossible to know how soon Paul began his public ministry after his "revelation of Jesus Christ" occurred. In Gal 1:15–24 he says he responded to his experience by going to Arabia and then Damascus in Syria, but he does not describe his activities during that three-year span. When the time ended, probably in the mid or late 30s, he actively proclaimed the gospel in Syria and Cilicia. Paul mentions a fourteen-year period of his early ministry, but none of his letters gives meaningful information about what he did during that time. Acts locates him in Syria and other nearby areas, where he conducted ministry, but says little more about that part of his life. All of Paul's surviving letters come from a later time; he wrote them between 50 and 58 CE, part of a span during which he conducted a relatively itinerant ministry in regions such as Asia Minor (modern Turkey), Greece, and Macedonia during roughly 47–58 CE. For portions of that time he was held in custody for unknown reasons, and his final arrest likely occurred between 55 and 58. Other ancient Christian writings say he was executed in Rome during the reign of Emperor Nero, probably sometime between 60 and 64.

Considering the long duration and geographical extent of Paul's public Christian ministry, any attempt to reconstruct the details of the man's activities, priorities, and thoughts quickly reveals itself as only a snapshot. It is a composite snapshot, constructed from a handful of surviving letters in which Paul responds to current and particular situations he perceives in a small number of Christian communities. No biblical material suggests Paul had any intention of writing documents that would equip the full Christian church to understand its theology for millennia to come. Paul did not expect his writings would finally be deemed scriptural alongside other revered documents such as the Law and the Prophets. Paul's lack of awareness about the eventual magnitude of his influence does not necessarily invalidate the way his letters would come to be treasured and used through history. The point about the letters' apparent ordinariness is instead to note how little access interpreters have into the fullness of Paul's life and experience. The letters express only a piece of a much more complex person. Nevertheless, it is the letters that came to influence Christian thought—and eventually Western culture as a whole—beyond any extent Paul could have imagined.

During that period of Paul's life about which most can be known, between 47 and 58 CE, it seems Paul rarely stayed in one place for long. In a rare mention of elapsed time, Acts describes him remaining in Corinth for eighteen months (Acts 18:11); that would have been an unusually long stay in one place, given the amount of miles Paul appears to have covered during a limited span of years. His letters frequently mention his journeys and his intentions for more travel. His itinerancy stemmed from his ambition to preach the gospel to new audiences (e.g., Rom 15:20; 1 Cor 3:6), for he generally preferred to establish new churches rather than to devote extensive time to leading existing ones into greater stability and maturity. He did not disdain the work of long-term leadership in a community; rather, his particular impulse was to reach out to others in new settings.

Paul's travels, evangelistic efforts, and ongoing communications with churches required him to rely on and expand a network of associates. Careful reading of his letters, as corroborated by the memories recounted in the stories Acts tells about him, reveals Paul as one who worked cooperatively with others. Paul was a piece—a particularly vocal and prominent piece—of a larger movement. He quotes and affirms traditions that originated within the wider church, such as hymns (e.g., Phil 2:6–11), confessional statements (e.g., 1 Cor 15:3–4), and liturgical formulas (e.g., 1 Cor 11:23–25). Most of his letters name coauthors. He mentions a number of partners whom he clearly trusted and admired. He occasionally commends leaders in the local churches to whom he wrote. Paul's network included women and men. Several letters name particular women who conducted public ministry and hosted churches in their homes; Paul expresses no embarrassment about that reality and no need to defend those women's efforts and authority. By all appearances, Paul regarded them as fully competent and fully authorized colaborers in the work of the church.

If Paul's ministry had an enduring hallmark, it was that he and his partners preached a message that invited gentiles to receive the benefits provided by the God of Israel without having to adhere to the Mosaic law. Paul viewed himself primarily as "an apostle to the gentiles" (Rom 11:13; cf. Gal 2:8), one distinctively directed by God to make known the good news of gentiles' full welcome into God's family without precondition and without relegation to a status inferior to Jews. Accordingly, Paul's surviving letters seem to have been written to churches that were composed predominantly of gentiles, although Romans may have been directed to multiple church communities composed of populations more evenly represented by gentiles and Jews. Even though Paul does not dwell on the notion of a law-free gospel in each of his letters, they all reflect his deep conviction that gentiles enjoy full participation in the salvation God makes possible. That is, even though Romans and Galatians contain the most extensive teachings about God's acceptance of gentiles through Christ, still even a letter like 1 Thessalonians does not hesitate to declare that its gentile audience has been "chosen" or elected by God (1 Thess 1:4), manifests "faith" (1 Thess 1:8), and now serves "a living and true God" (1 Thess 1:9). Nothing suggests that Paul's emphasis on gentiles meant he disparaged his Jewish identity and the well-being of his fellow Jews. When "a revelation of Jesus Christ" changed Paul, it changed his understanding of torah's role and his beliefs about exactly how God brings the whole world into a restored relationship with God, not his beliefs about God's certain commitment to the descendants of ancient Israel (e.g., Rom 9–11).

Paul frequently found himself amid controversy and the target of suspicion and opposition. The reasons vary, but they include disagreement over his teachings, occasional resentment directed toward his leadership, and perhaps public disturbances traced to his influence and reputation for divisiveness. In his letters he refers to his experiences of contending against the actions, counterassertions, and ire of various kinds of groups: people affiliated with churches he established, other Jewish Christ-followers who opposed his teachings about torah and the basis for gentile inclusion in the church, Jews outside the church, gentiles outside the church who resisted him and his message, and Roman authorities and their imperial propaganda. Something about Paul's zeal and tireless activity left him rarely lacking in opportunities to defend himself and his beliefs against criticism.

Partly because of his controversial character and teachings, Paul suffered hardships and persecution throughout his ministry. He frequently calls attention to the pain and shame he endured. When his letters focus on scars, bruises, or incarcerations, their purpose extends beyond garnering sympathy. Paul's public humiliations might have shamed him and thereby discredited his ministry and message in the eyes of his contemporaries, but he casts those ordeals as confirmations of his identity as an apostle, not setbacks. Paul did not embrace and celebrate his hardships as a perverted attempt to valorize victimization or to declare suffering a purifying or redemptive force. He instead characterizes his adversities as a means of participating in Christ's own sufferings (e.g., Phil 3:10). Paul regarded his life, which he understood as an attempt to live obediently to an apostolic calling to make Christ present to and within others, as an embodied reflection of what God had accomplished in Jesus Christ. In suffering, Paul did not just live like Christ; he lived in Christ, as if Paul was subsumed into Christ and his experiences. As one who suffered greatly yet nevertheless made known God's saving power through the Christian gospel, Paul presents himself in his letters as a canvas on which one can see the artistry of a God who brings new, resurrected life out of the horrors of death. For Paul, God—as seen working through Jesus Christ—accomplishes victory in places and situations that look like defeats to the unenlightened eye.

Paul's Legacy

Paul remained a controversial figure beyond his life span. A study of Paul's legacy can be conducted as a survey of the ways in which Paul's letters and personality have, throughout the church's history, fueled intense debates over theological doctrines, social norms, and the appropriate rhetoric for characterizing Christian identity. Some interpreters have portrayed Paul as the clearest and foremost interpreter of what God communicates and accomplishes through Jesus Christ. Others criticize Paul's theological and institutional legacy in the Christian church as a deviation from the movement Jesus of Nazareth initiated. Some esteem Paul's zealousness and confidence as inspirational, while others hear grating tones of imperious pretentiousness. Of course, countless views exist between those extremes. Only a few observations on this vast topic and complicated man can receive mention here.

During and soon after his life, Paul was influential beyond those individuals and communities that knew him most closely. Christ-followers continued to look back to Paul and let his reputation and example guide them going forward. Several other New Testament writings clearly refer to him or to teachings associated with him: Acts, James, and 2 Peter. In addition, as will be explored later, some letters that claim to be written by Paul might owe their existence to other authors, possibly Paul's followers or admirers. If so, those letters were produced as attempts to keep his ideas and legacy audible in ongoing conversations about churches' beliefs, practices, organizational structures, and priorities, even after Paul had died. Ancient Christian authors in subsequent generations respectfully recalled Paul's fidelity, while others lavishly celebrated his gifts as the stuff of legend. For some time after his death, his legacy revolved primarily around his renowned endurance, making him an exemplary expression of the life of faith, and not necessarily around the specific theological assertions he made in his letters.

As time wore on further into the second century, Paul's letters received more sustained attention. In some of the early church's battles over the definitions of orthodoxy and heresy, Paul's teachings played important roles. A few second-century writings—most notably one referred to as the *Kerygma Petrou*, or *Preaching of Peter*—indicate that some factions in the Christian church persisted in distrusting Paul because he did not uphold the importance of law observance and because they rejected his claims to be an apostle. Other writings from that century, such as the *Acts of Paul*, take a different view and lionize him as a wonder-working hero of the faith who modeled a form of Christian asceticism.

Obviously Paul remained both influential and controversial beyond the time of the ancient church. His writings, especially Romans and Galatians, deeply influenced monumental thinkers from Saint Augustine to Martin Luther and John Calvin to Karl Barth. Paul's teachings about church leadership and social issues continue to challenge and divide Christian communities. If Paul's legacy is a complex, multidimensional thing, so are Paul's own letters. Many people discover it is difficult to read Paul's writings free from excessively biased eyes because his legacy and reputation remain so influential and sometimes notorious in many quarters. It is common for people's preconceptions about Paul, his teachings, and his eminence to loom so large that his letters feel unapproachable or his teachings seem already decisively interpreted and firmly embedded in churches' institutional expressions. Paul's ideas have been used to do harm and to promote good; sometimes those results have stemmed from misappropriations of his letters. To guard against misunderstanding these documents, and to avoid confusing Paul's variegated legacy with the evidence housed in the letters themselves, readers benefit from taking steps to consider Paul in light of his own ancient sociopolitical and theological contexts. Interpreters do well to approach Paul first on his own terms, as a person inhabiting a first-century cultural and intellectual context. Then interpreters find themselves better equipped to grapple with the far-reaching transhistorical influence that Paul's letters have enjoyed.

Paul's Theology

Paul never wrote a complete exposition of his theological understanding. None of his letters comes remotely close to offering an A-to-Z account of his beliefs; nothing he composed resembles the systematic theologies that Christians produced during medieval and modern times. Romans might have much to say and put forth the most coherently integrated argument of all Paul's surviving letters, but even that illustrious book leaves unaddressed many theological ideas and dynamics Paul discusses elsewhere, such as the nature of Jesus' eventual return and Paul's expectations concerning a future resurrection of the body.

Paul did not write letters to impart a theological vision as if he was conducting a theoretical or academic exercise with no particular and direct connection to the lives of his ancient readers. He wrote to address specific, localized issues that churches were facing, to encourage churches undergoing difficulties, and to galvanize support for his ongoing ministry. Paul's letters convey his theological ideas as expressions of his work as a pastor: he addressed theological questions because he was a person guiding others into a deeper understanding and embrace of their identity and purpose as people who exist "in Christ," to use Paul's preferred expression. For example, when Paul wrote to the church in Thessalonica about Jesus' impending reappearance, he did so not because he wanted to guide them through a curriculum on eschatology or to speculate idly on God's future actions but because he had reason to believe his readers were losing hope since members of their community had died (1 Thess 4:13–5:11). His letter teaches the Thessalonians about Jesus' return primarily because he wanted to reassure them that their dead companions will nevertheless be present when Christ comes back to earth.

As attempts to relate and minister to communities from a distance, the letters betray a concern—sometimes a tender concern, sometimes a fierce one—for those churches' well-being. Such well-being was hardly assured given those groups' vulnerabilities as new communities without the foundations of much tradition or the good favor that comes from having an established and trustworthy public reputation. Some of the churches lacked knowledge about what it meant to be and live as believers. Others lacked cohesion and a climate of mutual belonging. Others needed help to recognize their collective purpose.

Because Paul's theological convictions emerge through his pastoral attempts to guide Christian communities, the most effective and appropriate ways of describing Paul's theological perspective do not squeeze his letters into a matrix of theological categories or discrete topics, such as what he believed about Christology, salvation, the Holy Spirit, and Christian conduct. Paul's theology reveals itself more sensibly through seeing it on display in individual letters addressed to specific audiences. Nevertheless, the following sketch of Paul's theology isolates a few dominant themes that manifest themselves when Paul discusses God, humanity, and the nature of the gospel in the letters he certainly wrote, restricting the discussion for the time being to those primary sources. No one can reconstruct from a handful of letters "Paul's theology," if that means a list of dogmas that he may have endorsed. Instead, this overview of several general themes aims to illuminate facets of Paul's basic theological outlook. It provides a basic orientation to the lenses that sharpened his vision of authentic ministry and faithful living and allows interpreters to take initial steps into Paul's world to experience how things looked from his perspective.

God

To consider Paul's letters as theological writings is to note that they are obviously interested in talking about God. Attention to God saturates the letters. Not only do Paul's writings reiterate God's connections to all aspects of existence, but they also express Paul's understanding of the character and activity of God. God's identity and deeds go hand in hand for Paul; each demonstrates and defines the other. Paul is not content, therefore, merely to assert that God is loving. Paul also insists that God acts in loving ways (e.g., Rom 5:5, 8; 2 Cor 13:11). A crucial expression of the dynamic relationship between God's character and God's activity comes to light in Paul's understanding of God's faithfulness to promises: through Jesus Christ God fulfills great promises made long ago in ancient Israel's history (e.g., 2 Cor 1:18–20; Gal 3:29; cf. Rom 11:29). God must remain true to what God pledges to do, for God is faithful, and vice versa. Paul sees evidence of God's fidelity woven through the good news he shares with his audiences.

Paul's confident regard for God's trustworthiness undoubtedly derived from the Jewish monotheism in the air Paul breathed his whole life. Further demonstrating his consistency with core Jewish beliefs, Paul held that God is the source of all that is (1 Cor 8:6). God's reliability and majesty depend ultimately on the power God possesses—a power God puts to work in reconciling a sinful world and empowering human beings to share in God's work and to remain holy and blameless (2 Cor 4:5–7; Phil 2:13; 1 Thess 5:23). Indeed, the whole of the good news, as Paul understood it, consists of a dramatic display of God's power manifested through Jesus Christ (Rom 1:16; 1 Cor 1:18–25), a power affecting all creation and not just individuals' consciences. Because of Christ's experience of humiliation and resurrection, Paul understood God's power on humanity's behalf as something other than sheer dominion or overwhelming force; in other words, God exercises power to fulfill divine promises in a paradoxical manner through Christ's submission and obedience (Phil 2:5–8). Divine power expresses itself through divine love, a self-giving love that dedicates itself to the well-being of others. Such love shows its truest colors through the cross and resurrection of Jesus Christ.

Since Paul's Jewish heritage taught him to have utter confidence in both God's power and God's resolve to fulfill longstanding pledges first given to the Hebrew people and later to the nation of Israel, Paul looks toward the future and sees the ultimate fulfillment of God's purposes as certain. God will, finally and fully, vindicate God's own faithfulness. God will save, and God will establish peace. God's commitment to humanity in the present, shown through the death and resurrection of Jesus Christ and the ongoing presence of the Holy Spirit, offers reliable evidence that God's promised future will certainly come to pass. Even now, God has already unleashed—and continues to unleash—"the righteousness of God" through Jesus Christ (Rom 1:17). The expression *the righteousness of God*, which Paul develops in various letters, refers to God's activity that secures, protects, blesses, and provides for people. The expression reprises Old Testament statements about God's unswerving commitment to creation and its inhabitants, a commitment seen in God's efforts to ensure justice and bring about the restoration of individuals and society. Paul insists that God is already in a process of bringing new realities into existence. The transformation began with Jesus Christ's death and resurrection. The complete realization of those realities is certain because God is trustworthy.

Jesus, Crucified and Raised

Each in its own way, the four Gospels present Jesus' crucifixion and resurrection as the climactic pieces of the story about him, yet those events remain only parts of much larger narratives about Jesus' life, teachings, and deeds. When Paul discusses Jesus and his role in God's activity on humanity's behalf, however, the cross and resurrection are nearly all he sees. Paul's letters hardly acknowledge aspects of Jesus' life and ministry. They contain nary a mention of the amazing deeds, parables, and sermons that make Jesus such a compelling figure to so many Gospel readers. It is possible that Paul did not know much about the events of Jesus' public ministry or did not talk about them in his interactions with the churches he founded and visited. Based on the evidence from his letters, he appears to have considered those stories—if he in fact knew them—as paling in significance compared to Jesus' death and resurrection. Those two ultimate events constitute the center of the divine drama Paul sees operating in the gospel about Jesus Christ. In the death and resurrection of the Messiah, God proves God's love, redeems humanity, and expresses grace.

The manner of Jesus' death—crucifixion—makes a big difference for Paul. Because Jesus' death radiated shame and ignominy—owing both to Roman conventions about honor, manliness, and seditiousness and also to Jewish notions of purity and accursedness—Paul believed the gospel inevitably creates offense and seems unworthy of people's attention (e.g., 1 Cor 1:18; Gal 3:13, 5:11). Yet Paul regards Jesus' putatively shameful death in a new light because God raised Jesus the Christ from the dead. The resurrection means more than a reversal of Jesus' death or a divine correction of a human error. Paul views Jesus' resurrection in various ways: as God's validation of Jesus' faithfulness, as a demonstration of God's power over death, as a guarantee of a future resurrection of all who belong to Christ, and as a clear statement of God's commitment to make new life possible now through Jesus (e.g., Rom 1:4; 6:4–10; 1 Cor 15:20–23, 42–45). The resurrection, as a divine act over what seemed to be an indomitable power, death, makes Paul regard Jesus' crucifixion not as ignominy and failure but instead as the vehicle of God's grace. What should have reeked of defilement instead brings blessing. What looked like powerlessness turned out to be a demonstration of God's power over death. The reality of a crucified and raised Messiah therefore disrupts and reconfigures many of the moral and religious values Paul previously held dear.

Jesus' death and resurrection together constitute the linchpin of God's salvation. As explorations of individual letters will reveal, Paul uses multiple terms and metaphors to describe the salvation that God accomplishes through Jesus' death and resurrection. A single characterization of God's accomplishments apparently could not do justice to the wealth of their significance, as Paul saw it. The most general way of characterizing the variety found in Paul's letters is to say that God, through Jesus' death and resurrection, has acted decisively to reclaim and reorder the world. In doing so, God has kept the pledge first made to Abraham—to bless Abraham's offspring (namely Israel) and also all the people of the world (Gen 12:1–3, 22:17–18). The nations of the world, gentiles, will be made "blameless" by their incorporation into Christ (1 Cor 1:8, Phil 1:10), and gentile believers now "serve a living and true God" as they escape "the wrath that is coming" (1 Thess 1:9–10). In Jesus' death and resurrection, God's grace extends to Jews and gentiles alike (Rom 3:21–26), upending any qualitative distinctions that Paul may have once affirmed between those groups (cf. Gal 3:28). Old systems and divisions have been demolished, not primarily as an expression of divine compassion but as a result of the dominion God exercises over sin. God's mastery over sin promises to end sin's ways of poisoning humanity's capacity for authentic devotion and self-understanding.

God further confirms the saving significance of the cross and resurrection, as well as the full union of Jews and gentiles, by bestowing the Holy Spirit. The Spirit, whom Paul calls "the Spirit of Christ" (Rom 8:9; cf. Phil 1:19), as well as more frequently "the Spirit of God," identifies Jews and gentiles alike as Christ's own people. Because the Spirit marks all of them as God's children, together they share the blessings that come from being the rightful heirs of Abraham (Gal 4:6–7; cf. Gal 3:29).

Jesus Christ's role in the theological drama Paul envisioned extends beyond the Lord's past experiences on the cross and in his resurrection from death. Paul expected Jesus to return, at which point God's work on behalf of humanity and creation will reach its full consummation. Paul characterizes this anticipated event—which in his earliest letters, such as 1 Thessalonians and 1 Corinthians, he expects to occur very soon—as the time when God will finally bless the whole world and transform people into imperishable beings (Rom 8:18–23; 1 Cor 15:51–54). Paul does not speak of Jesus' return as a time for the world's destruction or for transmigrating Jesus' followers into a distant heaven. Paul urges his audiences to live with an active awareness of Christ's imminent appearance and the promise of the divine judgment that will occur then (2 Cor 5:10; cf. Rom 2:16). He commends a life marked by hope, watchfulness, and action spurred by urgent readiness (1 Thess 5:6–8). The anticipation of Christ's return does not translate into withdrawing from society, engaging in antisocial behavior, or nurturing fantasies of vengeance against enemies or outsiders.

Jewish Apocalyptic Themes and Participation with Christ

As mentioned previously, multiple Jewish writings produced during the Hellenistic and early Roman periods envisioned God as engaged in a cosmic struggle that would eventuate in God's victory over various forces—whether understood in spiritual, political, or social terms—that harassed the people of God and kept them from experiencing the fullness of God's blessings. Those literary "apocalypses" or "revelations" each had their own emphases, but in general they shared an understanding that the fulfillment of God's promises would occur through dramatic divine activity, usually activity that would bring about the dawn of a new age. The literature's theological outlook therefore characterized God as determined to deliver God's people, certain to defeat God's opponents, and committed to judge the world for its rebellion and wrongdoing. Apocalyptic literature sought to encourage, or in some cases to warn, its readers with the knowledge that God was at work behind the scenes. It insisted God would not stay at a distance from human history or from the world's visible stage but would someday initiate a wholesale transformation, overcoming any impediments to the realization of God's holiness and God's promised security and blessing, God's *shalom*. Some of those texts promised new life to come after death. Paul's letters obviously do not share many of the formal characteristics of apocalypses like Daniel 7–12 or Revelation, but Paul's theology often shares some of their assumptions. Themes from apocalyptic writings evidently influenced not only Paul's outlook but also the perspectives of many other New Testament writings.

When Paul describes the Christian gospel to his audiences, he characterizes it in ways that resonate with themes that are familiar in the theologies and worldviews that animate apocalyptic literature. Paul emphasizes God's initiative, God's entrance into human experience, God's transformative presence, God's triumph over oppressive powers, and a divinely created new future for those whom God rescues. Paul's letters bristle with language and metaphors of warfare, oppression, liberation, redemption, and a transformed existence. Most notably, Jesus' death and resurrection, in Paul's view, constitute the key revelatory—or apocalyptic—moment; they are God's incursion into the world, an incursion meant to win a victory, create a new existence for God's beloved, and thereby reassert God's reliability and gracious character. Apocalyptic writings spoke of a future general, or corporate, resurrection from the dead that would coincide with the transition into a new age. For Paul, Jesus' resurrection sets this transition in motion. As Paul's letters describe it, the overall apocalyptic drama consists of more than a moment in time or the twin events of Jesus' death and resurrection. God's activity is unfolding, with Jesus Christ serving as a decisive pivot point or inauguration. The apocalyptic drama began in the past and persists now, after Jesus' death and resurrection; God's power and intentions continue to be revealed in Paul's own experience, Paul's ministry, and the life of Christian churches.

Jewish apocalyptic theology thus supplied Paul with an explanatory framework. It was a way for him to articulate the gospel with theological language and notions he and many of his contemporaries could understand. It allowed the Christian gospel that Paul and others preached to reaffirm core, established Jewish beliefs about God's power and trustworthiness. It offered a terminological and a symbolic reservoir for describing the effects and significance of Jesus' death and resurrection. Common apocalyptic themes provided the categories and mythic narrative by which Paul explained what made the story of Jesus a story of good news about what God has done and will yet do for the world. Individual letters provide various opportunities for interpreters to glimpse specific ways in which Paul's theology was nourished by common apocalyptic motifs. The current summary merely identifies some of the pervasive themes and gathers them together to illustrate how they contribute to a larger narrative about a faithful God who has revealed and continues to reveal the divine power and determination necessary to set the whole of creation on a new course.

The influence of Jewish apocalyptic themes further shows itself in Paul's understanding of God's character. If the gospel is a description of all that God has done and will yet do to reorder creation and the human condition, then the question of God's character becomes vitally important. It matters if the God who inaugurates a new age is trustworthy or capricious, capable or impotent. Paul's notions of God's fidelity and power, as described above, are quite at home in Jewish apocalyptic interpretations of Jewish Scriptures. Through Christ God reaffirms a faithfulness and power that are utterly effective and reliable expressions of divine love. God can be trusted; apocalyptic realities are therefore truly good news in Paul's perspective.

Apocalyptic themes also emerge in Paul's descriptions of the human condition. His letters frequently posit various dualisms and describe absolute divides between different conditions or camps, such as light and darkness, slavery and freedom, flesh and Spirit. What strikes some modern readers as a simplistic embrace of binary thinking or a naïve disregard for moral nuances actually finds its roots in Paul's conception of a war taking place throughout the cosmos. The war has two opposing sides, and it is waged by suprahuman and totalizing forces. A person lives in territory, so to speak, occupied and controlled by one or the other side, and therefore a person exists as either a slave to sin or a slave to God (e.g., Rom 6:20–22). Paul sees no middle ground, for either of those forces claims a whole person's existence and thus defines his or her identity.

Sometimes Paul refers to one of the forces in the cosmic battle, and humanity's central problem, as "sin." He refers to sin in the singular; very rarely does he mention "sins." It is insufficient to characterize sin as a moral stain; Paul sees it as a virulent enemy. Sin actively oppresses human beings as a power or disease that enslaves them. The discrete sins people commit are but symptoms of a deeper condition in which one is in servitude to a destructive, ungodly master. Paul therefore speaks of salvation as freedom and as the defeat of sin. Language that explicitly denotes "forgiveness" of transgressions does not appear in letters he wrote, except in a single case when he quotes a scriptural text (Rom 4:7, quoting Ps 32:1). In Paul's view, sin needs to be dethroned and eradicated, not painted over or offset.

The malicious forces God must defeat—sin, death, and Satan—do not surrender their power over the world without a fight, and so the gospel announces the news of God winning a battle and not merely doling out second chances and countering human ignorance. As a result of that contest, God has reclaimed humanity from God's adversaries. The apocalyptic turning point may have occurred in the past, at Jesus' cross and empty tomb, but God's victory will reach its certain and final conclusion in the future when death and Satan suffer their full defeat, a defeat assured because of God's decisive activity through Jesus Christ (e.g., 1 Cor 15:24–25; Rom 16:20). The effects of God's victory are all-encompassing; they set the whole of creation on a new trajectory (e.g., Rom 5:12–19; 8:18–23). God's triumph through the cross and resurrection brings an old age in cosmic history to an end and inaugurates an altogether new reality (e.g., Gal 1:4, 6:15; 2 Cor 5:17).

Even as Paul rejoices in the new age God has created, at the same time, Paul's theology hardly offers a utopian outlook on the world's current condition. The old age, where sin and death wreak destruction, continues in its twilight even as the new age has taken hold (e.g., Rom 8:18–25). The apocalyptic battle has been decided, but it currently remains unfinished. Paul therefore has much to say about how believers live faithfully and confidently now, as they wait for the full consummation of God's deliverance. The faith that characterizes Christ-followers unites them with Christ, expressing itself through trust and obedience in their day-to-day lives. For Paul, the primary meaning of faith is not about assenting to doctrines or choosing to believe in God's existence or in the plausibility of a yet unseen "new creation." Rather, faith represents a way of being and living with Christ. The new creation Paul promises is not about waiting to go to a distant heaven or channeling spiritual peace in the midst of volatile bodily existence. Paul insists that believers apprehend God's new creation now and participate in it as people who live "in Christ," united to him in a new existence established by faith.

The tides of Jewish apocalyptic theology possibly fed Paul's conception of believers' new condition as people who currently participate in the work and life of God. The phrase *in Christ* resounds across Paul's letters. When read in the contexts in which it appears in the letters, and when considered in light of Paul's understanding of Jesus as God's agent in an apocalyptic battle against God's adversaries, the notion of being "in Christ" signals a profoundly experiential dimension of Paul's theology. By virtue of their existence in Christ, believers find themselves in a coexistent union with Christ; located together in him, they therefore also share an existential union with one another.

For Paul, Jesus Christ was not merely God's weapon or resource in the battle against the cosmic powers that oppress the world. Jesus' own body was the place where that warfare was waged. What occurred in Jesus' body—a shameful death and a transformative resurrection—produced cosmic effects. Sin and death, according to Paul's graphically personified depiction of the cosmos, dwell within creation itself (Rom 5:12). Paul never exactly explains how God defeats sin, but he asserts that God does so through Christ, for God "condemned sin in the flesh" of God's Son (Rom 8:3). In the crucifixion and resurrection of Jesus' own self, God definitively disarms sin of its power over the created world. In Christ's own body, in his flesh and blood and then in his resurrected existence, grace and righteousness take sin's place and thus extend their new reign over the world (Rom 5:18–21). All who now find their existence "in Christ" are thereby included.

To encounter God's grace and righteousness, people do not escape from their existence in this world. As people in Christ, they share in Christ's own experiences. As Paul refers to it, people unite with Christ and benefit from his role in God's victory not as the result of a transaction or a stipulation of an agreement; rather, believers participate with Christ by joining him in the entire drama of the good news. Similar to how God, through Jesus of Nazareth, shared in all that it means to be a human being and to suffer human vulnerability and frailty (Phil 2:7), Paul describes his and his audiences' existence as a sharing in Christ's experiences: what happened to Jesus Christ, and what happened in him, happens to all. Paul's notion of believers' participation with Christ does not imply that people become assimilated into Christ so as to lose the particularities of their identity. Rather, in this participation they receive all of the benefits that God provides through Jesus Christ, including an intimate coexistence with the crucified and resurrected Lord himself.

Those who share in Christ's crucifixion will be raised as he was (Gal 2:19; Rom 6:3–8; cf. 2 Cor 5:14–15; Phil 3:10–11). Christ has not departed from the world but remains, living within believers (Gal 2:20;

cf. 1 Cor 6:17, 19), and therefore the collection of believers—the church—constitutes nothing less than "the body of Christ" (1 Cor 12:27). As such, believers possess a whole new identity, one defined by Christ. That identity involves more than receiving benefits from God as "joint heirs" with Christ (Rom 8:17). It means those in Christ together inhabit a whole new place of existence, a coexistence with Christ to share the new life God secures, a life from which sin's insidious presence and oppressive tyranny have been expelled. Paul's allusions to those realities imbue his theology with what later generations might call "mystical" elements, for he implies that he and his fellow saints in Christ enter into the life and experience of God. The existential union with Christ means that believers also share in Christ's ongoing work amid and for the sake of the world.

While much of Paul's theology, with its concentrated focus on Jesus' death and resurrection, looks back in time and declares God's decisive deliverance to have already begun, Paul also describes future elements of God's activity in ways that recall themes from Jewish apocalyptic literature. Paul's letters look forward to the return of Jesus Christ as another act in the unfolding apocalyptic drama. Jesus' return, according to Paul, will coincide with God's ultimate victory and will be the time when all of God's promises come to their full fruition (e.g., 1 Cor 15:20–28). At that time God's ultimate judgment will occur (e.g., 1 Cor 4:5; 2 Cor 5:10; 1 Thess 5:2–10). It will be the time when God resurrects the dead (1 Cor 15:20–23, 1 Thess 4:13–17). Paul looks forward to this future hope with utter confidence. In the meantime, the people of God live in expectation of the new age's full realization, even while that age has already established itself and has become a present yet still emerging reality (e.g., Rom 8:19–25). The community of people who exist "in Christ" keeps those apocalyptic convictions always in their vision, for they themselves provide a living demonstration of God's salvific activity. In their common life and in how they conduct themselves in public settings, they bear witness to God's transformative incursion into the human condition, even as they also embody a certain hope for the arrival of God's ultimate deliverance.

Greco-Roman Influences

Admittedly, it distorts the picture to treat "Greco-Roman influences" separately from the themes of Jewish apocalyptic theology that shaped

Paul's ideas. There was no such thing as a first-century Judaism that lived in total isolation from Greco-Roman thought patterns. For many generations prior to Paul, Jewish apocalyptic themes were forged and expressed in a Hellenistic cultural setting, yet that setting was itself fed by a wide array of influences from various lands and religious systems. Apocalyptic themes in Jewish writings, wherever all the precursors of those themes came from, appear to have made the deepest impact on Paul's theology. At the same time, the prominence of those Jewish themes does not mean that other cultural and ideological factors failed to leave their mark on the apostle and on how he arranged and expressed his thoughts.

Paul's theology does not necessarily reproduce common Hellenistic philosophical and religious ideas in stark terms as much as it shows the influence of Hellenistic currents through the ways his letters articulate his views. Paul's means of posturing himself as a teacher and his rhetoric bear the imprint of Stoic and Cynic emphases. Noting some of those imprints offers a reminder that Paul was, like his peers, embedded in the intellectual climate of his time.

Stoicism (originated by Zeno of Athens) and Cynicism (with roots in Diogenes of Sinope) were well established and wide-ranging philosophical and ethical movements that sustained themselves through their respective missionary impulses. Both groups included adherents who traveled, especially into population centers, and promoted their worldviews. Some of those wayfaring teachers, especially among the Cynics, advocated withdrawal from certain social practices and criticized conventional expressions of Greco-Roman cultural respectability. People who took time to explore the dominant lines of Paul's theology would certainly not have confused his theology with Stoic ideals about aligning one's life with a divine sense of reason and its associated virtues. Nor would they have concluded that Paul duplicated Cynic emphases on the virtues of ascetic, antiestablishment lifestyles that accord with nature. Yet Paul's manner of ministry resembled both of those groups' practices. Paul frequently notes that he worked to support himself during his itinerant ministry, not relying on handouts or coerced donations (e.g., 2 Cor 12:14–18, 1 Thess 2:9–10). He willingly made personal sacrifices to gain a hearing in various locales. Greco-Roman philosophers often pursued those same strategies to sustain themselves and simultaneously promote their teachings.

Paul's rhetoric also sometimes resembles Stoic and Cynic discourse. The similarities do not indicate direct links between Paul and influential philosophical figures, as if he deliberately patterned himself after specific people. The resemblances do suggest, however, that Paul crafted his theological message so it would resonate with conventional values and expectations. Frequently Paul describes his way of life as exemplary and a model to be followed, not necessarily because he was conceited, but because honorable and authentic teachers in his time were expected to manifest the values and ideals they taught (e.g., 1 Cor 4:16–17; 11:1; Phil 3:17; 1 Thess 1:4–6). In his letters Paul also sometimes boasts about the hardships he willingly endured in preaching the gospel (e.g., 1 Cor 4:10–13; 2 Cor 4:8–10, 11:23–33). He describes his travails and wounds as badges of honor and faithfulness because they reflect his participation in Christ's sufferings. Paul's efforts to construe experiences that might have earned him shame as instead events that legitimated him resemble the comments of Cynic philosophers who interpreted the scorn they received from conventional society as confirmation of that society's ethical bankruptcy. Finally, Paul's use of a rhetorical style called diatribe, which employs simulated dialogue to guide an argument and arbitrate its basic premises, makes parts of Romans resemble teaching tools used by Cynics and other philosophical movements from which Cynics drew inspiration. Those and additional aspects of Paul's rhetoric confirm that his teachings did not stand outside his cultural setting as entirely new or unrecognizable proposals. His theology spoke within that setting in ways that could make it understandable to, attractive to, and even sometimes set in relief against established values and intellectual foundations.

Social and Political Dimensions

The culture Paul inhabited recognized no strict separation between politics and religion, as many modern societies strive to do. A person's political and religious commitments were interlaced. Moreover, during the years when Paul wrote the letters that ended up in the New Testament, a Roman emperor cult was just beginning to emerge and would eventually gain momentum, especially in various parts of the empire's eastern regions. The cult consisted of socioreligious ceremonies and obligations that recognized the emperor as a divinity. Being considered an upstanding and loyal member of many communities would have obligated a person to participate in this cult or even in other Greco-Roman religious rites. Believers, as well as Jews who did not follow Christ, could stand out and perhaps attract the scorn and suspicion of their neighbors when they refused to participate.

In some settings, even in those where an emperor cult had yet to materialize, believers' conspicuous religious differences could incite backlash. Paul often refers to persecution in his letters—persecution afflicting other believers as well as himself. He rarely elaborates on the sources, motives, or nature of persecutions. Most of the hardship appears to have consisted of social ostracism or derision. Other evidence from the period suggests that violent and organized repression of Christ-followers occurred only very rarely during Paul's lifetime. Disdain for Christian beliefs and practices could have originated in reactions to believers' repudiations of imperially sanctioned religious rituals or simply in basic suspicions about Christ-followers' ill effects on social cohesion and communal prosperity. Anyone who refused to offer sacrifices to specific deities to relieve a crippling drought might have suffered social exclusion or lost customers when a regional harvest failed to meet expectations. Believers who opted out of religious ceremonies dedicated to promoting the emperor's vitality might appear more than strange; they might have looked potentially seditious in the wider population's eyes.

Paul's letters recognize the social and political implications of the message he preached. He did not understand his theology as politically neutral or dissociated from his imperial setting; indeed, he could not do so, since this theology directly affected the behaviors and values of individuals and communities who lived within that imperial context. Certainly Paul's letters never advocate a revolutionary stance over against the Roman Empire. On one occasion he even commends believers' subjection to governing authorities and the responsibility to pay taxes (Rom 13:1–7). At the same time, Paul does little to defend Christian faith and the gospel's central claims from those who might have seen Christian values as counter to Roman interests. Embedded in Paul's gospel is a belief in God's ultimate superiority over any and all constellations of political power, Roman and otherwise. Paul's ways of describing the good news summon his audiences to align themselves with a new theological order that implies the emergence of a new and very different kind of sociopolitical order. Or, to state it differently, the theological order created by God's accomplishments in Christ implies that people should view their political settings differently and with significantly rearranged priorities and loyalties.

An evocative theological vocabulary runs throughout Paul's letters—a theological vocabulary he shared with other Christian authors from the first century. The terms Paul uses resonate with other teachings and claims that his audiences would have heard in various settings. Paul's references to Jesus as "Lord," "Savior," and a bringer of "peace" echoed the use of those and related terms in Roman imperial propaganda's descriptions of emperors from the past, such as Augustus and Tiberius. Those imperial figures "saved" the world from its dangerous decline and instituted a lasting "peace." Even the term *good news*, or *gospel*, offered a contrast to other statements of "good news" about Roman military victories or benefactions provided by an emperor. The word for a "church" could also identify an "assembly" of civic groups, trade guilds, or other kinds of voluntary associations commonly found in any Roman city or village.

By not inventing novel, exclusively Christian terminology to express his theology, Paul effectively casts his descriptions of God and the gospel as comparable to, or as an alternative to, the sociopolitical status quo with which his audiences were very familiar. The language that expresses the gospel and fleshes out its meaning creates a counteridentity for Paul's readers who also heard that same language as part of their society's sociopolitical vernacular. With some of the same terminology and imagery that Rome deployed to define its citizenry's identity and shape popular values, Paul's letters subtly cast the gospel as an alternative to imperial pretensions. His theology asserts God's supremacy over all creation, including political systems.

As Paul's letters help his audiences discover and manifest who they are in Christ, Paul's rhetoric does not exactly depict churches as separate societies. They certainly are not groups that should see themselves as entirely isolated from the surrounding culture. Yet Paul does emphasize the gospel as a reality that brings individuals into a unique community with other believers. Belonging and integration are vitally important theological themes for Paul. He credits the Holy Spirit as a force that fosters corporate human flourishing. Paul also identifies the Spirit as the source of gifts that facilitate Christian community and the church's ability to express its faith in its common life. The social realities created as a result of God's actions through Jesus Christ depend principally on a Spirit-empowered love and mutual upbuilding (e.g., 1 Cor 12:4–26; Gal 5:22–6:2).

To help those church communities authentically express the new life God makes possible, Paul labored to promote their unity (e.g., 1 Cor 1:10). Unity provided, for Paul, a vital and tangible sign of God's activity, in which God creates the possibility of a unified relationship with God without giving preference to any individual's religious credentials, gender, ethnic identity, or socioeconomic position (e.g., Gal 3:28). Members of the church exist as relatives within God's own family, and so their common life must embody a deep-seated solidarity with one another. That allegiance, the letters insist, constitutes the core of a believer's political life—a life lived not in isolation from fellow Christ-followers but in close, cooperative relationship with them. Paul urges those communities to distinguish themselves from their imperial environment and ethos. They have a distinctive hope, and they belong to a different Lord. The members of Paul's churches were not separatists or revolutionaries, but Paul nevertheless implored them to understand their true loyalties as residing elsewhere than the Roman Empire (e.g., Phil 3:20). In every way, the gospel Paul preached called people to recognize that they belong to God, who had set them free to live lives pleasing to God (e.g., 1 Thess 4:1).

2

Paul's Letters

Those who pick up a Bible and read through the New Testament encounter Paul's letters without an accompanying clear explanation of where these documents came from or what to make of them. The book of Acts has much to say about Paul, celebrating his ministry and its importance, but Acts never describes him as someone who wrote letters to churches. Nor does the narrative of Acts offer much in terms of specific insights into Paul's enduring relationships with the multiple churches to whom he wrote his letters. Acts reveals next to nothing about the experiences of Christ-followers in Corinth, Philippi, Thessalonica, or other locations to which Paul wrote. The letters therefore endure as documents mostly dislocated from their original contexts. Each one represents only one side of a larger conversation between Paul and a church and only one or a few facets of a more complicated relationship between a community and the apostle. Even though people in some of those churches may have occasionally written to Paul (e.g., 1 Cor 7:1), only his words to them have survived. Interpreting Paul's letters therefore requires one to investigate the letters' contexts and to discern how the letters once contributed to larger conversations.

Paul's surviving correspondence to churches is not entirely disconnected from its original contexts. The letters themselves provide much evidence about a larger story—or stories—behind them and their origins, but sorting the evidence requires reading and comparing all the letters. The sequence in which Paul's writings appear in the New Testament provides little help, for their ordering is based, not on chronology or any reckoning of each letter's importance in relation to another one, but primarily on their length. Romans, the longest letter, appears first, and tiny Philemon closes the collection. The exceptions to this length-based ordering derive from an effort to keep paired letters next to each other, so, for example, the two letters to the Thessalonians sit side by side in the Bible, even though 2 Thessalonians is shorter than the letter that follows it, 1 Timothy.

The letters that bear Paul's name appear to be real letters, documents originally written and delivered to other people. With some exceptions that will be explored in due course, Paul composed the letters for actual flesh-and-blood people with whom he either had a pre-existing relationship or, in the case of Romans, people with whom he sought to build one. Understanding the letters requires interpreters to explore evidence about those relationships and to ask about the people Paul addresses in any given letter. The best way to investigate Paul's letters is to read them and examine the ways in which each one speaks to particular communities about particular subjects, for each letter was written to communicate distinctive things to a specific audience in unique circumstances. Interpreters must consider how Paul meant for each letter to communicate his ideas and to inform the beliefs, values, and practices of the people who first received them.

A Reading Experiment

To read an old letter is to examine a historical artifact from a distant time. To make sense of it, readers typically have to get a sense of its surrounding context, including to whom the letter was written, the nature of the relationship between author(s) and reader(s), the circumstances that prompted the author(s) to write, and the larger set of back-and-forth communications in which a particular letter participated. Even though an individual letter represents only one line of a more extensive dialogue, sometimes that one line can yield clues about the larger conversation.

The following short letter offers an example of what it takes to pay attention to the original context in which a document was originally written and sent. The letter is reproduced here exactly as it first read, except the date has been removed.

My dear Daughter:

Your letter was most welcome. I read it with a lot of appreciation. You evidently are just finding out what a terrible situation the President's daughter is facing. That was the main reason for my not wanting to be Vice-President. I knew what it would mean to you and your mother—to your Aunts and Uncles and Grandmothers and cousins particularly those named Truman if what has happened came about.

But you will have to try and bear it as best you can because it is a reality and as old Cleveland said you are facing a condition—not a theory. So you must face it, keep your balance and go along just as your dad is trying to go. People will be trying to find something in your conduct and in mine to talk about and criticize. If they really have something to find fault with then, of course, it is too bad. But if there is no truth in what they say we must go along, doing right and paying no attention to the dirt which is thrown at us.

That has been my policy since I was a little boy—and just look where it landed me! Maybe it was wrong. I am sending you a tissue of lies put out by Drew Pearson, which brought on the philosophical discourse. Had a lot of fun with Reathal about it. It is funny when you consider that your dad not only didn't chase you out of town but that he felt like weeping when you did leave—even in spite of that spell of bad humor.

I've always known that Washington is a hick town—in fact I don't know of a so called hick town that isn't a better and more friendly place—but I could never make you and your mamma believe it.

Hope Michael Joseph Casey has a grand summer and finally gets his private lodging properly placed. What does the fat Mr. Spot Wallace think of this interloper named Mike? I'll wager his opinion is not printable—if it could be expressed.

I hope you gave a nice time at home and I'll count the days until you return. I'm not going to San Francisco until next week. Had a nice boat ride Sunday with the newsmen who went the rounds with me on the V.P. campaign last fall. Glad you went to see Aunt Mary and Mamma.

Write your dad when you have time—kiss your mamma for me.

Lots & lots of love,
Dad

Because the names and historical referents in the letter are unfamiliar to many, some people find it difficult to situate the document in its historical setting. The letter's language and casual style may nevertheless allow readers to discern an affectionate tone and to judge the letter to be an informal and occasionally playful communication from a father to a beloved daughter. Readers with basic knowledge about American history can see more, however; they recognize the reference to political offices and the name *Truman* and conclude, correctly, that President Harry S. Truman wrote the letter. Revealing the online source of the letter also offers a clear hint about its author's identity, at least for those who can decipher a URL: http://www.trumanlibrary.org/whistlestop/ study_collections/personal/large/folder1/marg61145.htm. Building from those obvious clues, aficionados of U.S. presidential history, people of a certain age, or people who know their way around a search engine, may be able to supply more of the historical context. If they know that Harry and Bess Truman had only one child, Margaret, they can assume correctly that she was the letter's recipient. The letter's original date, June 11, 1945, tells readers that Truman wrote it two months after his succession to the American presidency during the final stages of World War II.

Even those who know next to nothing about Harry and Margaret Truman can make basic sense of the letter, even if the circumstances of the relationship between a new president and his adult daughter remain unfamiliar yet imaginable to most people. Those who can find ways to learn more information about the Truman family history position themselves to appreciate more details in the letter and confirm its tone as more lighthearted than severe. For example, the reference to a possible conflict between a certain "Michael Joseph Casey" and "Mr. Spot Wallace" suddenly comes into clearer focus when Truman historians report that those were pet dogs.

Readers can therefore infer information about the setting and tone of Truman's letter in a number of ways: from a careful reading of the letter itself, from considering its rhetoric and how that rhetoric compares to other communications between parents and children, and from historical data about both the individuals named in the letter and the wider culture they inhabited during their place in history. Gaining that information does not answer all the questions a curious reader might ask. For example, without evidence of a reply or reaction from Margaret, there is no clear way to know for sure what kind of effects the letter had. It could have made her smile, or it might have caused strain in her relationship with her father. Still, the historical information that can be gathered orients readers to the circumstances surrounding the letter. Oriented in that way, readers can formulate hypotheses about the letter's purposes and the relationship between its author and addressee. Interpreters then test those hypotheses by considering how well they help make sense of what the letter says.

Virtually the same interpretive dynamics operate when one considers Paul's letters. To make sense of the documents and how they figured in relationships between Paul and actual ancient readers, interpreters try to situate each book in a broader historical context to flesh out the larger story or conversations taking place between Paul and a given church community. Because Paul wrote mostly to people whom he knew and who knew him or things about him, the letters contain many assumptions and subtleties. Wise interpreters keep their eyes open for those details, even knowing that surely they will not detect or understand all the allusions or references.

Obviously the cultural and temporal distances between now and the composition of Paul's letters are much greater than the distances between the current day and Harry S. Truman's presidency. The amount of data researchers can gather about the United States of America's thirty-third president and his daughter is enormously greater than the specific information one can learn about Paul and the people in Philippi who first heard his letter to them. Other than what Paul's letters reveal about specific people, no additional information is available about almost every individual Paul names. At the same time, a wealth of literary and material information about the ancient world informs general hypotheses about Paul's writings. The more interpreters know about the cosmopolitan culture of ancient Corinth, the more they might see in Paul's communications with the fractious Corinthians. The more interpreters know about slavery in the ancient world, the more they might understand Paul's elliptical rhetoric in Philemon, a letter written to a man, his family, and his wider church community about how he should treat a slave he owns.

Paul's letters do not record the whole range of Paul's theological thoughts, nor do they represent the whole of Paul's ministry. They nevertheless reveal very much about Paul's interactions with a handful of Christian communities, helping modern interpreters understand Paul's contributions as an influential leader during the Christian churches' earliest decades. The letters also provide a lens to view many of the controversies, developments, aspirations, and struggles that led those churches to grapple with the issue of how they should live in conformity with the good news about Jesus Christ. First-century churches possessed no owner's manual, and Paul's letters were not attempts to provide a comprehensive guide to Christian beliefs and Christian behavior. Reading the letters allows interpreters to listen to snippets from larger, ongoing conversations in which Paul instructed, encouraged, and corrected churches as they considered what it means to be "in Christ" and what it looks like to live lives shaped by the gospel of God.

Pastoral Care from a Distance

Paul did not write letters out of a desire to create theological treatises that would articulate timeless explanations of foundational or theoretical topics. Rather, his letters have a situational quality about them; they address particular needs, crises, opportunities, and issues that Paul perceived as relevant in his efforts to tend to the spiritual vitality of different churches. Each of Paul's letters has a particular tone. Sometimes gently and other times fervently, the letters exhort members of churches. They answer questions people have posed. They offer support. They intervene into specific conflicts. They greet friends and coworkers. They issue reminders. Paul portrays himself to his audiences as not just a friend who shares a long history with Christian communities but as one charged to provide them ongoing nurture. Several of his letters refer to visits he hopes to make to the communities, suggesting he uses the letters as substitutes for his own presence and as pieces of a larger strategy of providing support and care. The letters allow him to inject his voice into ongoing debates, struggles, adventures, and victories that particular Christian communities experienced.

While each letter shows only a small part of who Paul was and what he believed, together they paint a rough sketch of a pastorally minded leader who aimed to promote the welfare of specific Christian communities. Little evidence exists to indicate whether his audiences appreciated or heeded everything Paul wrote to them, but nevertheless, some of his letters survived and eventually circulated widely among Christian groups, suggesting that at least some of Paul's contemporaries found his teachings helpful, true, or inspirational.

Paul's letters cohere with one another in ways beyond their shared attempt to make Paul and his pastoral voice present among Christian communities. All the letters pursue the same general purpose, in that they all aim to influence readers so they might better understand and express their Christian identity according to how Paul understood that identity. Paul's letters also cohere and speak in complementary ways because they follow a basic form. Exploring the form affords greater insight into how Paul endeavored to make his case to audiences in persuasive, compelling ways.

The Form of Paul's Letters

Since not many modern readers have read personal correspondence from the ancient world, they easily miss the ordinary character of Paul's letters. The form that the documents follow is roughly consistent with letter-writing practices that were common in Paul's cultural setting. Just as a reader's ability to detect certain mannerisms and rhetorical cues in President Truman's letter allows one to understand it as a personal letter meant to express encouragement and love, gaining familiarity with the basic conventions that Paul's letters incorporate permits a better understanding of what he attempted to communicate to his original audiences.

Salutation

In the Greco-Roman world, letters usually began with a declaration of the author's name. Likewise, each of Paul's letters begins with the word *Paul*. Occasionally Paul identifies himself as an apostle as well, perhaps to enhance a sense of his authority as a church leader. Several of his letters also note cosenders, such as Timothy or Sosthenes. Next, ancient letters named their recipients, just as Paul address letters to "the church of the Thessalonians" (1 Thess 1:1) or "all God's beloved in Rome, who are called to be saints" (Rom 1:7). An epistle's salutation typically concluded with some sort of greeting or blessing. For example, Paul was apparently fond of wishing "grace" and "peace" upon his readers.

Thanksgiving

While other letters from Paul's era ordinarily followed their salutations with expressions of thanks to the gods in general or to particular deities, Paul's practice was to render gratitude or praise to God in light of

God's accomplishments through Jesus Christ. Often his letters express thanks to God for the faithfulness or well-being of the audience. Paul's thanksgivings are more than rote expressions of piety, for they reiterate the common ground Paul shares with the churches to whom he wrote. Perhaps Paul knew his readers would be more inclined to respond positively to his letters if he first reminded them of the shared identity they possessed in Christ. A thanksgiving in a Pauline letter also usually foreshadows material and motifs that will come in the full epistle, setting the table for themes Paul will later serve his audience. For example, when Paul elaborates the basis for his thankfulness in 1 Thess 1:6–10, he mentions the expectation of Christ's return and the endurance of the Thessalonians' faith in the midst of persecution; both topics reemerge as key themes before Paul concludes the letter.

Body

The body is the heart of a letter—not the only place where a letter accomplishes its purposes and communicates its messages, but the place where persuasion and explanation occur most plainly and with most detail. A letter's body might serve a variety of functions, depending on how much an author wants to address and exactly how an author plans to make an effective case. Paul's shortest surviving letter, Philemon, arises from one major concern: the fate of a man named Onesimus. In that letter's body, Paul expresses his opinion on the matter and attempts to persuade his audience to respond in the way he deems best. In 1 Corinthians, Paul addresses a variety of issues, at times moving from one to the other as if working through a list of things he believes the Corinthians need to know for them to function as a healthy church community.

There is great variety in what an author might do in a letter's body. Depending on the specific correspondence and the circumstances that prompted him to write it, Paul might explain his understanding of the situation behind the letter, reflect theologically on the issues his recipients are facing, make requests of his audience, urge them to persevere, admonish them, or exhort them to live in particular ways.

Closing Exhortations

A letter is more than its body and the communication that occurs there. Sometimes final commands, requests, or greetings help reaffirm the relationship or shared values between the author and recipients. When Paul exhorts his readers, often his words echo themes he has already addressed or subtly anticipated previously in the letter. Usually he encourages his fellow believers to live consistently with what he has taught so their lives will conform to the gospel just as their attitudes and beliefs do.

Conclusion

Paul's letters conclude in various ways, depending on the setting and the mood of the letter. Often he extends greetings, expressed generally or to specific people among his audience. In some letters he instructs recipients to greet others, occasionally commending "a holy kiss," which was an expression of church members' kinship or their shared spiritual union in Christ. He sometimes offers a final blessing to express his confidence in God's ongoing work among the letter's original readers.

Paul's Use of the Form

Not every ancient letter adhered to a single prescribed format. Official governmental correspondence and personal notes did not read in precisely the same way, just as they do not today. Paul's letters do not read exactly like either of those types, but the general contours of their form are nevertheless very recognizable and consistent with this broad overview.

Examining the form of Paul's letters indicates that they were easily identified as letters. Paul used a relatively ordinary and familiar medium of communication to facilitate his theological and pastoral efforts. Leading churches from a distance did not require him to invent a new or unique form of communication. He gives no indication that he might have considered a letter an inappropriate means or technology, as if letters were somehow profane ways of communicating something as profound as the truths of Christian teachings. If sending a letter could allow Paul to instruct, correct, or encourage, he would do so.

To state that Paul's letters conform to a general format should not imply that Paul followed a rigid template. Like any thoughtful author, Paul relied on the form as a general guideline and knew how to treat the form as flexible, adapting it as necessary to make his points. Some of the greatest rhetorical force in his letters comes in instances in which he departs from his ordinary form. For example, Paul's letter to the Galatians includes no statement of thanksgiving or blessing; instead, it transitions immediately from its salutation into a rebuke of its audience that begins, "I am astonished that you are so quickly deserting the one who called you" (Gal 1:6). The lack of a conventional thanksgiving might have surprised the Galatians and immediately communicated Paul's anger and urgency, a tone that the rest of the letter sustains. For another example, 1 Thessalonians includes an opening thanksgiving and then returns to render thanks to God multiple times in the letter's body (1 Thess 1:2–10; 2:13; 3:9–10). Paul's refusal to keep the thanksgivings relegated to a specific section of the letter adds to the effusive and at times tender quality of the document. Paul uses every section and nearly every paragraph of the letter to build up the Thessalonians' ability to remain faithful and thus to encourage other Christian communities. Paul was obviously thankful for God's role in their contagious faithfulness.

To study the form of Paul's letters is to recognize that Paul wrote to shape the thoughts, convictions, loyalties, and behaviors of his contemporaries. For Paul's letters to be persuasive, he had to compose his communications in ways that would be familiar to his original readers. Like any form of communication, the letters depend on their rhetoric, their ways of conveying a message to persuade an audience. Paul's use and adaptation of his letters' general form offer only one example of the letters' rhetoric. Others examples of rhetorical dynamics emerge through investigations of each letter itself.

The Sequence of the Letters

Given the relatively arbitrary sequencing of the Pauline Letters in the New Testament, one can choose to read and study them in a number of different orders. Following the traditional canonical order, as this companion does, is obviously one way. While it makes sense that one might instead desire to study the letters in the sequence in which they were written, that task is complicated because there is no clear consensus about the chronological order. Reconstructing the chronological sequence must involve a degree of speculation. While noting that clarity about the letters' original dates and sequence is not essential for understanding and situating most of the letters individually and as a collection, the following proposed sequence is not particularly controversial:

1 Thessalonians
1 Corinthians
2 Corinthians
Galatians
Philemon
Romans
Philippians

Readers who do not want to follow the canonical order might choose to move back and forth among the respective chapters in this volume of the companion if they want to walk through the letters following the proposed chronological sequence. The companion's design and approach aim to allow readers to do that without generating confusion.

As for the other letters in the New Testament that bear Paul's name, they may come from a later period, as explained in upcoming chapters. They were composed probably in this sequence:

Colossians
Ephesians
2 Thessalonians
The Pastoral Letters (Titus, 1 Timothy, and 2 Timothy)

3

The Letter of Paul to the Romans

Romans has earned a reputation as Paul's heftiest letter. The document's length and rhetorical intricacy explain only part of that distinction. More important is the letter's theological gravity, which weaves its way through Paul's sustained explanation of the Christian gospel, the news of what God has accomplished through Jesus Christ. Romans devotes considerable attention to describing God's activity: through Jesus' death and resurrection, God has set people free from the power of sin and death so they might experience new life, both now in the power of the Holy Spirit and in a coming time when God will finally redeem the whole creation. Paul's relentless focus on what God has done and what God will yet do imparts a strong confessional flavor to Romans. In other words, the letter moves forward through a series of declarative statements about God and the human condition, making it speak like a preacher's attempts to disclose theological truths to hearers. Yet Romans is neither an attempt to convert an unbelieving audience nor Paul's try at composing a comprehensive theological manifesto. Rather, Paul pronounces and elaborates theological convictions because he aims to equip the Christian congregations in Rome with the foundational beliefs on which they should base their understanding of their essential identity—as a unified and mutually accountable fellowship. Paul speaks theologically so the Romans might live faithfully.

Written near the end of Paul's life, probably between 56 and 58 CE, during the same general period as Philemon and Philippians, Romans

distinguishes itself among the other surviving Pauline Letters especially through its diplomatic tone and its relatively sustained focus on
the question of what God accomplishes through Jesus Christ. Few subjects in this letter seem ancillary or secondary; Paul keeps his eye on
what God has done and on what God's gracious activity means for a
now-liberated humanity. The document's rhetoric clearly marks it as an
encouraging letter, seen in Paul's eagerness to commend the Romans
and to foster their willingness to express the belonging they share with
one another. As with all of his letters, in Romans Paul ruminates on
theological matters precisely so his audience's theological understanding will contribute to their ability to live out the gospel in authentic and
vibrant ways. In particular, Paul urges the congregations in Rome to
devote themselves to being welcoming communities, places where true
fellowship and generous forbearance flourish, because part of the good
news is the delcaration that God has mercifully embraced and adopted
Jews and gentiles alike. The church therefore should exemplify nothing
less than the new realities God has established.

Even though Romans eventually came to be regarded as nearly
indispensable for researchers and Christians who want to make sense
of Paul's theology, Paul did not set out to write a letter that would be
remembered long into the future and celebrated for its heftiness. The
document's origins and purposes were much more unassuming and
focused on a particular task at hand. The letter's original task—really,
one of its tasks—comes to light when interpreters note that Romans
possesses a unique characteristic in comparison to the other letters Paul
wrote: Paul addresses it to a collection of churches he did not found. The
letter first went to people who, with a few exceptions, did not know Paul
except perhaps by reputation. This means that in Romans Paul cannot
and does not appeal to a relationship he has developed with his readers
or to any visits he has made to Rome; he cannot reassure the Roman
believers of his genuine concern for their spiritual vitality by recalling
how he has conducted himself among them in the past, as he does in all
the other letters he wrote. Paul composed Romans as a letter of introduction to particular groups of ancient Christ-followers. Undoubtedly
the letter did not stand or fall solely on its own words, for the believers
in Rome would already have known some information or hearsay about
Paul and his ministry. In addition, when at the end of the letter Paul
greets many people in the audience by name, he confirms that a handful

of people in the church did indeed know him personally. Paul had advocates among the Roman believers.

Of course, the letter's influence over time expanded beyond the neighborhoods of ancient Rome and beyond the hopes Paul had for the congregations there. Although Romans is not a detailed exposition of Paul's overarching theology or his final word on every subject, still the letter sometimes is regarded as the fullest expression of Paul's ideas, which is a reputation the letter may not deserve. In any case, Romans has proved to be one of history's most influential pieces of literature—taking all literature, not just religious literature, into account. Nearly all major Christian thinkers have immersed themselves in this book and its soaring theological vision. Prominent and far-reaching theological disputes have been won or lost over interpretations of this letter. Even thinkers who may have never read Romans have felt its influence. Since it has exerted such a heavy sway in Christian thought over two millennia, its theological and anthropological assumptions have deeply shaped Western societies and intellectual history. Given the extent of Western colonialism and Christian missionary efforts, interpretations of the letter have indirectly left their mark on countless aspects of cultures around the globe. Studying Romans takes interpreters deeper into Paul's history and his pastoral efforts to instruct specific congregations about their understanding of the gospel, even as analyzing the letter allows interpreters also to explore theological claims and imagery that have been key pieces of Christianity's two-thousand-year-long influence across the world.

The Letter's Origins and Ancient Audience

The story behind Romans and the people to whom Paul sent the letter is part of a larger story about Christian faith taking root and gradually growing in Rome. The history of the Roman churches exemplifies some of the challenges and opportunities that Christ-followers encountered in the first century as they endeavored to put their new beliefs into practice and to organize their common life and worship. That history is interesting in its own right, but it also matters for interpreting Romans, for the history provides an important foundation for understanding who the letter originally addressed and why it says what it does.

The New Testament itself provides a smattering of hints about that history, even though no biblical text explains how Christian churches first came into existence in Rome. Nothing in Romans suggests Paul ever had a hand in preaching the gospel there, and he does not comment on the Roman congregations' origins. As Acts tells the story about Paul's relationship with believers in Rome, when that book's action finally reaches the area around the imperial capital, Christ-followers journey from the city to meet Paul as he travels toward them as a prisoner; he does not bring the gospel to Rome for the first time (Acts 28:14b–15). Likewise, the New Testament as a whole reveals almost nothing about the people who composed the churches in Rome. Paul mentions several of those men and women by name in Romans 16, but in doing so he provides very little description.

Other parts of Romans supply interpreters with additional clarity about the letter's audience. Most notably, Romans suggests that Paul wrote to an audience composed of both Jews and gentiles. Early in the letter, Paul takes care to explain how "all, both Jews and Greeks, are under the power of sin" (Rom 3:9). Later in the letter he helps his audience navigate differences of opinion related to the choices they make about foods they will or will not eat. The references to dietary scruples that derive from a person's conscience do not necessarily mean that Paul has in mind Jews in the church who still observe dietary practices prescribed by torah; there are reasons why gentile Christ-followers might have abstained from certain meats too. Nevertheless, some of the differences Paul describes could have originated in traditional dividing lines between Jews and gentiles. Moreover, one of the letter's rhetorical and theological crescendos calls attention to God's longstanding commitment to bring Jews and gentiles into harmony as people who worship and glorify God together (Rom 15:5–13).

Additional evidence supports assumptions that Paul had good reasons to worry about the possibility of divisions among the Christian communities in Rome, including divisions springing from tensions between Jewish Christ-followers and gentile Christ-followers. Acts includes a brief statement of why the couple Priscilla and Aquila, two Christian teachers, had to leave Rome: because Emperor Claudius (who ruled 41–54 CE) "had ordered all Jews to leave" the city (Acts 18:2). A similarly brief segment of the ancient Roman historian Suetonius' book *Lives of the Caesars* provides context for that decree: Suetonius, writing over seventy years after the event, mentions an edict issued in the late 40s CE by which Claudius expelled from Rome those Jews who were participating in disturbances created by an instigator named Chrestus.

It is plausible that Suetonius or his sources confused the common name Chrestus as a Latin equivalent for the Greek *Christos,* meaning Christ. If so, then Claudius' edict could indicate that Jewish communities in Rome during the late 40s experienced notable dissension sparked by the claims of the Christian gospel, and the emperor responded by banishing those individuals he deemed responsible for the public unrest. If that event actually happened, barring influential Jewish Christ-followers from the city, then subsequent Christian gatherings in Rome could have been, for a time, led or energized more by gentiles than by Jews. Indeed, even if the one whom Suetonius called "Chrestus" refers to an actual man with that name who lived in Rome, and not to Jesus Christ and the church's claims about him, still an expulsion of certain Jews from Rome, for whatever reason, could have disrupted the Christian community there. In any case, it is unwise to venture especially detailed speculations about the possible disruptions or their extensiveness since no one knows exactly how large was the Christian community in Rome at that time or how many Jewish believers Claudius might have temporarily banished from the city.

Once the expelled Jews were allowed to return to Rome, as Priscilla and Aquila apparently were, according to Rom 16:3, Paul might have feared the possibility of divisions or at least tensions arising when gentile believers and returning Jewish believers suddenly reencountered one another after several years of separation. Whatever the real or imagined roots of those tensions and whatever specific issues could have strained relationships in the Roman congregations, Paul wrote to the believers in Rome to promote unity and understanding. His letter sets forth the theological basis for gentiles' and Jews' unity as children of God and coinheritors of God's blessings because of Jesus Christ.

Romans never mentions Claudius, Chrestus, or an expulsion. It is not clear that Paul meant for the letter to speak to divisive conditions that were created or exacerbated as a direct result of Claudius' edict. But the historical background about the edict and the potential for strained relations among Roman Christ-followers are important to keep in mind regardless. Rome was a large, diverse, crowded, and sometimes contentious setting. The Christian gospel often disrupted social norms and challenged religious values in the places it went. Paul wrote to Christian communities in Rome that could have been hampered by strained relationships caused by a multitude of factors.

Archaeological investigations indicate additional details about the conditions in Rome. The Roman Christ-followers tended to be concentrated in certain neighborhoods in the city during the first century. A couple of those particular locations suffered economic strain because of their very high population density. Manual laborers lived there. Many of those people had emigrated to Rome from the east. Poverty was the rule. In the other quarters of the city where Christ-followers dwelled, the population represented a greater range of social strata. Not all of the people who received Paul's letter lived the same way, therefore. Geographical, cultural, and economic differences likely distinguished and even separated the Roman believers and their individual congregations in such a large and busy city. Nevertheless, Paul wrote to all of them, for he addressed the letter to "all God's beloved in Rome, who are called to be saints" (Rom 1:7). To reach all of them, the letter would have been read to members of house churches in various demographic settings.

Many factors might therefore have contributed to an uneasy unity or a diminished sense of shared identity among the Roman churches. Divisions or factions could have arisen from Jewish-gentile tensions, economic and cultural differences, or the social and political burdens of people taking on a new religious identity in an imperial environment. Whether Paul had reliable information about discord among the saints in Rome, perennially worried about the possibility of such problems developing, or simply intended to address certain matters as a preventive measure finally does not matter too much for understanding Romans and the people who first received it. The salient point for studying Romans is to know that Paul almost certainly did not write to a homogeneous audience. Likely he hoped to eliminate bickering and grave divisions among the Christ-followers scattered in different parts of Rome. Paul also expected his pastoral letter would unify his audience to him, for he encourages them to support him as he forges ahead in his ministry.

A person may resolve to write a letter for more than just one reason, of course. Paul likely had multiple intentions for using his correspondence to introduce himself to the saints in Rome. Some parts of Romans intimate Paul's desire for the Roman believers to support him in his plans for future ministry. He evidently hoped his fellow Christ-followers would rally around his ongoing efforts to preach and model a gospel of unity in places beyond Rome. He informs his readers in Rom 15:22–24 that he expects to visit Rome on his way to Spain, indicating his intention to ask the Romans for material support for a missionary venture to a place where Christian teachings had not yet been proclaimed.

Additionally, Paul tells his audience that he will soon deliver funds he has collected to the church in Jerusalem (Rom 15:25–27, 30–32). By mentioning his plan, Paul apparently aimed to secure the Romans' support for his efforts to maintain a friendly and generous connection between his itinerant ministry among gentiles and the predominantly Jewish church in Jerusalem. Paul therefore urged the Roman churches to know and take comfort from what he teaches, leaving them convinced that he himself lived out a gospel that rules out the possibility of either Jewish or gentile believers claiming independence from one another. If neither of those groups can be independent of the other, then neither one can assert an inherent superiority over the other. That vital theological reality animates the whole of Romans. In this letter Paul celebrates the salvation God has provided as a salvation that initiates new life and establishes new relationships for people to enjoy with God and also with one another—whether Jews or gentiles, settled or transient, economically comfortable or vulnerable.

Overview

Romans introduces Paul to the believers in Rome mostly by introducing contours of the gospel as Paul understood it. The letter says little in terms of personal information about Paul. The theological presentation in Romans unfolds in a sustained, integrated manner. It does not jump erratically from point to point. In places, Paul employs a dialogical technique characteristic of diatribe, in which he simulates a conversation with an imagined conversation partner. That form of steering an argument allows Paul to communicate an awareness of objections or mistaken inferences that might result from what he says. It also permits him to avoid addressing additional criticisms that might be raised against him. The occasional use of a diatribe style mostly allows Paul to defend himself and his claims against misunderstandings or erroneous rumors. If Paul suspected that some in his Roman audience had heard negative reports about him or might have been mistrustful about his way of articulating the gospel of God, the diatribe provides him a tool for making his way through potentially contested issues both strategically and congenially.

Salutation and Thanksgiving (Rom 1:1–17)

Paul composed this letter alone; he names no coauthor. When his self-introduction morphs into a short summary of "the gospel of God," Paul gives an initial hint that the letter will aim for more than acquainting his audience to him; it will introduce them to his understanding of the gospel. The long salutation draws connections, both syntactical and theological, between Paul and the Romans, for God has "called" all of them to participate together in the blessings made possible through Jesus Christ. Even in its opening sentences the letter seeks to build a sense of mutuality between Paul and churches he has not yet visited.

True to conventional form, the letter then turns to render thanks to God. Specifically, it rejoices over the Romans' reputation for faith. Faith, Paul says, motivates him also to ask God for the opportunity to visit Rome, for he expresses eagerness to nourish the Romans' faith in person while their faith does the same for his.

Having named so much common ground with the Roman believers in the letter's salutation and thanksgiving, in Rom 1:16–17 Paul gives a thumbnail description of the gospel that provides the basis of their shared identity. What he calls "the gospel" extends beyond the specific beliefs or the theological ideas they share; rather, Paul makes a statement about the God he and the Romans both know, the God who makes salvation available to all who have faith, the God who acts in the gospel. Not merely a message, "the gospel" as Paul describes it "is the power of God" to accomplish salvation. As the divine activity that makes salvation available and effective, the gospel reveals "the righteousness of God." Based on its use in the Septuagint, that expression refers not to God's moral purity or to an abstract divine attribute but to God's activity that accomplishes salvation for God's people. "The righteousness of God" encompasses all that God does to bring about salvation and then to sustain those whom God saves. In speaking of that "righteousness" at the beginning of Romans, Paul lays a foundation for the whole letter with his assertion that the good news concerning Jesus Christ expresses God's ongoing and effective determination to deliver and protect people.

The Indictment of All Humanity (Rom 1:18–3:20)

Even as Paul identifies "the gospel" as God's righteousness in action, he also sees "the wrath of God" being revealed in humanity. The sketch of the gospel thus begins by describing the problem that God addresses through Jesus Christ: sin, which manifests itself in "ungodliness," "wickedness," and lawlessness. Apparently looking first at the gentiles of the world, Paul notes various types of abusive, predatory, and self-serving behaviors. The specific details in the latter half of Romans 1 have fueled much discussion and generated differing opinions regarding how to interpret Paul's views, especially in recent discussions about human sexuality. In particular, interpretive debates consider what makes something qualify as "natural" for Paul. Interpreters also explore the apostle's cultural presuppositions about different varieties of same-sex sexual activity, for his audience would have recognized moral distinctions among various kinds of behaviors and motives. Scholars' debates are too extensive to summarize here. Many interpreters agree, however, that Paul's critical comments about sexual activity in Romans appear to have in mind, specifically, predators who target children.

Any discussion about Paul's controversial statements in Romans 1 must not overlook the issue of how they function within the larger argument of the letter. All of the specific vices Paul singles out represent, in his perspective, a more fundamental form of sinfulness and perversion: an abandonment of God. Even though God has been revealed through the natural order, people did not acknowledge God but instead opted for forms of idolatry. Paul's argument is not primarily about sexuality, then, but about the nature of sin as rebellion against God and estrangement from God.

People's rejection of God incurs God's "wrath," which Paul characterizes not as revenge or castigation but as a response in which God "gave up" people, handing them over to the inevitable alienation and damage that result from their idolatrous choices. Experiencing the consequences of sin's destructiveness, gentiles therefore find themselves without a way out. They live engulfed all the more deeply in sin and certain to perish as a result. Paul asserts that this is the case not only for the gentiles who brazenly participate in evil but even for others who unctuously pass judgment on them. The problem, as Paul describes it, is universal.

Not content to indict only gentiles or humanity in an indistinctive sense, Paul also shines a spotlight directly on Jews' culpability. Even the law of Moses cannot protect them from sin's power, for, in fact, the torah that confers Jewish identity and guidance for Jewish living also judges Jews' sinful behavior. Even though Jews may possess what Paul calls an "advantage" insofar as God has long been revealed clearly in their midst through the benefits of Scripture and traditions, still Jews find themselves precisely where gentiles, or "Greeks," are: literally, "under sin." That means everyone dwells "under the power of sin," as the NRSV renders the expression in Rom 3:9. All people are enslaved to sin, compelled to do its bidding. Whether this power called "sin" manifests itself through idolatry, selfishness, debauchery, or any sort of shortcoming denounced by the law, in the end sin holds sway over all humanity and provides a warrant for God to condemn anyone.

Justification by Faith (Rom 3:21–4:25)

After such sweeping indictments about humanity's captivity to sin, one might expect Paul to call people to change their ways. He does not do so at this point in the letter, because people who exist entirely under the power of something stronger—namely, sin—lack the ability to free themselves or to improve their way out of their circumstances. Paul focuses, instead, on what God has done and is doing to address the human plight. The letter thus undergoes a dramatic shift, moving from humanity's transgressions to God's intervention. The words *But now* begin the new movement, announcing the arrival of a new time. God has initiated the new time, bursting into the scene of human enslavement to manifest "the righteousness of God," God's saving activity, recalling Paul's brief summary of the gospel in Rom 1:16–17.

Paul describes God's "righteousness" in connection with "faith." English translations of Paul's letters usually speak of the noun *faith* (instead of "belief") and the verb *believe* (instead of "have faith"). In English the words *faith* and *believe* do not appear to have a direct lexical connection, but they both translate what is essentially the same word from Paul's Greek. When Paul speaks of "*faith* in Jesus Christ" and "all who *believe*," his contemporaries would not have missed the clear verbal link between the noun and verb. As previously discussed in the overview of Paul's theology, Paul's references to faith indicate more than people's cognitive disposition toward Jesus; the term includes a sense of the connection people share with Christ. In Paul's diction, faith represents *trust* and a lived solidarity with Christ more than a form of intellectual belief or assent. That faith has an active, existential character to it, for it involves the commitment of oneself to the reliability of another. Elsewhere Paul refers to Christ as one who exhibits faith himself, for Jesus faithfully trusted God's promises and died as an act of obedience to God's intentions (e.g., Rom 5:19; Phil 2:5–8).

Paul has much to say about how God's righteousness manifests itself, but he takes little space to say it. He offers brief claims, not extended explanations. God justifies those who have sinned. God redeems them. God provides Jesus as a means of purification, like a ritual that marks the cleansing of a place and a people that were previously defiled. The various ways of describing the salvation God accomplishes recall passages and themes from Jewish Scriptures, evoking, for example, God's act of redeeming the Hebrew people from Egypt through the exodus and God's intention to dwell among God's people in a holy sanctuary or temple. By likening God's righteousness through Christ to other actions God has taken in the past, Paul emphasizes God's determination to preserve God's people and to remain present among them. Paul never draws a schematic diagram to explain the precise mechanics of *how* salvation comes to pass or *how* God liberates people from sin. Instead, he states, repeatedly, *that* God has done so through Jesus' death and resurrection. Paul hardly regards salvation as a one-dimensional act of God, capable of a single description or characterized by a single metaphor. The variety of language he uses to refer to God's activity betrays his wonder even as it reveals the multifaceted nature of what God has done.

In Romans, however, Paul's attention falls most frequently on one particular way of talking about God's salvation: through Christ, God justifies people. The verb *justify* could also be translated "make righteous," just as the English words *justification* and *righteousness* both translate the same Greek noun. "Justification" refers to aligning oneself—actually, in Paul's theology, it refers to having oneself *be* aligned—to the activity of God's righteousness as it discloses itself through Jesus Christ. To be thus aligned with God means that one becomes a full beneficiary and ongoing partner in God's resolute and decisive activity to reclaim the world. Justification implies freedom from sin and the creation of a new or renewed existence that corresponds to what God desires for humanity and all creation.

God reclaims all who are under sin, Jews and gentiles alike, because justification happens through faith and not the Mosaic law that Jews received. To support that claim, which might have struck some Jews of Paul's time as scandalous because it could be heard as a threat to the importance of Israel's history and priority, Paul looks back to the example of Abraham. In Abraham Paul finds a man whose faith ("Abraham *believed* God"), according to Gen 15:6, led him to share in God's "righteousness." By anchoring the Christian claim of *justification by faith* in the history of God's original election of the Hebrew people, Paul frames the gospel of Jesus Christ as a continuation and fulfillment of God's prior activity among Abraham's biological descendants, as traced throughout the history of Israel and Judah. Paul's argument to the Romans, which resembles though does not reproduce another one he wrote earlier in his life (Gal 3–4), considers Abraham more than just a handy illustration. Abraham's story is critical for Paul because the patriarch is "the ancestor of all who believe."

As that ancestor, the premier man of "faith," Abraham serves as a kind of prototype for how God's righteousness operates. Paul insists that the blessing and inheritance God promised to Abraham would finally be realized for all people, Jews and gentiles, in the same manner that God originally became Abraham's benefactor: through faith. Abraham's justification came through faith. Justification through Christ, encountering God's righteousness in the gospel, likewise comes through faith. Abraham's justification did not occur through any power the torah might or might not possess. Instead, Abraham's faith came first. The law—and even God's command that Abraham be circumcised—came after Abraham's faith. As Paul recounts it, Abraham's story establishes that faith was always at the heart of God's longstanding intention to bless all the peoples of the world.

What It Means to Be Justified (Rom 5–8)

The form of Paul's argument upholds his desire to foster closer ties both among his audience and between himself and his audience. In other words, the syntax of Romans supports the purpose of Romans. The indictment early in the letter spoke in the third person about gentiles and their depravities, and then it shifted to the second person when discussing those who pass judgment on that behavior and Jews, whose torah cannot shield them from sin. Paul thus indicted all of his audience along with the rest of humanity. References to "all" dominated the indictment's conclusion and the description of what God has done in justifying people by faith. Chapter 5 begins, following the lead set in Rom 4:24, with another shift, as Paul's rhetoric employs first-person plural syntax. Paul now addresses a unified group of justified people as one of its members, describing what "we"—he and the Romans, as fellow believers—can expect as a result of "our" justification and reconciliation with God. The Romans share connections with each other and with Paul. This section of the letter speaks of many benefits for justified people, benefits they enjoy corporately. In the opening paragraph alone, Paul mentions a few key benefits: peace with God, access to God's grace, a "hope of sharing in the glory of God," the promise that suffering will not leave "us" finally discouraged, hearts full of God's love, the gift of the Holy Spirit, and deliverance from God's wrath.

Paul takes care not to characterize those benefits as tools to empower people in a struggle *they* must wage to defeat the sin that had previously overwhelmed them. Instead, the gifts signal people's entrance into a different kind of existence; they represent the outcome of a victory *God* has won over sin. Paul communicates this by contrasting the consequences of Adam's sin with the results secured by Christ's "act of righteousness." Inspired by the primeval history told in Genesis 3, Paul says sin entered the world and brought death with it, resulting in death reigning over humanity (cf. 1 Cor 15:21–22). But that reign ends because of Christ, for now those who benefit from Christ will "exercise dominion" that death once had. Likewise, sin's "dominion" has been supplanted by grace's "dominion." The salvation Paul describes entails a movement from death to eternal life, a movement made possible by God's defeat of sin, death, and the power those forces possess to afflict humanity.

In chapter 6 Paul continues to dwell on the cosmic scope of the gospel as a declaration of God's victory. The victory eventuates in the "newness of life" in which "we" walk, as well as in the expectation of sharing "in a resurrection like [Christ's]." The newness has already begun. Paul does not tell the Romans that their sins are forgiven; he tells them that sin has been dethroned. Believers' enslavement under sin has ended. They have died to it and been freed from its power. The key theological insight behind those claims lies in the idea of believers' union with Christ. Corporately, "we" participate, Paul says, in Christ's own death. He speaks as if believers were all present in Jesus' crucifixion and likewise raised from the dead to demonstrate their newfound freedom from death's power.

That freedom, however, does not mean sin no longer poses a threat. Paul warns of sin's potential to regain control over one's self and one's passions. Nor does freedom equal utter self-determinism, for

Paul describes freedom from sin as a transition into a new enslavement: Christ-followers "have become slaves of righteousness" (Rom 6:18). That new slavery to God's righteousness ensures sanctification, or holiness, and eternal life—much more favorable outcomes than the death that comes from enslavement to sin. Just as slavery in the Roman world was totalizing, claiming a person's whole identity and denying a person's basic rights by rendering an individual as property, those whom God has justified belong entirely to God (cf. 1 Cor 6:15–20).

Having referred several times in the letter to the law of Moses and its inability to deliver people from sin's power, Paul makes a stronger statement in Rom 7:4–6 when he says that believers are dead to the law, which once "held us captive." By suggesting such a close association between sin and torah, or at least an association between the effects they both have—namely, enslavement—Paul finds himself compelled to offer more information about the law. He insists that the law is "spiritual," holy, not sin, and not the source of death. However, torah played a role, an unwitting role, in sin's dominion, for Paul speaks of sin appropriating God's law for sin's own destructive ends. Sin incites rebelliousness against God and leads people to overestimate the law's power to restrain sin and keep a person in fellowship with God's goodness. Sin provides the true agency that produces evil; the law does not do so, for sin creates desire and a lack of self-control that the law cannot ultimately suppress. As a result, sin ends up corrupting the law, making the law a facilitator of sin's ability to enslave and wreak destruction. So insidious is sin's power, it deceitfully makes even God's torah its catalyst and tool.

Through Jesus Christ, however, and not through any impaired power of the sin-perverted law, God has set people free. The law no longer condemns. Paul also appears to indicate, by speaking of "the law of the Spirit of life in Christ Jesus" (Rom 8:2), that God has also redeemed or purified the Mosaic law by overthrowing the sin that had once so treacherously manipulated it.

In Romans 8 Paul returns to focus on what life looks like as a result of the freedom God has secured. Images of transformation, present and future, weave their way through this part of the discussion. The Holy Spirit transforms believers from existence "in the flesh" to existence "in the Spirit." The expression *in the flesh* does not refer principally to one's embodied, flesh-and-blood existence; Paul does not disparage human bodies as essential limitations to one's spirituality and does not construe salvation as an escape from the world. "In the flesh" refers to a life lived under sin's power, for even though sin has lost its mastery over people, it remains an active and destructive force in the world (cf. Gal 5:13–26). The Holy Spirit, however, empowers the people of God to live differently, for the Holy Spirit allows the God who raised Jesus from the dead to live within believers. The transformational presence of the Spirit offers yet another expression of Paul's focus on participation, on believers' coexistence with Christ. Possessing the Holy Spirit, Jews and gentiles alike discover their identity as children of God. Even more, as people joined to Christ, all believers are heirs, "joint heirs with Christ," in line to receive all God's promises and all that belongs to God (cf. Gal 4:4–7).

Other transformations remain in store as well. Paul's outlook on the life believers live holds a number of claims in balance; people are definitely free from sin, yet sin still poses a threat; believers confidently expect to share in Christ's glory, yet suffering still encumbers current existence. The letter acknowledges not only personal sufferings, another piece of what it means to be united to Christ in his death and resurrection, but also the sufferings and struggles that creation endures. Only rarely do Paul's letters address the implications of the gospel for the whole of creation, beyond human beings, but in the middle of chapter 8, Paul personifies the current creation as waiting, even groaning in labor pains as it does so, for new life to spring forth and for God's victory to become absolute and final (cf. Rom 16:20). The Holy Spirit plays a role in the expectant longing for transformation, for the Spirit, too, groans through "sighs too deep for words." God does not stand apart from a beleaguered and restless creation, as if waiting at a comfortable distance before swooping in to fix everything. Rather, through the Holy Spirit, God participates even now in the world's arduous yearning for God's intentions to reach their fulfillment.

One transformation that will never occur is for God to abandon God's people. Paul describes the Holy Spirit as certain proof of believers' adoption and a pledge that God's future will come to pass. Nothing, Paul insists, can "separate us from the love of God in Christ Jesus." Such a claim might sound like wishful thinking, if not for the fact that the whole of the letter up to this point has emphasized salvation as something God alone has accomplished through a decisive display of grace, love, inclusion, and power.

The Faithfulness of God (Rom 9–11)

When Paul wrote Romans, Christian churches by and large had not established an identity that rendered them fully distinguishable from Judaism. Nevertheless, as he wrote in the mid-first century, Paul observed the Christian gospel as increasingly unable to attract his Jewish contemporaries. Intractable differences of opinion between the church and Jews who rejected Christian claims prompted Paul to inquire in this section of Romans whether "the word of God had failed" (Rom 9:6). The question matters for reasons other than idle intellectual curiosity, for neither Paul nor his audience could be expected to trust that the salvation God provides through Jesus Christ is permanent and reliable if the gospel or the experience of the church simultaneously implies that God has rejected or somehow passed over Jews who do not follow Jesus as the Messiah. If the gospel entails the expiration of God's promises made to people God had already chosen, then God's new promises have little basis for anyone to believe them. Paul therefore spends three dense chapters explaining that the gospel he preaches does not invalidate God's faithfulness to Jews, and that Jews' general reluctance to embrace the Christian message should not be a cause of disillusionment concerning God's plans or God's reliability.

These theologically rich chapters spawn a wide variety of interpretations, for their argument is not easy to follow. They, along with other parts of Paul's letters, have been used by Christians throughout history who declared that the church supersedes the Jews, collectively considered, as God's chosen people. Those interpretations suffer from a number of flaws, yet they remain part of the church's and the letter's legacy. More convincing interpretations of Romans 9–11 contend that, even though Paul does not claim to be able to explain the situation with great clarity, he nevertheless reasserts God's unflagging commitment to Jews as God's chosen people.

While these three chapters undeniably affirm the ongoing validity of God's original promises to ancient Israel in a general sense, they leave other, more specific questions unanswered. Paul does not pretend to be capable of discerning God's mysterious intentions. In the end, he leaves the issue up to God, for Paul does not offer a detailed explanation or proof as much as he strongly affirms that the Jewish people's salvation remains securely in the hands of an utterly trustworthy God. Buoyed along in the discussion by numerous quotations from various

Septuagintal texts and clearly pained by the fact that so many of his fellow Jews remain unconvinced by the gospel, Paul declines to entertain the possibility that God is fickle or capricious. Nor is God surprised by what has occurred. Nor is God a failure. Paul cannot see the situation as anything other than a piece of God's inscrutable plan. Paul makes his case in a manner that resembles many of the Old Testament's prophetic writings. To be more specific, Paul labors to give a theological reckoning of the disobedience he sees among Abraham's descendants and at the same time to offer confident hope for their eventual restoration.

Paul refuses to diminish the importance of God's previously pledged commitment to Jews. This section of the letter even names them as "Israelites" (Rom 9:4, 6; 11:1), which calls attention to the Jews' connections to ancient Israel's adoption, glory, covenants, law, worship, and promises. God's choice, not any faithfulness or unfaithfulness on their part, defines who the Jews are and gives them their distinctive value. That calling, which is the result of God's free choice, cannot be revoked. Paul therefore, almost by a process of elimination, proposes that the Jews' unwillingness to embrace the gospel evidences disobedience on their part as well as a hardening or a stumbling that has come upon them presumably on God's part. Yet the situation remains temporary, Paul insists. In an odd claim that certainly history has not borne out, Paul asserts that the salvation of gentiles during the period of hardening will make the Jews jealous (cf. Deut 32:21). In time, after "the full number of the Gentiles has come in," then at last "all Israel will be saved" (Rom 11:25–26).

Paul avoids any suggestion that the existence of the church in Jesus Christ nullifies God's promises to Israel. He would probably be appalled by anyone, living in any era, who would suggest that Christianity somehow replaces Judaism or renders it obsolete. For when Paul refers to Christ as "the end of the law" in Rom 10:4, the wider letter suggests he means Christ brings the law to its fulfillment (cf. Rom 13:8–10) or restores torah's intended purpose by breaking sin's hold over it. Nothing about Romans supports an idea that Christ terminates or invalidates the Jewish law. Additionally, Paul uses the image of grafting to characterize gentiles in the church as vitally connected to and sustained by their Jewish spiritual kin. Paul calls gentile believers "wild olive shoots" who have been grafted "to share the rich root" of Israel's history, which exists like a cultivated olive tree. Paul understands that history as an ongoing demonstration of God's longstanding graciousness and God's commitment to bring promises to their fulfillment. Branches need a root; therefore, the church's existence and confidence cannot survive separately from Israel's history and apart from God's ongoing commitment to the promises God has made to the Jewish people. Sharing in that root does not imply that a gentile church somehow *appropriates* Israel's rich heritage or God's unique calling. In an essential way made possible through Christ, gentiles *participate* in the adoption and promises God first declared to the ancient Israelites and their descendants.

It seems proper for Paul to end his winding and occasionally anguished discussion with a doxology in the final four verses of Romans 11. Just prior to the doxology Paul confesses that Israel's "hardening" constitutes a "mystery," meaning that it makes no sense on the outside but will finally become transparent when God's purposes are realized. Paul's final statement of trust in God paired with an expression of humble wonder concerning God's mysterious ways makes for a fitting last word to Paul's attempt to wrestle a difficult theological question.

Life in Christ (Rom 12:1–15:13)

Nearly all of Romans 1–11 focuses on God's activity, for it lays out ways in which "the righteousness of God" becomes effective, known, and utterly reliable through Christ. Beginning in Romans 12, Paul turns attention toward how believers should live in response to what God has done. The chapter's opening appeal calls for a commitment of one's whole self—treating one's whole person as "a living sacrifice" to God. Such a way of life constitutes freely given "worship," not obligation or adherence to ethical principles and religious duties. Indeed, Paul calls such a self-sacrificial life "reasonable" (which is a better translation of the Greek word *logikos* than "spiritual" in Rom 12:2)—meaning that such an outlook on life is the obvious, fitting response to God's initiative and goodness.

Paul's specific encouragements revolve around, first, behavior that enriches Christian community: love, cooperation, and a willingness to forgo retribution in reaction to wrongs suffered. He next commends a willingness to seek harmonious existence with governing officials by respecting their authority and paying taxes. When Paul refers to those authorities as people appointed by God, he lends to governments and even despots a theological legitimacy that strikes many modern people as dangerous. Debates about this passage need to consider that

Paul's perspective is not unique, for it aligns with the teachings of other ancient Jewish authors. Also, it makes sense that Paul would appreciate some aspects of the Roman state's muscle since his ability to prosper and travel safely depended on the stability the empire provided. On the other hand, and lending irony to the passage, Paul himself would, in his martyrdom, eventually suffer the empire's brutality and intolerance.

Perhaps, in his comments about respecting those who govern, Paul has in mind ways in which the Roman churches could have attracted negative attention from local officials, such as the incidents that led Claudius to expel some of the city's population. It is also possible that Paul had a reputation for sparking social unrest in the places he ministered, and so with those words in Romans 13 he attempted to assuage any anxieties his audience might have had about him and his motives for a future visit to their city. When he follows this passage with instructions about living with a sense of apocalyptic struggle and readiness (Rom 13:11–14), Paul reminds his audience that they have more pressing matters requiring their attention, given that they live in expectation of the imminent dawning of God's new day. Protesting tax burdens, which was a regular occurrence in some Roman neighborhoods, or engaging in behaviors that would prove socially disruptive and would attract unwanted opposition from authorities, might prove distracting from the efforts Paul thought were more vital for Christ-followers as they awaited what God would soon do next.

The longest discussion in this section of the letter instructs the Roman believers not to pass judgment on one another over dietary preferences. Paul evidences his desire to promote unity among the Roman churches and perhaps also his worry that harmful divisions could have already formed among his audience. He does not say whether the dividing lines about diet have caused distinctions between Jews and gentiles or between the rich and the poor. Whoever might have composed the specific groups he has in mind, Paul refers to those with dietary scruples as "the weak" and sets them in contrast to people whose consciences do not interfere with their food choices. His concern speaks to this particular issue's potential seriousness. Divisions over diets could have inhibited the intimacy of table fellowship among Christ-followers, or they might have led to one group holding the other in contempt or impeaching the spiritual commitment of another. At the heart of the issue is the overriding need for members of a community to support one another, even if it means surrendering one's personal prerogatives. Paul therefore calls on "the strong"—a group with which he associates himself—to forgo their freedom for the sake of their neighbors' conscience (cf. 1 Cor 8:1–11:1). Although he believes no food is unclean in and of itself, he still does not tell the scrupulous eaters to get over their inhibitions. He commends unity, empathetic forbearance, love, and a sense of mutual accountability at the expense of personal freedom, for both groups live as God's servants.

In the end, Paul characterizes unity as more than kindness or what makes for an orderly community. Unity expresses the gospel of Jesus Christ. The discussion of dietary scruples opens with a summons to all the Roman churches to "welcome" one another, and it ends in Rom 15:7–13 with another call to welcome, precisely because "Christ has welcomed you, for the glory of God." Unity therefore models the example of Christ, who committed himself and sacrificed his comfort for the sake of benefiting others. As a result, gentiles and Jews share fellowship in every way because of Christ, just as together they share fully in God's salvation (e.g., Rom 1:16, 10:12). Paul thereby implies that every other arrangement of groups that could emerge within Christian communities, including his "weak" and "strong" people, must recognize that same essential unity and share the same high regard for their neighbors in faith.

Paul's Plans for Mission and Travel (Rom 15:14–33)

As Paul begins to bring the letter toward its close, he briefly alludes to some of his purposes for writing and mentions his future plans. Paul's statements about his anticipated travels imply that he is eager to motivate the saints in Rome to support his efforts to preach the gospel someday in Spain.

Paul probably never realized his desire to travel to Spain. Even his arrival in Rome likely did not occur as he expected, if Acts correctly describes his actual journey to Rome as a prisoner in military custody. Other Christian writings tell of Paul's execution in Rome during the reign of Nero, who ruled 54–68 CE. But Paul does not foresee such an end to his life when he addresses the Romans and seeks their support for ongoing mission. More immediately, Paul solicits the Romans' prayers for his imminent journey to Jerusalem "in a ministry to the saints." This involves delivering a financial gift he has collected by soliciting offerings from other churches, a project he describes more extensively in 2 Corinthians 8–9 (cf. 1 Cor 16:1–4).

Exactly why Paul asks for his audience's prayers concerning his trip to Jerusalem remains unclear. Apparently he knew about opposition to him and his ministry from "unbelievers in Judea," and the narrative of Acts suggests he had good reason to be concerned about the possibility of suffering slander and rejection (e.g., Acts 21:17–23:15). By expressing to the Romans his desire that the church in Jerusalem receive his support favorably, Paul possibly betrays a concern about his relationship with the Jerusalem church. The tensions on display in Galatians may have intensified into animosity toward Paul by the time he wrote Romans (e.g., Gal 2:1–14). Paul may have developed a reputation for preaching a message that was antitorah, a reputation that his argument in Romans could combat (e.g., Rom 7:7–25; cf. Acts 21:20–22). It would have been the kind of reputation that could turn the Jerusalem church against him entirely. In any case, Paul informs the Romans of his plans and his uneasiness about going to Jerusalem. By being forthright in the letter, Paul seizes an opportunity to strike a sympathetic pose in his audience's eyes, which might help him retain the Romans' support if somehow the Jerusalem church were to discredit him by rejecting him and his offering. No sources tell whether Paul's gift to the financially strapped Jerusalem church was successfully received or welcomed. All that one can know for sure is that the prospect of delivering the gift evoked cause for concern in Paul.

Greetings, Closing Exhortations, and Benediction (Rom 16)

Unique among Paul's letters in this regard, Romans closes with a rather long list of greetings Paul extends to twenty-six specific people. He identifies some of them as Jews. Presumably others of them were gentiles. Judging from comparative studies of ancient materials, the majority of names on Paul's list would have been recognized as appropriate for slaves or freed slaves. The list therefore suggests that these individuals in the letter's audience belonged to one of those categories or were descendants of freed slaves. Paul also mentions a couple of full families, which could indicate that some of the audience consisted of people with greater economic and social status. For Paul to know so many people in congregations he had not visited speaks to the relative ease of emigration and intercontinental commerce in Paul's day and perhaps also to the extent of the apostle's personal networks. The length of the list and its references to some of Paul's coworkers strengthens the letter's ability to introduce Paul to other believers whom he had never met in person. The list demonstrates the connections that already existed between Paul and the Roman saints, and it identifies certain individuals in Rome who might have vouched for Paul's credibility.

Although nothing else is known about almost everyone Paul names, still the list provides important evidence about aspects of life in these early Christian communities. Most noteworthy are the women Paul identifies. The first on the list, Phoebe, is actually an outsider to the Roman churches, for she delivered this letter to Rome for Paul. Paul commends her to his audience and also refers to her as a deacon and a benefactor. What Paul means by "deacon" is not entirely clear, but the term's appearance in other letters obviously indicates public and influential contributions to the work of Christian ministry. Even if Phoebe did not hold a specific office called "deacon" in her church in Cenchreae (a city near Corinth), Paul uses the same term in other literary settings to describe himself and other associates as public and influential "ministers" or "servants" of the gospel (e.g., 1 Cor 3:5; 2 Cor 3:6, 6:4, 11:23; cf. Phil 1:1; 1 Tim 3:8–13). Paul clearly trusted Phoebe and her abilities, for he charged her both to bring the letter to Rome and probably also to answer any questions the Romans might have had about what Paul wrote.

Paul greets Priscilla, calling her by the shortened name *Prisca*, along with her husband, Aquila. Paul speaks approvingly of this couple and their work also in 1 Cor 16:19 (cf. Acts 18:1–3, 18, 24–26). They hosted a church in their house, as they did also in Corinth, and had offered vital support to Paul. Paul also greets someone named Mary, "who has worked very hard among" the Romans, along with several other women: the mother of Rufus, Julia, and the sister of Nereus. He singles out Tryphaena, Tryphosa, Persis, and people who work diligently "in the Lord." Precisely what kind of work they performed remains undescribed, but Paul recognizes their valuable contributions to the Roman churches' ability to thrive as communities of faith. Additionally, Paul mentions a woman named Junia alongside a man called Andronicus and refers to both of them as "apostles," the same distinguished title with which Paul introduces himself in Rom 1:1.

The Letter's Themes and Theological Emphases

Romans has been the source of interpretive debates probably since the letter was first read aloud to congregations in Rome. It is a richly theological document, with much to say about the nature of God and the character of the Christian gospel. Some of the letter's more notable themes are not exclusive to Romans but appear also in other letters Paul wrote. Explorations of those books will, therefore, also enhance one's understanding of Romans.

Justification and Faith

Some of the liveliest conversations that have arisen from analyses of Paul's letters, especially Romans and Galatians, address the questions of what Paul means by "justification" and what it means to say that justification depends on "faith." The conversations must take account of a number of factors, including the ways in which Paul's thinking reflects the influence of theological currents fed by a Jewish apocalyptic worldview, Paul's manner of interpreting Scripture, and Paul and his Jewish contemporaries' understanding of God's gracious election of Jews as descendants of Abraham and inheritors of God's promises. Only a brief overview of some basic aspects of the relevant terms and theology can be provided here.

As mentioned, a single Greek noun can be translated as, among other things, both "righteousness" and "justification." Most English translations of the Bible make their choice between those two options depending on how translators interpret a sentence's wider context. Those who read Romans in English understand the letter better when they keep in mind the fact that Paul's discussions of God's righteousness share a close semantic connection to Paul's notion of the justification God renders to humanity. The contextual nuances that distinguish those two ideas differ only slightly.

The Greek word that is translated as both "righteousness" and "justification" (*dikaiosunē* and cognates) appears relatively frequently in the Septuagint with reference to God and God's activity on behalf of people and all creation. Undoubtedly Paul understands God's righteousness based in large part on how those scriptural texts present it. The word has a wide and rich semantic range when used to describe God in those contexts. Just a few examples of the word's use in the Septuagint convey a basic sense of the range. The following examples help illustrate the backdrop for what Paul means by "righteousness." Together, the examples characterize the word by providing a sampling of its connections to certain divine activities and their consequences. For simplicity's sake, the examples reproduce translations from the NRSV, which itself translates from the Hebrew texts from which the Septuagint was derived. These particular translations nevertheless capture well the wider context of the passages, since both the original Hebrew version and the later Greek translations of these verses speak of divine "righteousness." The words in italics represent translations of the biblical term in question:

> I will declare to you all the *saving deeds* of the Lord that he performed for you and for your ancestors. (1 Sam 12:7b)

> In you, O Lord, I seek refuge; do not let me ever be put to shame; in your *righteousness* deliver me. (Ps 31:1, which corresponds to Ps 30:2 in the Septuagint's rendering)

> Your *righteousness* is like the mighty mountains, your judgments are like the great deep; you save humans and animals alike, O Lord. (Ps 36:6, which corresponds to Ps 35:7 in the Septuagint's rendering)

> The effect of *righteousness* will be peace, and the result of *righteousness*, quietness and trust forever. (Isa 32:17)

> I bring near my *deliverance*, it is not far off, and my salvation will not tarry; I will put salvation in Zion, for Israel my glory. (Isa 46:13)

> Thus says the Lord: Maintain justice, and do *what is right*, for soon my salvation will come. (Isa 56:1a)

The examples ascribe an active quality to God's righteousness. In other words, to speak of God's "righteousness," "saving deeds," or "deliverance" is to describe God's activity and power more than to define God's attributes or moral excellence. The references to righteousness provide a sketch of the kinds of actions God performs that provide salvation and therefore also a sketch of what salvation consists of: refuge, exaltation, rescue, peace, security, deliverance, judgment, justice, vindication, and comfort. When Paul therefore summarizes the gospel of Jesus Christ as the revealing of God's righteousness (Rom 1:17, 3:21), he characterizes the gospel as an instance, the fullest instance, of God's power to save, claim, protect, and renew. "The righteousness of God" stands for the complete expression of God's commitment and power to accomplish salvation from the power of sin and death and to preserve those whom God saves.

When God reveals God's righteousness and thus justifies people, God therefore does more than change people's status by pronouncing them not guilty or repairing their relationship to God. Paul writes, rather, as if justified people come to share fully in God's saving activity. To be justified is to be brought into a new space, so to speak, into the sphere in which God's salvific and active righteousness holds sway and remains at work to reclaim the world. Believers belong to this divine effort of righteousness as if they are its slaves (Rom 6:18). In another letter Paul says that believers live so fully in God's security that they "become the righteousness of God" (2 Cor 5:21).

Justification is only one of the terms Paul uses to describe what God does to break the reign of sin and death. In Romans Paul speaks also about redemption (Rom 3:24, 8:23), a transfer of slavery from living under sin and the law to becoming God's own slaves. Reconciliation (Rom 5:10) and purification (Rom 3:25) also each make an appearance. Additional letters mention, among other things, a new creation coming into being (2 Cor 5:17, Gal 6:15) and a future experience of divine glory (e.g., Rom 5:1–2, 8:17–18; 2 Cor 3:18; Phil 3:21). The various themes of salvation all speak about God establishing something new. In addition, Paul sets statements about God's salvation in contradistinction to sin's power. He frames God's activity as a victory in a battle against forces that oppress creation (e.g., Rom 5:18–21; 6:6, 14; 8:1–3). Animated by a basic worldview that pictures God in conflict with opposing forces, yet certain to win battles against those rival powers, Paul's theology employs themes also seen in Jewish apocalyptic writings. Accordingly, he characterizes the righteousness revealed in the gospel as a transformative demonstration of God's fidelity to all creation. In the gospel of Jesus Christ, God asserts and actualizes God's indomitable commitment to bring about an ultimate, complete state of affairs in which God stands victorious.

Paul connects faith to God's righteousness and to humanity's justification, as seen in his repeated efforts to distinguish the power of faith from the power of the law. Faith, not the law, accomplishes justification. The connection also comes to light in Paul's reliance on the scriptural story of Abraham believing God. Paul takes Gen 15:6, as a piece of God's election of Abraham, as a prototypical expression of God's determination to have faith be the vehicle or power by which God's promise to bless the world will prove effective.

Paul's references to Abraham's faith lead interpreters to consider the question of what faith is. When Abraham believed God, it was more than his cognitive assent to what God had told him. It involved a lived obedience on Abraham's part, committing himself existentially to God's reliability and the promise of blessing to come (e.g., Gen 12:1–9, 15:1–21). Similarly, Jesus committed himself to an act of obedience (Rom 5:19). Faith, for Paul, involves obedience (Rom 1:5) and trust because faith entails a sharing in Christ's own life and Christ's commitment to be the means of revealing God's righteousness. The Greek word translated "faith" also means "faithfulness," a word that perhaps better captures Paul's sense of a person's experience of coexisting with Christ and relying on God.

Christ's own faith, or faithfulness, therefore occupies an important place in Paul's theology (see also Phil 2:5–8), for Christ was one who actively dedicated himself, even his whole existence, to the realization of God's righteousness. Paul's grammar subtly expresses the notion of Jesus' commitment to God's intentions, when Paul occasionally speaks of Christ and faith side by side. As the footnotes in many recent English translations of the Bible indicate, the Greek expression Paul uses behind the translation "faith in Jesus Christ" (e.g., Rom 3:22) could also be rendered "the faith(fulness) of Jesus Christ." This indicates, in the wider context of Rom 3:21–22, for example, that Jesus himself initiated the revelation of God's righteousness precisely through his death. The alternate translation "the faithfulness of Jesus Christ" makes sense in this setting according to what the Greek grammar allows, what the context of Paul's larger sentence indicates, and what Paul's wider theological argument contends. Speaking of Christ's own faithful commitment to God's purposes allows Paul to characterize the gospel, first and foremost, in terms of what God has done to address humanity's captivity to sin. Jesus Christ, in his death, obediently and faithfully surrendered himself to play his critical role in God's determination to reclaim the world. By trusting God in this way, Jesus Christ also made a statement about God's trustworthiness to deliver humanity. A key piece of God's own character—namely, God's reliable commitment to act on humanity's behalf—is therefore the ground of all faith.

This understanding of Christ's faith does not rule out the importance of believers' faith. They are, after all, rightly called "believers" or "those who believe." To return to the example of Rom 3:22, Paul speaks in the same sentence both about the decisive reality of Christ's faithfulness and about God's righteousness being for the benefit of "all who believe." Paul makes a similar statement in Gal 2:16, where he declares justification occurs through "the faith[fulness] of Jesus Christ" and then immediately notes that "we have come to believe in Christ Jesus" (cf. Phil 3:9). The point Paul pursues in those passages is that believers, who participate in Christ's faithful act that brings them to share in God's righteousness, come to possess the resolute faithfulness that Jesus, like Abraham, first exemplified. Just as believers become coparticipants in Christ's sufferings, death, resurrection, inheritance, and glorification, so also they participate with Jesus' faithful embrace of God's righteousness. Believers become like Jesus Christ in every way, thanks to faith.

The Holy Spirit

Paul's relentless focus on Jesus' death and resurrection as the centerpiece of the good news sometimes makes it easy to overlook the large amount of attention his letters, particularly Romans, devote to the Holy Spirit. The presence of the Holy Spirit provides utter confidence in the effectiveness of God's actions through Jesus Christ, according to Paul. The Spirit serves as the hallmark of believers' new identity and existence (Rom 7:6). The gift of the Holy Spirit guarantees a future resurrection (Rom 8:11). Because the same Spirit indwells gentiles and Jews, Paul insists that both groups, together, constitute the children of God (Rom 8:14–16, Gal 4:6–7). The Holy Spirit is the source of power for believers (Rom 15:13), enabling them to live in ways that express their newfound freedom from sin and their joyful servitude to God and to one another. In other letters, most notably 1 Corinthians 12–14, Paul describes the Holy Spirit as the source of gifts given to believers to allow them to bear witness in diverse ways to the essential unity they share in Christ (cf. Rom 12:3–8).

As Paul presents the subject, then, the sheer reality of the Holy Spirit at the heart of the church's identity and experience indicates the fulfillment of God's promises and the arrival of a new existence. Likewise, in other writings Paul connects the Holy Spirit to the promise God made to Abraham to bless all the nations of the earth (Gal 3:14) and speaks of the gospel as inaugurating God's "new creation" (2 Cor 5:17, Gal 6:15). Paul recognizes that sin persists as a destructive force and death remains a reality in the present, so the Spirit actually indicates the *emergence* of a new and certain future and not the complete and final realization of that future.

The Spirit remains, nevertheless, a reliable pledge for believers as they await the fullness of God's purposes to arrive: the Spirit bears to believers the "first fruits" of God's bountiful harvest (Rom 8:23; cf. 2 Cor 1:21–22; 5:5). Moreover, through the Holy Spirit, God remains present in God's people. Not only have the benefits of God's righteousness—that is, believers' justification—become real within human existence, but God remains among believers too. When Paul describes the Spirit interceding for Christ-followers with inaudible groans as they await God's full redemption (Rom 8:26–27), he implies that God knows well the struggles that inflict all of creation. In addition, Paul's metaphorical language about creation's labor pains (Rom 8:22), which creation suffers alongside a groaning Deity, implies that God also expresses intense longing for completion, deliverance, and new opportunities for the whole cosmos. Through the Holy Spirit, therefore, God continues to experience in God's own person the realities of a frail yet expectant world.

Women Leaders in the Roman Churches

When Paul praises Phoebe as a "deacon," Priscilla as his coworker and the cohost of a house church, Junia as an "apostle," and other women who perform valuable work on the Lord's behalf, he opens a door ever so slightly for interpreters to observe the leadership roles some female Christ-followers performed in Rome and elsewhere during the first decades of the Christian church's existence. Throughout much of church history, however, the evidence from Romans 16 has been ignored or disparaged, treated as if Paul could not really have thought those women were fulfilling the same kinds of roles as their male counterparts. Junia the apostle, for example, was long overlooked. Most interpreters casually assumed Paul really refers to a man, someone named Junias, which reliable Greek manuscripts of Romans now make clear was not the case. Paul's mention of Junia, a woman's name, offers an important example of Paul's willingness to credit female saints for performing vital and visible work of ministry. While the common Greek term *apostolos* was widely used to designate any kind of an envoy, in Paul's writings it refers particularly to people who minister on Christ's behalf, people whom Jesus directly commissioned to do so. Therefore Paul regards himself as an apostle just as much as Jesus' original handpicked disciples were (1 Cor 9:1, 5; 12:28; 15:7–9; 2 Cor 8:23; Gal 1:1, 17). Most likely, then, Junia was one of Jesus' earliest followers and someone who encountered the resurrected Christ, for Paul refers to a large number of such people in 1 Cor 15:6. All the other people called "apostles" in the New Testament engage in very public and occasionally risky acts of ministry, for they are people who proclaim the word of God, teach, organize communities of faith, and provide a bedrock for the churches' ability to bear testimony to Jesus and his resurrection (1 Cor 12:28; cf. Acts 10:39–42). Even though nothing else about Junia is known, Paul defined her for posterity as someone "prominent" among this distinguished group of pillars in the early churches. Whatever specific work she did and whatever practical authority belonged to her would appear to be no less, and no less valuable, than any other apostle's.

When Paul greets Junia alongside Phoebe, Priscilla, and others, Romans therefore provides important evidence to demonstrate that women contributed in significant and various ways to the public and recognized leadership of first-century churches and their ministry. Paul expresses no embarrassment in referring to certain women as coworkers and even one as an apostle. The absence of any defensiveness on Paul's part suggests he did not consider those women and their contributions as unusual or scandalous. Their names and Paul's affirmations remain important to note, for the letters Paul certainly wrote rarely say much about women even in a general or abstract sense. He usually fails to single out women for special attention. Occasionally he raises the question of whether there are distinctions that affect how men and women operate with each other "in Christ" (e.g., 1 Cor 11:2–16; Gal 3:28). In Romans, however, Paul provides brief yet very clear evidence of his attitudes toward—and gratitude for—the contributions of a handful of specific, individual women who served God by providing leadership within Christian communities.

Other New Testament writings, such as the Pastoral Letters, indicate that, within just a few decades after Paul's letter went to Rome, women in churches found themselves deprived of opportunities to serve in those kinds of public leadership roles. That development appears to represent a decisive departure from how Christian churches organized themselves in their earlier generations, however.

Christian Living, Unity, and Dietary Scruples

Paul's instructions in Rom 14:1–15:13 about "strong" and "weak" believers give interpreters a good opportunity to examine Paul's views on what Christian living and unity should look like in practice. For Paul, theological foundations nearly always provide the principles that shape his vision of how Christ-followers ought to live. In this specific case, wherein he discusses dietary scruples and charitable community, Paul's practiced instructions proceed from a theological conviction that believers do not belong to themselves but to the Lord Jesus (Rom 14:7–9; cf. 7:4; 14:4; 1 Cor 6:15–20; 2 Cor 13:5). Believers' existence in Christ has a mutual or corporate character, meaning that they share an organic connection to one another as well (Rom 12:4–5). Because of those principal theological realities, Paul goes on to speak about dietary choices and mutual forbearance as he does.

Paul's concerns about divisions erupting over dietary practices may appear quaint to modern people who have become familiar with gluten-free and vegan options on menus alongside steaks and pork chops, but many cultural factors made the first-century experience different. The issue, as Paul understood it, extended far beyond matters of taste or choice. Shared meals and hospitality carried greater significance for ancient communities in Rome than they typically do today. Questions of legal propriety also might have weighed heavily on a person's conscience: if one has lived for decades believing that certain foods defile a person before God, that conviction does not go away easily just because Paul teaches that "nothing is unclean in itself" (Rom 14:14; cf. Mark 7:18–20). Additionally, the vast majority of meat available for purchase in Rome, for those who could afford to be picky about where to buy their food, or who could afford meat at all, would have come from animals that were involved in some kind of religious sacrifice. Although in Romans Paul does not explicitly call attention to meat sacrificed to other gods, or "idols," as he does in a similar conversation in 1 Corinthians 8 (see also 1 Cor 10:23–11:1), still the same dynamics could have been an issue for some believers in Rome, where public festivals, professional gatherings, and dinner parties commonly involved religious honors given to a particular deity. For certain Christ-followers, eating food associated with the worship of other supposed gods might have resembled the idolatry Paul denounces elsewhere in the letter (e.g., Rom 1:20–23; cf. Rev 2:14, 20).

Paul therefore recognizes that participating in those kinds of events or eating meat would strike some Christ-followers in Rome as returning to the lifestyles or identities they sought to leave behind, while others in the congregations would experience no compunction. The issue, therefore, might have had great potential to cause resentments and divisions. Paul addresses the matter out of a desire to steer the Romans away from denying their fundamental corporate identity as siblings in Christ. To do so, he guides his audience toward a theological understanding of unity and how to pursue it in their life together.

As Paul instructs the Romans, he gives great weight to an individual's conscience. Ethical absolutes do not solve the problem as Paul describes it; rather, a person's motivation and desire to please God take center stage in Paul's discussion (Rom 14:4, 10, 14, 22–23). At the same time, accountability to God (Rom 14:12) and to one another (Rom 14:13, 15, 19–21; cf. Gal 5:13–14) always have to direct and sometimes constrain an individual's freedom, because causing another person to violate his or her conscience and thus to sin violates a believer's core identity as someone who now exists as a member of a fellowship that coexists with Christ himself. Paul therefore tells the strong, those whom he considers more spiritually mature, to avoid meat in settings where eating meat would offend or damage the more immature, or weak, believers. For if the strong insist on following their freedom at the expense of the weak, they fail to love (Rom 14:15; cf. 1 Cor 8:12).

The love among believers expresses their unity. Unity repeatedly emerges as one of Paul's primary emphases when his letters describe the Christian life. For Paul, the importance of the church's unity does not derive from a sense of mutual tolerance as a cardinal virtue. Rather, through its unified existence, rooted in love, the Christian church declares its theology. A unified church makes manifest the unity Paul sees at the heart of the gospel. The gospel itself is a declaration of newfound unity, for through Christ God has brought gentiles to share fully with Jews in the promises God first gave to Abraham's physical descendants (cf. Rom 15:7–13). Paul's letters recognize that unity rarely comes easily. Perhaps, then, it should come as little surprise to modern Christians that churches even today find it challenging to figure out how to embrace and to model in concrete ways their identity as communities of mutual welcome. Paul would perhaps tell them to remember Jesus, who himself first welcomed all (Rom 15:7).

4

The First Letter of Paul to the Corinthians

In 1 Corinthians, Paul urges a young Christian community to recognize that no one can be united to Christ without also being united to other believers. The unity Paul has in mind exceeds casual expressions of affinity and an appreciation for a group's shared interests; Paul describes a solidarity so comprehensive that it is existential. The church's members exist as a corporate, living being because each of them has been united to Christ in his death and resurrection. The church's identity as a community fully integrated with Christ cannot help but influence how Christ-followers should live.

When read on the heels of Romans, 1 Corinthians shows noticeably different dimensions of Paul's theological perspective. While Romans devotes considerable attention to God's "righteousness" and God's commitment to bring about the "justification" of "the ungodly," 1 Corinthians mostly refrains from those themes and terms (e.g., 1 Cor 1:30, 6:11). Instead, in this letter Paul focuses on the newness God has brought into being through Jesus' death and resurrection. Those pivotal events have inaugurated a new age and therefore a new existence: a former era has come to an end (e.g., 1 Cor 10:11), and God's final victory over death is awaiting its full and certain consummation (e.g., 1 Cor 15:20–28). The momentous, even world-altering, events of cross and resurrection provide the theological basis for Paul's earnest appeals for unity among the Corinthians. The cosmic newness God has set into motion demands new ways of living and new ways of understanding one's relationships with fellow believers. Paul therefore composed this letter to communicate his vision for how the church rightly lives during this pivotal moment in history, in light of the new age God has begun to reveal.

First Corinthians addresses a variety of issues that relate to how the Corinthian Christ-followers should understand themselves as a community and how they should conduct themselves in both public and private settings. The sheer number of different issues Paul treats does not indicate that Paul's purposes for the letter were disjointed. Rather, the letter covers a diversity of specific subjects for one simple reason: Paul knew the Corinthians well. First Corinthians is not Paul's letter of introduction to this church. They likewise already knew him well. He sent the document to the Corinthians in response to a letter they had sent him, in which they apparently named a number of issues, either to seek Paul's opinions or to explain their motives for acting in certain ways. In 1 Corinthians he offers his reply, sometimes treating the issues one at a time. The letter provides insight into what was a much more complicated and extensive relationship Paul shared with the Christian community in Corinth.

With both letters and visits, Paul conducted extended conversations with the Corinthian believers. In 1 Cor 5:9 he refers to a letter he had written to them previously, and in 1 Cor 7:1 he explicitly begins to address the topics named in the correspondence they had written to him. No copies of either of those documents have survived. In 2 Corinthians, Paul refers to yet another letter he wrote to the church (2 Cor 1:23–2:4; 7:8). The amount of letters, as well as the contents and moods of Paul's surviving letters, testifies to a longstanding and occasionally boisterous relationship between the apostle and the church he founded with the help of others, according to 1 Cor 2:1–5 and 3:1–6 (as well as Acts 18:1–18). The letters that were preserved and eventually found their way into the New Testament suggest that Paul considered the Corinthians in need of his ongoing guidance if they were going to express their new Christian faith in authentic and apt ways. Taken together, 1 Corinthians and 2 Corinthians reveal that Paul and the Corinthians' relationship changed over time, exhibiting frustration as well as approval, opposition as well as commitment, and solidarity as well as rivalry. The letters offer reminders that Paul frequently had to contend for his views about the gospel and the nature of Christian identity, as well as reminders that internal strife and disagreements about the appropriate contours of Christian living have characterized Christian communities for a long time.

The Letter's Origins and Ancient Audience

Corinth sat on an isthmus connecting Greece's southern and northern landmasses. The city had access to two major seaports. Two miles to its north, providing access to the Ionian Sea, sat the city of Lechaeum. Four miles east of Corinth, Cenchreae overlooked a gulf that touched the Aegean Sea. Wide-ranging travel, culture, and trade flowed in and out of Corinth, as if the city were situated in the neck of an hourglass. Like many Roman-controlled population centers near seas and over-land trade routes, Corinth's geography and reputation for commerce, shipping, and industry attracted people from many cultures and back-grounds. Part of Corinth's enduring honor came from its role as a host of the Isthmian Games, a major collection of athletic contests held every other year. When the letter uses athletic imagery in 1 Cor 9:24–27, Paul may be acknowledging those games, which were a key element of the Corinthians' cultural identity.

Long before Paul arrived there, the city had acquired a reputation for wildness and excess, as confirmed when the playwright Aristo-phanes (ca. 400 BCE) coined the verb *corinthianize* to describe a per-son's descent into materialism and depravity. By the time Paul wrote 1 Corinthians, however, the city's ethos and morals were no more exces-sive or noteworthy than any other urban center in the Roman Empire.

According to Acts 18:11–12, Paul spent eighteen months in this cosmopolitan environment, and his stay overlapped with the time when a Roman proconsul named Gallio was in office. If those details are accurate, they would locate Paul's arrival in Corinth in the year 50 CE, since Gallio served only a very short time in the region. It is more dif-ficult to affix a firm date to the writing of 1 Corinthians, but the letter itself suggests it was composed not long after Paul left Corinth, proba-bly between 53 and 54 CE, which probably makes it the second of Paul's surviving letters, following 1 Thessalonians.

Along with a coauthor named Sosthenes (1 Cor 1:1; cf. Acts 18:17), Paul wrote the letter from Ephesus (1 Cor 16:8). Despite his physical separation from the Corinthians, still Paul maintained connections with the church there before he composed 1 Corinthians. In addition to the previous letters from him to them (1 Cor 5:9) and from them to him (1 Cor 7:1), Paul had sent his trusted coworker Timothy to instruct the Corinthians face-to-face (1 Cor 4:17; cf. 16:10–11). In addition, Paul received information about the Corinthian church from "Chloe's people," perhaps slaves, business associates, or family members of an otherwise unknown woman who might have been a prominent member of the church. Paul also refers to a trio of people who might have been a delegation sent to him from Corinth (1 Cor 16:17–18). In sum, it is reasonable to assume that Chloe's people, the delegation, or both delivered to Paul the letter that he mentions in 1 Cor 7:1. All of those details about correspondence, travels, and reports do not have a major effect on interpreting the letter, but they nevertheless underscore the fact that Paul maintained close connections with the Christ-followers in Corinth. The details also suggest that either Paul or the Corinthians or both parties had a strong interest in having Paul continue to serve as a key leader and adviser to the church, even as he resided very far away when he wrote.

First Corinthians offers no real data on which to base a reliable estimate of the size of the Corinthian church. When Paul addresses the letter to "the church of God that is in Corinth," he probably does not mean a single house church, since the rest of the letter speaks so frequently about divisions and factions in the church and about the wide variety of spiritual gifts on display when this church gathers for worship. The singular "church" in the salutation reaffirms the notion of Christian unity that constitutes one of the letter's central themes; *the* single church in Corinth comprises the multiple subcommunities of Christ-followers that might have existed there and occasionally assembled in larger groups (e.g., 1 Cor 11:18, 14:26), although there is no reason to suspect there was a notably large number of these house churches.

The overall community to whom Paul wrote appears to have consisted mostly of gentiles who had no meaningful connections to Judaism prior to when they first heard the gospel (1 Cor 12:2). Some of the audience members, however, could have been Jewish or somehow affiliated with Judaism, based on a reference to circumcised men among them (1 Cor 7:18). The letter's addressees spanned a modest range of social classes, including slaves (e.g., 1 Cor 7:21–24), poor laborers (e.g., 1 Cor 11:22), and a few who enjoyed much more social capital (e.g., 1 Cor 1:26; 11:21–22). Paul offers general instructions in the letter, directed toward the Corinthian church at large, as well as occasional comments aimed exclusively at groups of men (e.g., 1 Cor 7:18, 36–38) and women (e.g., 1 Cor 7:8–9, 25–28, 39–40; 11:2–16).

Paul addresses the young church as a community that exhibits a lively spirituality yet suffers from divisions and internal competitiveness. Exemplifying the immaturity and misunderstandings that Paul repeatedly criticizes, some members of the Corinthian church identified with certain leaders or schools of thought to the exclusion of others (1 Cor 1:11–12). Paul detects a dangerous smugness in their factionalism. His letter aims to reorient their understanding and behavior, not because their attitudes and rivalries equate to rudeness, but because such conceit and presumption ultimately contradict "the message about the cross," the good news declared and actualized by Jesus' death and resurrection.

Overview

Paul and Sosthenes' letter addresses a variety of subjects that pertain to the Corinthians' conduct. The catalog of topics owes itself in part to what the Corinthians have written to Paul (1 Cor 7:1; cf. 7:25; 8:1; 12:1; 16:1, 12); perhaps their previous letter to him posed direct questions or advocated for certain positions on specific points of controversy. Because 1 Corinthians moves swiftly from issue to issue, it strikes some readers as a jumble in comparison to a crisper letter like Romans, with its more sustained theological progression. Yet 1 Corinthians is hardly without its organizing themes. Certain theological convictions hold the letter together, as Paul kicks off his correspondence with a foundational call for unity in the church (1 Cor 1:10) and follows up on that appeal by frequently reminding his audience that the gospel affects all dimensions of their corporate lives, for all aspects of their existence participate in what God makes possible through Jesus Christ's dying and rising.

Salutation and Thanksgiving (1 Cor 1:1–9)

Even though Paul does not explicitly state his concern about the divisions afflicting the Corinthian church until 1 Cor 1:10, the very beginning of the letter underscores the unity that all believers share in Christ. Paul refers to the Corinthians as "saints," people whom God has designated as holy, or set apart for God's purposes. They possess that identity through their corporate existence, for they share it "with all those who in every place call on the name of our Lord Jesus Christ." When Paul turns to give thanks to God, he also commends the Corinthians' rich array of spiritual gifts. He tells them they are a community fully equipped to grow stronger and thrive as they await the approaching day of Jesus' "revealing" (his *apokalupsis*, in Greek).

Unity Derived from the Power of the Cross
(1 Cor 1:10–2:16)

Paul wastes no time before appealing directly to the Corinthians to "be in agreement," steer clear of "divisions," and "be united in the same mind and the same purpose." His exhortation expresses the letter's primary purpose as a summons to the Corinthians to understand who they are in Christ. As the letter continues, Paul will not describe a united community as a uniform community in which all members are interchangeable parts, everyone lives exactly the same way, or the church holds to a set of doctrines with absolute certitude. Rather, Paul calls the church to an integrated existence characterized by an ethos of unity and a sense of shared belonging. Throughout the letter, whether Paul addresses a specific issue that would probably contribute to schisms in Corinth or not, Paul consistently directs his efforts toward helping the Corinthians become more integrated among themselves in how they function as a community. He guides them toward integrating their eager—if not downright arrogant—embrace of their spiritual identity and spiritual gifts with their understanding of how to live in the present tense as Christ's people. Most foundationally, Paul speaks of the Corinthians' integration with Jesus himself as he characterizes the church as a community invariably marked and shaped by the Messiah's scandalous death and transformative resurrection.

Paul builds the letter's main theological foundations right away, for he devotes the rest of this section to a discussion of God's activity through Christ—a discussion launched when Paul expresses dismay over quarrels among the Corinthian Christ-followers. At least some people in the church had divided into factions based on allegiances to various teachers or schools of thought: Paul, one of Paul's associates named Apollos (1 Cor 16:12; cf. Acts 18:24–19:1), Cephas (the Aramaic equivalent of Peter), and simply Jesus himself. Paul will return to some of those divisions in 1 Corinthians 3–4, but for now he does not defend or refute anyone's doctrines but instead emphasizes Christ's indivisibility.

The gospel Paul preaches—a "message about the cross" and a proclamation of "Christ crucified"—contradicts the snobbery and jousting that Paul associates with the factions in Corinth. An expression of good news about a crucifixion constitutes a paradox of sorts: the gospel has salvific effects as a powerful divine act while at the same time it expresses itself in the guise of scandalous foolishness. A crucifixion offers no cause for pride. By every conventional metric, it makes Jesus and his followers losers and laughingstocks in the eyes of uninitiated observers. No Jew could be expected to see a crucified and therefore cursed and discredited man as God's promised Messiah. Further, no gentile in the Greco-Roman climate would be inclined to view as a savior a man who died in such a contemptible and shameful manner, branded as a threat to the Roman Empire. Everything about crucifixion appears to Jews and gentiles as incompatible with the notions of advancing either the work of God or the good order of the universe. Yet the gospel Paul preaches follows a different line of vision: Paul sees God's power at work in Jesus' experience of utter weakness.

Along with God's power, wisdom also operates in Jesus' crucifixion—not wisdom as information or intelligence, but wisdom as divine agency. Wisdom actively expresses and brings about God's intentions for the world's well-being (cf. Prov 8:22–31; Wis 7:22b–8:1, 9:9–11). The cross, however, manifests God's wisdom through an apparent expression of wanton foolishness—an ignominious execution. God's active wisdom confounds common Greco-Roman assumptions about how any god should act effectively, just as that divine wisdom runs counter to conventional assumptions about virtue, honor, success, and how to identify God's righteousness and holiness. Paul insists that both sides of a paradox therefore remain true: God's power shows itself at work through the crucifixion, although the presence of divine power in that event does not negate the ugly and painful realities of Jesus' death. The cross does not excuse anyone's subversive arrogance; instead, Jesus' execution always exposes and condemns human pretention. That manner of death, as an unexpected expression of God's power, leaves all of humanity, the people who scorned God's Messiah, with no basis for boasting in their values, traditions, progress, or cleverness. They can boast in nothing but God, for God alone proves to be the source of true life. Paul's implication is clear: no one can participate with a crucified Christ while simultaneously adopting a smug or self-satisfied outlook. For those who attempt to do so, the conduct contradicts the theology.

Even Paul's own preaching conforms to the odd and paradoxical dynamics of divine wisdom, for he first presented the gospel in Corinth with simplicity and fearfulness. Neither brilliant rhetoric nor an impressive presence allowed the gospel to take root there; rather, "a demonstration of the Spirit and of power" proved convincing. Paul does not describe what he means by that expression. The "demonstration" could refer to impressive signs and wonders Paul performed or to some kind of public religious experience. It could also be Paul's way of characterizing the gospel as something other than a message to be heard, understood, and deliberated. Perhaps something about Paul's own preaching about the cross summoned his audience into a mystical encounter with God (cf. Gal 3:1–5). Whatever the case, Paul roots the power of the gospel solely in *God's* ability to reveal God's wisdom. Human insight cannot discern such things. It is the Spirit, who knows "even the depths of God," who has "revealed" (1 Cor 2:10, using the Greek verb *apokaluptō*) God's truths and the new realities God has instituted. No teacher and no faction in any church can therefore claim credit for their perception or gifts, for those come from the Spirit of God.

Not Leaders, but Servants (1 Cor 3–4)

In this section of the letter, Paul returns to the question of divisions arising from people's affiliations with certain leaders. He criticizes the Corinthians for their spiritual immaturity as evidenced by their desire to identify with various factions over against others. The persistence of sectarian divides creates more than a disconnected community; it also implies competition and the creation of hierarchies since different groups might have claimed particular prerogatives for themselves. Paul therefore criticizes his audience for a lack of true spirituality and for their inauthentic spiritual understanding. Having received the Holy Spirit, they should be keenly aware of their dependence on God, yet Paul accuses them of having become self-satisfied, perhaps too enamored of their own knowledge, freedom, or spiritual potential.

Even Paul and Apollos, recognized leaders in Corinth elsewhere, have no basis to elevate themselves, for they understand themselves as God's servants, people who minister on God's behalf. God, not human agents, produces spiritual growth. The contributions of individual leaders have their value, but those efforts reveal themselves to be dross if they do not conform to Jesus Christ and the grace of God. Paul therefore holds himself up as an example to the boastful Corinthians; his role as an apostle does not make him independent or exalted over others. His language in 1 Cor 4:1 describes him and his associates as Christ's helpers or assistants and as supervisors in the ministry of God's mysteries. Paul sarcastically yearns to have it all like the self-assured Corinthians think they do, to share in their self-importance, to seek honor, and perhaps to enjoy a life with few worries about the repercussions of bad behavior. Instead, as an apostle whose experience actually conforms to Christ's example, an example forever defined by the crucifixion, Paul finds himself more familiar with disrepute and hardship.

Encouragement rises to the surface from time to time as Paul offers criticisms in 1 Corinthians 3–4. Even as he scolds his audience for their immaturity, he reassures them of their identity and security in Christ. Because God's Spirit resides in them, in their corporate existence they are God's temple: God does not shape them from far away but from within their own communal life. Furthermore, Paul reasserts his commitment to the Corinthians by characterizing his relationship with them as a father with his "beloved children." Paul's initial efforts to introduce his audience to the gospel created an intimate familial bond between them (cf. Phlm 10). Finally, he promises to make his associate Timothy available to the Corinthians—to teach them and perhaps also to serve as Paul's eyes and ears in Corinth until he can return to the city and address the believers there in person.

Sexual Immorality, Lawsuits, and Marriage (1 Cor 5–7)

Beginning in this section and continuing beyond it, Paul addresses various issues that he knows are affecting the Corinthian church's public witness about the gospel and the church's ability to maintain an ethos of unity. The first of the discussions concerns sexual immorality, stemming from a report Paul has received and following up on a topic he treated in a previous letter to the Corinthians. Paul expresses dismay about an ongoing sexual relationship between a Christ-follower in Corinth and his stepmother, identified as "his father's wife." Paul wants this man disciplined, hoping that his expulsion from Christian fellowship might lead to a change in behavior and might protect the rest of the church from an influence that, like yeast spreading through dough, has potential to corrupt the whole community. The letter makes no mention of disciplining the woman; perhaps she had little choice in the situation or was not affiliated with the church. Paul's disappointment extends also to the wider church community, for he interprets the Corinthians' tolerance for the pair's sexual relationship as an expression of arrogance and a boastful attitude. This particular criticism of the Corinthians could indicate that they understood their Christian freedom (cf. Rom 6:1–7:6; Gal 5:1, 13–15) as license to live as they pleased or to withhold judgment on others' morality. Against such a view, Paul instructs the church to avoid contact with members who exhibit various forms of openly immoral behavior (cf. 1 Thess 4:3–8).

In chapter 6 the discussion turns to lawsuits, suggesting that some in the Corinthian church had initiated legal complaints against other Christ-followers instead of settling their differences on their own or having their fellow believers mediate their disputes. Although Paul does not give a detailed explanation of his objections to the lawsuits, it appears he fears either that the church's reputation will suffer or that allowing judges from the wider society to have such authority potentially violates the community's holy, separate identity. The broader context of the discussion, which is preceded by criticisms of sexual immorality and followed by admonitions against "fornication," suggests that Paul does not want the church's common life and public image to resemble his stereotyped assessment of the Corinthians' native values. The church should be distinctive in how its members conduct themselves and treat one another, even if the distinctiveness translates into a willingness to forgo restitution for a wrong suffered at the hands of another Christ-follower. Members of the church should not position themselves against other members of the same "body" (to anticipate the metaphor coming in 1 Cor 12:12–27). By reminding the Corinthians of "what some of you used to be," Paul thus calls attention to the transformative nature of the gospel. The leading edge of Paul's exhortations about Christian conduct is theological, not ethical, for his instructions appeal to the Corinthians' new identity. The people in his audience are not the same people they were prior to their introduction to the gospel of Jesus Christ.

When the NRSV and other modern Bible translations put certain sentences in quotation marks in 1 Cor 6:12–13, the punctuation reflects the opinion that Paul quotes slogans or teachings that were popular among the Corinthians, perhaps taken from a letter they wrote to him (see also 1 Cor 10:23). Paul restates the sayings so he might add his own nuance to them. The idea that "all things are lawful" has a ring of truth, but Paul quickly qualifies the statement by endorsing self-control as a complementary value. Food may have no deep significance for questions of holiness and defilement, but later in the letter Paul will take seriously the potential for dietary convictions to divide a community. Paul therefore advocates for limits to how far Christian freedom can go (cf. Rom 14:1–15:13, where Paul addresses the issue of dietary scruples).

The limits Paul places on sexual behavior and dietary choices both connect to how people treat their bodies. Paul insists that what one does with one's body is not an insignificant matter, for Christ dwells in that body. Those who emphasize their spiritual identity to the point that they deliberately denigrate their embodied existence—either through deprivation or through careless excess—have missed the point, for in doing so they disregard the opportunities available in their current existence for manifesting God's Holy Spirit. One's whole existence matters, for one's whole bodily existence provides a locus for encountering God. That theological foundation undergirds much of what Paul says in this letter in which he expresses concern about how the Corinthians' behaviors may be undermining their ability to give expression to the gospel itself.

When Paul explicitly mentions, in 1 Cor 7:1, his intention to address issues from a letter the Corinthians sent to him, his overarching focus remains as it was, on offering theological rationales for how Christ-followers should rightly understand and conduct themselves. His discussion of marriage and sexual relations resumes themes and emphases he introduced already in 1 Corinthians 5–6.

Paul supports marriage and discourages divorce (cf. Jesus' words in Mark 10:2–12; Matt 19:3–9). Although he endorses marriage, he does so as a concession, seeing marriage as a legitimate outlet for sexual desire and thus a defense against the sexual promiscuity that he regards as contrary to the character of Christian identity. Paul implies that he lives chastely, a manner of living he commends over marriage, although he describes his asceticism as a gift from God.

Despite Paul's own choice to remain celibate, his instructions to married couples avoid prudishness, for he supports the "conjugal rights" of each partner. Mutuality should characterize their sexual relationship, for neither the husband nor the wife enjoys absolute authority over his or her own body. Probably Paul's point here is not to allow one partner to exploit the other but to emphasize the equal status and responsibility of both partners where it comes to the health of a marriage relationship, or at least that relationship's sexual expressions. The egalitarian impulse in Paul's instructions imparts an authority and value to wives that might have surprised some of Paul's contemporaries, given ancient patriarchal mores.

At the same time, the overall view of marriage described in these few verses has little to say about mutual devotion or love. Because Paul regarded Christ's return as imminent and believed "the present form of this world is passing away" (1 Cor 7:31), his letter does not focus on marriage's potential beyond its utility in promoting an orderly exercise of people's sexual appetites. Because "the appointed time has grown short" (1 Cor 7:29) and Paul aims to prepare the Corinthians for "the impending crisis" (1 Cor 7:26) brought on by the collapse of the former world order when Christ reappears, Paul does not advocate major changes in the Corinthians' social arrangements. Married people should therefore remain married, single people should remain single, and slaves should remain slaves. Paul shows little interest in changing certain established social structures; instead, he counsels the Corinthians to focus their energies on the question of how they can "please the Lord" in the little time they have left before God brings history to its consummation. If Paul's ways of viewing all of those social institutions appear to be peculiarly determined by his expectation of Christ's imminent return, that is because they were. It remains unknown, then, how Paul might have instructed the Corinthians differently about family structures, love and marriage, or the merits of slavery had he known that Jesus would not return and bring an end to the current state of the world anytime soon.

Food Sacrificed to Idols, Individual Freedom, and Idolatry
(1 Cor 8:1–11:1)

When Paul offers teachings about food that has been "sacrificed to idols," he indicates that one of the points of division or confusion within the Corinthian church stemmed from dietary issues, specifically how those issues relate to the proper exercise of Christian freedom. Evidently some of the Corinthian Christ-followers opted to abstain from certain foods out of a desire to avoid all appearances of showing devotion to other deities. Most meat sold in a city like Corinth came from temples or similar sites, for it was the product of animal sacrifices to various gods. Moreover, even though many of the church's lower-class members might not have been able to afford meat on a regular basis, still meat would have been available to them without cost from time to time at major city-sponsored festivals in honor of a god or goddess.

Surely some Corinthians wondered whether it would offend Christ or discredit their Christian witness if they partook in the festivals, bought meat for their own consumption, or enjoyed it when they were guests in someone else's home. The debate therefore extends far beyond matters of personal taste and politeness. The issue might have touched the consciences of some believers deeper than others, depending on their background in certain religious communities and their former participation in certain rituals. The controversy ultimately extends to questions about exactly how separate the church should keep itself from common social norms and how the church should avoid creating divisions among its own members.

Paul's discussion of the issue resembles what he wrote to the Romans, at a later point in his career, in Rom 14:1–15:13 (cf. Rev 2:14, 20). In 1 Corinthians, however, he provides a more extensive theological foundation for understanding that sacrifices to other deities do nothing to diminish the lordship of Jesus Christ and the supremacy of the one true God. Paul approves of anyone's efforts to "flee from the worship of idols" because he understands the devastation idolatry causes, as seen in his references to the trials of the ancient Hebrews according to the books of Exodus and Numbers. Yet Paul also insists that ultimately idols are powerless, for sacrifices to them are essentially sacrifices to demons. Demons oppose God, but they cannot make food defiled, since that food belongs to God, for "the earth and its fullness are the Lord's" (quoting Ps 24:1).

Nevertheless, even as Paul insists that a believer's conscience should not balk at consuming food sacrificed to other deities, he also instructs the Corinthians to exercise great care in protecting other people's consciences. Some Christ-followers apparently remained unable to dissociate certain foods or ceremonies from acts of devotion to other gods. The responsible response to this, Paul says, is for their fellow Christ-followers to avoid meat and thus avoid giving offense. He prefaces the entire discussion by elevating love over knowledge, meaning that he values an active concern for other members of the community over the freedom of conscience that comes from knowing that eating meat sacrificed to idols brings no dishonor to Christ. A right understanding of the knowledge, strength, and authority Christ provides does not constitute a license to trample other believers' sensibilities or shortcomings. Eating meat may be *lawful*, for Paul teaches that the law of Moses cannot limit or diminish a believer's freedom (1 Cor 10:23; cf.

Rom 7:4–6; 8:2; Gal 3:23–26), since believers now serve Christ and not the law. But eating certain foods may not be *beneficial* to the Corinthian believers in certain contexts, however, since they now find themselves obligated to seek the well-being of others (cf. Rom 6:15–22; Gal 5:13). To insist on one's own freedom to eat anything with a clear conscience in a setting that confuses and wounds another's conscience is to sin against Christ. Such disregard for another person's well-being is what diminishes God's glory, not the meat a person ingests.

Lest the Corinthians assume that Paul's comments only arbitrarily or unfairly limit their freedom to do whatever they want, in chapter 9 Paul embarks on a tangent to underscore his and his associates' willingness to relinquish their own rights and comforts for the sake of promoting the gospel. Paul claims he has not asked the Corinthians to provide him the financial support he deserves as their spiritual leader, a right he describes as based in the Lord's own command, because Paul does not want to erect "an obstacle in the way of the gospel of Christ" (1 Cor 9:12). Paul would rather fund his ministry through his own labor and austerity than risk being confused with unsavory people who profit from disseminating their philosophical or religious instructions. The apostle claims he regularly renounces his liberties so he can serve the gospel effectively and so others might not be deterred from sharing in the gospel's blessings. He promotes and practices self-control because it eliminates confusion and therefore serves the gospel's ability to attract others and keep them in the fold, just as later in 1 Corinthians he will for similar reasons promote orderliness in how the letter's audience conducts their worship services.

Proper Worship Practices (1 Cor 11:2–34)

Repeatedly Paul commends orderliness to facilitate the unity he seeks to inculcate in Corinth. Disorderliness may confuse how outsiders understand the church and its beliefs, and moreover, some undisciplined behaviors risk violating cardinal tenets of the gospel itself. Paul considers the Corinthians' worship practices as important contexts for maintaining order. Two particular issues occupy his attention in this section of the letter.

The first one concerns how women wear their hair, apparently with specific regard to the hairstyles they choose in contexts of public worship. Perhaps no other passage in Paul's letters is as cryptic as

1 Cor 11:2–16, for Paul employs, deliberately in some cases, language with multiple meanings and arguments of dubious validity. Although it is relatively easy to tell what Paul wants—he wants women to cover or style their hair in certain ways while praying or offering prophetic pronouncements in public worship—it is quite difficult to decipher what drives that desire or what cultural assumptions influence his understanding of what makes for either disgraceful or praiseworthy behavior in this setting. The confusing aspects of Paul's rhetoric should not detract from a basic truth about this passage: Paul acknowledges and does not disapprove of the fact that in Corinth women were actively praying and prophesying in settings of Christian worship.

The Greek terms Paul uses in this passage express his desire that these women avoid having their hair fall loosely from their heads in worship services, lest they bring dishonor to their head. Some interpreters think Paul associated women wearing loose hairstyles with prostitutes, but more likely he has in mind other Hellenistic religious cults in which prophecy was delivered by female prophets who contorted their bodies and emerged from spasmodic trances with disheveled appearances. Such frenzied rituals occurred in the worship of Dionysus, Cybele, and Isis, and so perhaps Paul aimed to avoid confusion with those religions.

Paul's rationale for policing women's public behavior and hairstyles extends beyond the question of what a woman's appearance might communicate. Paul also expresses concerns about implications for authority and honor. The passage becomes especially difficult to decipher when Paul reveals those concerns and expounds on the significance of one's "head," for that word ends up taking the argument in many directions. The word, in Greek as in English, means more than the top of one's body; it also refers to an authority figure or a person's source. Paul plays on the multiple meanings of "head" to equate what he considers to be a dishonorable hairstyle with a woman's capacity to disgrace her husband and, by extension, with a potential to disgrace Christ and God. Paul supports his assertion by citing the order of creation as described in Genesis 2, although he ignores the more egalitarian creation story recorded in Genesis 1. He makes an obscure reference to angels. Like some Stoic and Cynic thinkers of his era, he appeals to norms he observes in the natural world. In the end, Paul constructs an ambiguous argument that relies on presumptions about subordination and superiority, even though he also acknowledges that "all things," women and men alike, ultimately "come from God" in a more equal sense.

In 1 Cor 11:17–34, Paul turns to a second worship-related issue when he addresses the Corinthians' manner of observing the Lord's Supper, which he criticizes for reifying and confirming the divisions in the church. Following the ancient custom of celebrating the Lord's Supper as a full-fledged common meal (see Jude 12), the Corinthians nevertheless discriminated along lines of social status and wealth, for some people ate full meals separately while others remained unfed and hungry. In response, Paul recites a liturgical rubric concerning the Supper, echoing traditions also found in the Synoptic Gospels' accounts of Jesus' final night with his followers. The words of the rubric define the church's celebration as a shared, common participation in the remembrance and proclamation of Jesus' death—a death Paul understands as being for all and as forging the foundations of Christian unity. Because the Lord's Supper expresses the church's connection to Christ and his death, it is patently wrong for the meal to reiterate distinctions among its participants or to make some participants appear more privileged than others. Therefore Paul castigates the Corinthians for worshiping "in an unworthy manner" when their celebrations reinforce disparities in individuals' resources and social status. The church's violation of a core principle embedded in the Supper's setting and symbolism even makes some of its members liable to divine judgment, which Paul implies is already being experienced in the sicknesses and deaths of some Corinthians.

Spiritual Gifts and Worship (1 Cor 12–14)

Paul introduces this section of the letter as about "spiritual things" and not necessarily "gifts," as the NRSV and other translations put it. The distinction is important, for the main focus of this section is the Holy Spirit and the kind of spiritual identity the Spirit imparts. Paul's focus on "gifts," introduced in 1 Cor 12:4 with the Greek word *charisma*, remains secondary, for gifts given by the Spirit are meant to be expressions of the Spirit and the foundational unity the Spirit creates. In other words, the gifts point to the Spirit; they do not exist for their own sake. The core conviction that animates this entire part of the letter concerns the Holy Spirit as a cohesive force. The Spirit incorporates all believers into "one body" of diverse members who function in interdependent ways. Because "one and the same Spirit" activates different gifts, all aspects of Christian existence, including corporate worship, must express love and unity.

When Paul offers lists of various spiritual gifts, he does not give an exhaustive inventory but a representative sampling. Those gifts represent more than a person's talents, for Paul describes them as given and activated by God through the Spirit. All of them support Christian ministry in one way or another. Believers exercise those gifts out of their identity or location within an interconnected "body of Christ" (cf. Rom 12:3–8). Speaking of a "body" whose parts must work together so as not to harm their collective whole, Paul deploys a metaphor that was already very common among Greco-Roman authors, including some Jewish authors, who used it to warn against the corrupting dangers of social and political factions. The analogy of a body and its functions allows Paul to emphasize differences among believers and their various roles even as he assigns value to those differences based on their ability to contribute to a unified, organic, and healthy whole. No one can therefore claim greater status or honor than another, for God chooses to give "the greater honor to the inferior member" of the body. First Corinthians does not name Christ as "the head" of this body, as Ephesians and Colossians do (Eph 4:12, 15–16; 5:23, 29–30; Col 2:19), suggesting that Paul sees the entire church, in its corporate unity, as the full and cooperative expression of Christ and the physical embodiment of his presence. The body suffers as a unit and rejoices as a unit. As a result, such a body cannot tolerate dissension among its members.

When Paul cites apostles, prophets, teachers, and other roles people perform, he recognizes that some gifts and members of the body have more prominent or perhaps more indispensable roles. Yet he immediately moves to celebrate love as the most valuable and central characteristic of Christian community. Love, according to Paul, takes primacy.

Love is a vital force that does things; the love Paul describes is not a feeling but an agent. In the Greek syntax of 1 Cor 13:4–8, love is the subject of active verbs; it animates Christian witness and contributes to Christian unity. This passage's description of love complements other passages from letters Paul wrote; all of them together place love at the heart of the gospel. In Jesus Christ God demonstrates love for humanity (Rom 5:8, 8:39; 2 Cor 5:14, 13:11; Gal 2:20; 1 Thess 4:9). The love God shows through Christ represents the fullest expression of God's love, as the torah discloses the centrality of that love (Rom 13:8–10, Gal 5:13–14). Paul presents love not as a spiritual gift but as the end toward which all spiritual gifts and Christian ministry are deployed. Love is the fitting response to God's work through Christ (Rom 12:9–10; 1 Cor 16:14; Gal 5:6; Phil 1:9; 2:1–2; 1 Thess 3:12). Finally, Paul associates love with spiritual maturity, for love provides a way of living amid the incomplete knowledge that characterizes life in the waning old age. While Christ-followers wait to see God "face to face" (cf. 1 Cor 15:50–52) and then to realize full knowledge of God, they abide in the meantime in faith, in hope, and, most crucially, in love. Those three powerful forces allow the church to represent Jesus Christ and the gospel most completely and authentically as believers await the fullness to come. For love will not lose its energy or give up before that time arrives, since "love never ends" (1 Cor 13:8).

Having provided a theological assessment of spiritual gifts as expressions of both a unifying Spirit and a unified body of Christ, and having clarified the gifts as subordinate to love, the letter moves to explain the proper use of gifts in corporate worship. To the fragmented Christian community in Corinth, Paul declares that mutual "upbuilding" must be the indispensable condition for how believers make use of God's gifts for ministry. Paul declares that gifts such as prophecy and speaking in tongues, apparently familiar practices in the Corinthian church, should always "build up the church" (cf. 1 Cor 8:1). Those whose gifts allow them to reveal knowledge of God but who do so in ways no one else can hear or understand actually detract from the purpose of public worship and the goal of encouraging and strengthening the corporate church. Paul therefore commends orderly ways of exercising those gifts so others, including outsiders, will understand what is being said. Paul directs the Corinthians to conduct themselves in ways that will avoid giving outsiders the impression that Christian worship resembles the more mantic and unrestrained practices associated with certain forms of Greek and Roman religion.

The Resurrection of the Body (1 Cor 15)

A long reflection on Jesus' resurrection and believers' future resurrections may seem at first like an appendix attached to a letter focused on the church's unity and conduct in the current age. However, once readers appreciate the letter's underlying theological basis, Paul's comments on resurrection appear much more integral to the letter as a whole. Over and over again through the letter, Paul has helped the Corinthians understand what kind of living best corresponds to the gospel. The principles guiding those discussions did not arise from reflections on ethical virtues or on cultural foundations of proper behavior as much as they stemmed from Paul's theological conviction that through the death and resurrection of Jesus Christ, God has begun to transform the world and human existence into whole new realities encompassed by a whole new age. In a sense, the idea of a future resurrection reiterates the entire letter's main theological outlook, for the new realities that should define and influence the church's identity and common life now are about more than the expectation of a *different* or *improved* era. It is an altogether *new* era that God's people have entered, and that era brings with it a promise of ultimate transformation. Resurrection is a piece of what is coming, an embodied participation in that transformation God is accomplishing.

The church, while it waits, must live in the meantime in ways that reflect and announce that emerging newness, for the church resides at "the ends of the ages" (1 Cor 10:11). In line with an outlook he likely adopted from emphases in Jewish apocalyptic theology, Paul understands Jesus' death and resurrection as world-changing events, for they herald the arrival of the new age. Paul therefore uses this part of the letter to assert that Jesus' resurrection ensures the future resurrection of "those who belong to Christ." The future resurrection will come when Christ returns, accompanied by trumpet peals, a stock apocalyptic image (cf. Matt 24:31, 1 Thess 4:16, Rev 11:15). Following the final resurrection, Christ will hand over "the kingdom to God the Father, after he has destroyed every ruler and every authority and power." The ultimate power he will defeat is death itself. Such a hope for a majestic future informs the ways Christ-followers ought to live now.

At the beginning of this section, Paul vouches for Christ's resurrection by reciting confessional statements he knew from the wider church's liturgical or catechetical traditions (1 Cor 15:3–7) and by recounting his own encounter with the resurrected Christ. The reality of Christ's resurrection supplies Paul with the assurance that there will be a future resurrection of the dead, which aligns with a hope deeply embedded in Jewish apocalyptic writings and in Paul's identity as a Pharisee (e.g., Phil 3:5; Acts 23:6–9, 24:14–15, 26:4–8). Situated as they are, in part of a larger letter that repeatedly appeals for unity, Paul's statements of confidence in the coming resurrection offer one more reason why his audience should temper their spiritual smugness: they have hardly yet arrived into the fullness of God's blessings for them. The best is yet to come.

In the second half of the chapter, Paul turns to discuss the nature of the coming resurrection. He insists that it will be a bodily resurrection, contrasting his understanding as different from various Greek notions of the afterlife. Many Greek philosophies taught that death would free a person's soul from its imprisonment within a body. A few philosophical movements, such as some that were informed by Stoic currents, held that a person's immortal self would journey toward a new horizon of existence, which might involve reincarnation or transmigration into a new body. Paul, however, describes the transformation of one's body from "a physical body" to "a spiritual body," an undefined term that likely refers to a body fully quickened or transformed by God's Spirit. In any case, that new body will take on imperishability and immortality when it is changed at a time when God finally defeats death and accomplishes the final victory in the cosmic apocalyptic drama (cf. 2 Cor 5:1–5; Phil 3:21).

Paul's notion of resurrection therefore involves both continuity and discontinuity. The continuity resides in his insistence that the resurrection involves bodies. Paul says nothing about a spirit or soul departing to take on an ethereal existence. In God's promised future, a person's body remains, as it is in this life, a locus for encountering, experiencing, and expressing divine grace. That reality dignifies human beings' current existence as embodied creatures even as it also reaffirms Paul's instructions about treating one's body—and one's neighbors' bodies— honorably, for bodies are places wherein God dwells (e.g., 1 Cor 6:13–15, 20; 8:12; 12:12–27). Yet because human bodies are corruptible, derived from "dust" and destined to return to "dust" (cf. Gen 2:7, 3:19), resurrection must also entail a discontinuity: human bodies cannot stay the same and must undergo a transformation, for they are not *returned* to life but raised to *new* life. Paul briefly characterizes the transformation as "a mystery," something inexplicable now but that in time believers will come to know and experience in its fullness. Although Paul does not make an explicit connection to stories in the Gospels, the dynamic he describes concerning continuity and discontinuity bears resemblance to scenes in Luke 24 and John 20, in which Jesus' resurrected body remains wounded from his execution yet has also been transformed by his resurrection, for the risen Christ does things in those parts of the

Gospels that he did not do previously, such as being unrecognizable to others, disappearing, and materializing within locked rooms.

Future Plans, Closing Exhortations with Greetings, and Benediction (1 Cor 16)

Paul's discussion of his future plans begins with brief instructions about his fund-raising efforts on behalf of "the saints" in Jerusalem. Paul says much more about his ongoing collection to support the Jerusalem church, a project that evidently aimed to provide relief to that church's impoverished members in particular, in 2 Corinthians 8–9 (cf. Rom 15:25–32). Paul's additional comments about his and others' impending travels, along with the greetings he extends to his audience, reaffirm his commitment to the Corinthians and keep in view his and the Corinthians' membership in a more extensive network of Christian ministry and fellowship. Paul and the Corinthian believers share vital relationships with others engaged in ministry in distant places, meaning the body of Christ is more than local. It encompasses a widespread, vibrant unity.

The Letter's Themes and Theological Emphases

First Corinthians hardly offers a comprehensive description of what Christian living entails. Like Paul's other letters, it aims to provide pastoral leadership with attention to specific shortcomings, opportunities, or questions that he believed were present in the community to which he wrote. In all of Paul's letters, an underlying pastoral goal is to remind his audience who they are, for the letters all aim to form communities of faith so they become more consistent with the gospel as Paul understands it. Paul's leadership is therefore theological leadership insofar as his letters' instructions and exhortations emerge out of how he understands what God has done and will yet do through Jesus Christ.

Theological convictions permeate the letter. Because Paul thought the Corinthian church was suffering from a malformed conception of what it means to live as spiritual people "on whom the ends of the ages have come" (1 Cor 10:11), he addresses questions of unity, regard for one another's conscience, and the function of spiritual gifts. Because Paul thought the Corinthians' enthusiastic embrace of their Christian freedom had led them to mistreat one another or damage the vitality of their public expressions of the gospel, his letter addresses questions of self-control, orderliness, moral purity, and the importance of embodiment as an integral aspect of what it means to participate in God's presence and activity. Because Paul thought the Corinthians did not fully appreciate the gospel's searing ability to reveal and criticize the pretense embedded in conventional values about power and self-sufficiency, the letter addresses the scandal of Jesus' crucifixion and the basis for Christian unity. Just as 1 Corinthians guides its audience to a more integrated existence, relating realities at the heart of the gospel to the Corinthians' conduct, so also several of the letter's theological emphases relate closely to one another.

The Public Witness of the Body of Christ

Several of the issues Paul addresses in this letter relate to the Corinthians' ability to navigate their cultural landscape in ways that rightly express the new realities God is bringing into being. Paul does not want the church in Corinth to conduct itself in a manner that will confuse outsiders or will contradict the wisdom, righteousness, sanctification, and redemption that correspond to the new life made available in Christ (1 Cor 1:30). An urgency fuels the fire in Paul's specific instructions about believers' conduct, for he assumes the church has little time remaining before Christ returns (1 Cor 7:26, 29, 31).

Paul's positions on certain issues might have been difficult for his readers to predict. He tells them that eating food sacrificed in ceremonies honoring Greek and Roman gods will not necessarily defile one's body or dishonor Christ (1 Cor 10:23–27), yet a man who has sex with a prostitute is guilty of doing precisely those things (1 Cor 6:12–20). Yet for many—but definitely not all—Corinthian freemen, the cultural norms with which they were raised would have not frowned on either of those activities. Perhaps some men in the church had shared a bed with prostitutes regularly throughout their lives as a socially acceptable outlet for their sexual energies. Paul forbids some prevalent behaviors and permits others, while not always providing detailed rationales.

Paul's criticisms of the Corinthians' celebration of the Lord's Supper also involve discerning which common cultural practices have no place in the body of Christ (1 Cor 11:17–34). When the Corinthians do not share equally in the food served at these meals, they conduct those gatherings as one might have been expected to host an ordinary dinner party. In most Corinthian households and shared meals, the higher-status attendees would be served the better food and have access to more of it. Slaves, most women, children, and other lower-status persons might not even eat in the same room or at the same time as the more honorable men in attendance. The more socially prominent members of the Corinthian church probably were not conspiring to be rude or selfish when partaking in the Lord's Supper with other believers; the way those meals were apparently conducted conformed to conventional patterns. Paul will have none of that behavior, however. No matter how acceptable those patterns might appear in other homes around Corinth, Paul sees them as articulations of a hierarchy. In particular, the hierarchy makes distinctions according to people's purported value, thus allowing social status to occlude the unity of the church, which is a community in which all of God's people share equally in the same one Spirit (1 Cor 12:12–13).

Paul's solution instructs the Corinthians to engage in a truly shared meal in which all are present together and all partake of the same food, no matter how odd such a practice might appear in the general scheme of social mores. Paul requires that solution not as an attempt to exhort the Corinthians toward greater politeness; he commands them to order their communal life in a way that prevents some people from dominating others, for all members of the community share in the Lord's death and benefit equally and fully from that death. Declaring those pivotal truths about Christ's death is the point of the Supper in the first place.

Every Christian community must determine how its cultural context rightly or wrongly shapes that community's common life, governance, and behavior. Not all conventional assumptions and practices contradict the gospel, and not all of them have a place in God's new age. The Corinthians had to modify some of their habitual behaviors because, according to Paul, they no longer lived in the same old world. Paul does not reject Corinthian culture entirely; he even quotes a Greek playwright approvingly in 1 Cor 15:33. But Paul also does not let the church indiscriminately import every conventional value and assumption into its common life. He negotiates those complicated judgments guided by a few basic principles. He rejects prerogatives and hierarchies and contends for an ethos of mutuality. Paul insists that a person's whole self, including one's body, participates in God's salvation, and so people cannot denigrate the worth of their bodies or their neighbor's body. Paul regards the church as set apart to embody and proclaim

God's holiness, for the Holy Spirit resides among God's people (1 Cor 3:16–17; cf. 1 Thess 4:1–8, 5:23–24). Paul also demands that people, especially the smug Corinthian believers, consider the well-being and needs of other people as more important than their own. The death of Jesus Christ, a supreme act of self-giving love, offers a transformative expression of all of those principles and therefore places them at the heart of the church's identity. Paul would undoubtedly contend that what was true for the Corinthians is true for all: the church in every generation should be a community shaped by the cross of Christ and by the anticipation of a future resurrection, for those events necessarily influence how believers understand themselves and live as a *community* of faith.

The Crucifixion of Jesus and the Shape of Christian Community

Ask most ancient Corinthians about what it would mean for them to be able to participate in the life and deeds of a deity and they might have answered, the opportunity to share in power, prominence, and enlightenment. Those virtues were greatly prized in the Roman world, and they were considered characteristics of gods; common beliefs held that a worthy deity could grant gifts that would provide clout and advancement. By contrast, when Paul discusses Jesus' crucifixion, he makes no attempt to hide foolishness, weakness, and lowliness at work there. The God of Jesus Christ acts rather differently than the other gods in the Greco-Roman religious marketplace were purported to act. Therefore, when Paul expresses his concern about those Corinthians who suffer from an inflated sense of their own significance, he calls attention to the crucifixion of Jesus, not because Paul wants to counsel humility for its own sake, but because the crucifixion provides the key to understanding who God is and how God operates.

Through Jesus' crucifixion, God shows strength, but it is strength couched in weakness. Wisdom, something much discussed and much valued in Greek writings produced by ancient Jews and gentiles, likewise expresses itself in what appears to be foolishness (1 Cor 1:18–2:16). In the death of Jesus on a cross, God acted in unexpected ways; even more, to say that the crucifixion expresses God's wisdom means the crucifixion divulges what God knows to be true. In other words, Jesus' humiliating death speaks a divine verdict by issuing judgment on those who use their power to dominate their rivals. At the same time, Jesus' execution ironically declares the value of who he was and how he both lived and died: devoted to helping others. The church must therefore live and present itself in similar ways, for the church exists as the collection of people who participate in the salvation that springs from the crucifixion. The church discovers God's power at work only when it finds itself aligned with Christ's particular experience of weakness.

Paul's claim extends beyond saying that Christ-followers should embrace and rejoice in their sufferings, although he says more about that subject in other letters (e.g., Rom 5:3–5; 2 Cor 1:3–7, 7:4–7, 12:1–10; Phil 1:29; 3:10–11). His more fundamental point in 1 Corinthians is that believers, like Christ, should demonstrate a willingness to put others' well-being above their own. It is a mistake to interpret Paul's words about the cross as a call to invite victimization or to tolerate abuse as though it is somehow a redemptive or virtuous thing to suffer oppression at the hands of another. Paul directs his appeals in 1 Corinthians instead to those who possess power and to those who exalt themselves over others. Those are the specific people he enjoins to surrender their advantages in order to assist others. The cross for Paul is primarily a story of power relinquished, not a story of powerlessness imposed (cf. Phil 2:1–8). To align with Christ's weakness means willingly accepting the scorn that inevitably falls on those who devote themselves to elevating others.

True spirituality, according to Paul, involves conforming to Christ. It means a person identifies fully with Christ by being united with him in his death (e.g., 1 Cor 1:13–15). As a result of that unity, people "belong" to Christ (e.g., 1 Cor 15:23; cf. Rom 7:4, Gal 5:24). Therefore, they anticipate an embodied resurrection like his (e.g., 1 Cor 15:20–22, 45–49). Paul's notion of spirituality does not entail a flight from this existence as a form of world denial, for in Christ God acted through a human body, even as the Holy Spirit now dwells in believers' bodies (1 Cor 6:19; cf. 6:13–15). Bodies are more than placeholders for the Spirit to occupy temporarily, for one day they will be transformed, shaped by the Spirit to make them spiritual and imperishable (1 Cor 15:42–46). They will continue to be the locations in which Christ-followers encounter new life from God.

Spiritual Gifts and the Holy Spirit

Unity occupies a crucial position in Paul's understanding of how any Christian community must function. Unity was created and guaranteed by God, for through the death and resurrection of Jesus Christ, God extends welcome, belonging, and salvation to all people, no matter who they are (1 Cor 12:13; cf. Gal 3:28). The Holy Spirit confirms this new corporate identity and creates unity, for the Spirit indwells all who belong to Christ. As a result, the Holy Spirit's work always has corporate and cohesive dimensions.

This foundational unity adds a creative tension to Paul's discussions about both spiritual gifts and the ways of organizing the church's work. Paul affirms the value of certain gifts, like prophesying, and certain roles, like apostles (1 Cor 12:27–31; 14:1). Yet Paul refuses to let any gifts and roles imply the existence of qualitative distinctions among believers. The one Spirit gives a diversity of gifts and calls people to diverse ways of using those gifts; the diversity is essential for the Spirit to foster the church's common, corporate health. But diversity should not become a license for value judgments among the body of Christ's constituent parts. No believers can claim superiority over others or dominate someone else.

Paul speaks about the Holy Spirit and spiritual gifts with regard to their connections to Jesus Christ. The presence of the Spirit serves as the ground for the Christian testimony *Jesus is Lord* (1 Cor 12:3). The Spirit's gifts therefore empower and embolden that testimony. In addition, the Spirit enables believers to participate with Jesus Christ, initiating them—literally, "baptizing" them—into Christ's living body (1 Cor 12:13). Through the Spirit Christ remains present to the world, embodied in and as a church that shares a united identity and a united purpose.

Different Christian traditions have sought, in various ways, to organize themselves and express the potent unities Paul describes; in the process, churches often show how much more difficult it is to live in true unity than it is to give it lip service or simply to settle for mutual tolerance. The problems the Corinthian believers had with conceit and divisiveness are really not so unusual, especially when they are considered from a modern vantage point, during the contemporary period in which countless congregations are dividing themselves or separating themselves from meaningful fellowship with other ones. Churches' current divisions along lines of race, worship aesthetics, faith practices, social class, hospitality, moral presuppositions, and too many other factors speak to the never-ending difficulty of incorporating God's new realities into the lives of believers who find it so difficult to rid themselves of attachments to the old age's tyrannizing hierarchies and factions.

The Unity of the Church and the Women in Corinth

Despite Paul's insistence that the unity at the heart of the gospel pro-hibits individual believers from elevating their intrinsic value or their importance to the church's work over other people and their contri-butions, inconsistencies arise when the letter itself draws distinctions between the men and women in Corinth. Different passages tell differ-ent stories. For one thing, when Paul addresses the hazards of sexual immorality, his focus usually falls solely on men and their complicity. For example, when Paul discusses prostitution, he has nothing to say about the prostitutes or the wider families of both a prostitute and her john (1 Cor 6:15–20). More specifically, when Paul gives attention to men and women inside the Corinthian church, on one hand he offers a remarkable affirmation of the mutuality that should characterize a sex-ual relationship between a husband and wife (1 Cor 7:3–5), while on the other hand he reaffirms that a husband is "the head of his wife" (1 Cor 11:3), meaning a husband bears a kind of innate authority over his wife and even possesses a kind of primal superiority. The former passage endorses a sexual relationship that is more egalitarian than what many Corinthians would have known, while the latter assumes, without the aid of a strong supporting argument, that men possess a natural, even God-given superiority over women (cf. 1 Cor 11:7–9).

In general and across his letters, Paul's comments about women's behavior, as well as his tendency to address explicitly only the men in his audiences, suggest that his theological convictions sometimes took a back seat to the cultural conventions that informed his understanding of what qualifies as acceptable gender and social roles. For one thing, Paul held that all believers share fully in God's blessings through Christ and therefore possess equal value before God (e.g., Gal 3:28). Yet Paul also occasionally reasserts traditional gender-based hierarchies; for example, in 1 Cor 11:2–16, he implies that women remain subordinate to men in some essential fashion. In that passage, despite its many ambig-uous terms and claims, Paul roots the subordination of women to men in the natural order, the design of creation according to Genesis 2, and familiar social customs. In instances like those, when Paul insists on maintaining distinctions between men, women, and their respective roles, hierarchy and subordination slip back into the conversation. As a result, Paul's explicit and implicit judgments about men and women eclipse the unity Paul elsewhere identifies as an innate aspect of the body of Christ. Paul's teachings thus appear conflicted, for reasons that are hardly easy and perhaps impossible to dissect.

First Corinthians extols Christian liberty and calls for the abolition of certain biases and forms of favoritism that endangered the Corinthian church's unity. Yet in this letter Paul holds back from making a clear statement about women and men possessing equal status in their relationships and their functions in the church. In a document so devoted to celebrating the unity made possible through Christ, Paul does not contend for the full realization of a new social structure and a new view of humanity that might more fully express the theological realities he values so highly. It is impossible to determine whether Paul's apprehension represents malice or a more innocent unawareness of the presuppositions about gender that he inherited from his cultural context. Interpreters are wise, however—and more than justified—when they allow some of Paul's most sweeping theological statements about unity and equality (e.g., 1 Cor 12:12–13; Gal 3:28) to speak more loudly than both his silences and his occasional appropriations of particular cultural values (e.g., 1 Cor 11:14–15). Paul's theology and its emphasis on unity in Christ might have sowed the seeds for a more egalitarian ethos of gender and society than he evidently ever sought to cultivate himself. Paul's unwillingness or inability to seek greater change in his own cultural context surely contributed to those seeds' very slow—and sometimes thwarted—growth throughout church history. Modern interpreters can nourish the theological roots that Paul helped establish, however, and thus help Christian communities tend to this plant, encouraging it to grow and bloom into a fuller expression of the unity that the body of Christ must exhibit in all its functions.

Further complicating the issue of how to analyze Paul's views on women and how women should conduct themselves as believers is the inability to reconstruct the conditions in the Christian community that 1 Corinthians originally addressed. This letter's comments about women's roles in worship services might have been specifically directed toward particular Corinthian women whom Paul considered disruptive. Some interpreters have hypothesized that a group of women in the congregation might have struck Paul, whether justifiably or not, as key contributors to either this particular church's divisive ethos or the church's negative reputation among Corinth's wider population. There is not enough evidence in the letter to establish the credence of such proposals. At the same time, since so much of 1 Corinthians devotes itself to steering the church away from creating confusion or offending outsiders, it remains reasonable to suppose that Paul aimed at least in a general sense to stifle the activity of women who he thought could appear scandalous in the eyes of the wider population. The letter's efforts to curb the influence or enthusiasm of women in public worship do not necessarily represent Paul's assessment of women's value and his opinions about their legitimate contributions for all times and all places. In any case, his teachings about the women in the Corinthian congregations have been construed as normative.

Difficult interpretive questions arise from Paul's apparent inconsistencies, the ways in which ancient cultural presuppositions evidently influenced Paul's perspective, and the ambiguity of his teachings in certain parts of 1 Corinthians. The difficulties should not lead interpreters to resignation but should remind them to consider the parts of Paul's letters in light of the whole body of evidence concerning Paul's theology. Individual passages need to be put into conversation with each other so interpreters do not imagine they can construct a comprehensive account of "Paul's view of women" based on a single passage from one of his letters. A notable example of this interpretive principle presents itself in 1 Cor 14:33b–36, where the letter forbids women from speaking when the church gathers. The translators who produced the NRSV inserted parentheses around this notorious passage, thereby noting that it represents a jarring disjunction from the surrounding argument. When one reads the wider passage without the words of 1 Cor 14:33b–36, Paul's rhetoric flows relatively seamlessly from 1 Cor 14:33a directly to 1 Cor 14:37. In addition, the prohibition expressed in 1 Cor 14:33b–36 creates a contradiction with 1 Cor 11:2–16, which discusses acceptable conditions for women to speak, even to provide leadership, during public worship. So the prohibition of 1 Cor 14:33b–36 can hardly be considered the main focus of Paul's discussion or an absolute, normative interdiction against all women speaking in a worship setting.

One possibility is that 1 Cor 14:33b–36 has in mind a specific group of women in Corinth whom Paul attempts to censure. More likely, however, these verses constitute an interpolation, meaning they are an addition to the letter written by someone other than Paul at a later time. Irregularities in existing Greek copies of 1 Corinthians, as well as a possible scribal notation in one manuscript, suggest that ancient copyists had reason to doubt the authenticity or originality of 1 Cor 14:33b–36 as part of this particular letter. In addition, these verses' clear similarity to 1 Tim 2:8–15 gives a basis to suppose that someone writing after Paul added the material in 1 Cor 14:33b–36 in a deliberate attempt to make 1 Corinthians echo 1 Timothy, a letter that Paul probably did not write. When interpreters compare 1 Cor 14:33b–36 to other parts of 1 Corinthians and other parts of the New Testament, they therefore cannot consider these verses as Paul's full and final word on the subject of women's participation in public worship. This is especially true since these verses might not even be Paul's own words at all. Any responsible and generous investigation into Paul's views about women's roles in church leadership must look widely across his letters and weigh many passages.

No single letter tells the whole story of Paul's views. No one letter can plumb all the depths of what it looks like to live in light of the gospel as Paul understood it. Each of his letters has its own things to say, and he found himself compelled to focus on different subjects at different times and places. What remains most consistent across the span of Paul's surviving correspondence is his conviction that through Christ God has brought forth a transformed existence. The practical realities of that transformation are always multiple and complex. Sometimes they are difficult to see because of the blinders worn by all people—both Paul and the Christian thinkers who have read his writings over time. Those new realities therefore do not always come to pass all at once. If Paul's churches needed encouragement, clearer vision, and the benefit of other perspectives to perceive the full extent of the transformations embedded in God's new age, maybe Paul himself was in a similar situation. Modern interpreters are perhaps not so different, either.

5

The Second Letter of Paul to the Corinthians

Paul's determination to see the gospel of Jesus Christ made manifest in the lives of Christ-followers in Corinth expressed itself in more than a single letter. In 2 Corinthians he continues to reach out and offer guidance to the community, yet his words betray a palpable sense of misgiving and frustration as his relationship with the Corinthian church continued. Despite the contentious atmosphere, Paul's writing expresses his deep commitments to his audience and to his own ministry. Paul displays a passionate desire to contend for the Corinthians' well-being, a desire he communicates repeatedly even as he acknowledges many hardships that threaten to erode his trustworthiness and derail his attempts to provide spiritual leadership. Nevertheless, those hardships, which Paul experiences both in his dealings with the Corinthians and in his apostolic ministry in general, hardly shake his convictions about the new creation God has brought into being through Jesus Christ. Paul asserts that the difficulties he and the Corinthians face actually provide them opportunities to exhibit the grace of God through their efforts to support one another and through the power of God they encounter as they endure various adversities.

Second Corinthians occasionally has an emotional and rhetorical intensity that is easy to notice. At the same time, several characteristics of the book make it challenging to understand. For one thing, 2 Corinthians indicates that Paul's relationship with the church in Corinth deteriorated after he and Sosthenes sent 1 Corinthians, but the book neglects to recount exactly why things turned sour. Although 2 Corinthians does not detail what went wrong, it does refer to a visit Paul made and a letter he sent, suggesting that both of those acts contributed to strain in the relationship. Possibly 1 Corinthians was poorly received in Corinth and therefore it also increased the audience's aggravation. The complexity of 2 Corinthians suggests that multiple issues and grievances required Paul to fight on several fronts to re-earn the Corinthians' trust. Whatever the exact sources of the problems between the apostle and this church, through the subject matter and tone of 2 Corinthians, Paul presents himself as one seeking reconciliation while he also vigorously defends himself. He eagerly hopes that the Corinthians will once again open themselves to him and his teachings.

Related to the challenge of determining what evoked the irritation and contrition Paul expresses in 2 Corinthians, several rapid shifts in this letter's rhetoric have led many interpreters to propose that the book 2 Corinthians is not a single letter but actually a composite document comprising pieces of multiple letters Paul wrote. Whether 2 Corinthians has always been a single piece of correspondence or is an amalgam of multiple letters, the book includes a range of rhetorical techniques, recording Paul speaking in voices that are alternately impassioned, caustic, determined, sarcastic, and exasperated.

Second Corinthians resonates with 1 Corinthians in several ways. As mentioned, both books exhibit Paul's deep regard for the Corinthians and his occasional vexation with them. Furthermore, like 1 Corinthians, 2 Corinthians speaks to a church that, according to Paul, needs instruction about how to live in light of the new age God has brought into being through the death and resurrection of Jesus Christ. Although the fullness of God's glory has yet to emerge in its entirety, Paul assures the Corinthians that God transforms people in Christ as they confidently await the time of God's ultimate judgment.

The Letter's Origins and Ancient Audience

Generally speaking, the audience of 2 Corinthians was the same audience that received 1 Corinthians, insofar as both letters address themselves to "the church of God that is in Corinth." Second Corinthians explicitly directs itself to a more expansive readership by including also in its salutation "all the saints throughout Achaia," the region surrounding Corinth. The passage of time since 1 Corinthians made the audience's conditions different, of course, since the Corinthians' relationship with Paul had changed in the short period since he wrote that letter. What looks like an amicable exchange in 1 Corinthians, despite the document's occasionally critical and sarcastic tone, strikes enough of a contrast with the more fretful 2 Corinthians to suggest that the believers in Corinth had grown more disaffected with Paul by the time he wrote 2 Corinthians or any of its parts, which probably happened during the span 54–56 CE.

Paul, writing with Timothy as a coauthor, mentions other encounters with the church in Corinth. He refers to a letter he wrote that grieved the Corinthians (2 Cor 7:8). Elsewhere he speaks of a letter he wrote in lieu of visiting Corinth, a letter he composed "out of much distress and anguish of heart and with many tears, not to cause [the Corinthians] pain, but to let [them] know the abundant love" Paul had for them (2 Cor 2:4). If those two passages from 2 Corinthians refer to the same letter, all indications suggest it expressed Paul's pain over his frustrations with the Corinthians and further damaged his relationship with them. The kind of hurtful letter Paul alludes to in those passages does not appear to describe the relatively innocuous tone of 1 Corinthians. Likely, instead, in 2 Corinthians he refers to a different letter or perhaps a pair of them. Paul also mentions a "painful visit" he made to Corinth (2 Cor 2:1), presumably sometime after sending 1 Corinthians. Paul refers again in 2 Cor 12:14 and 13:1 to an earlier visit he made to Corinth, which could be this same "painful visit" and also the same visit he had promised to make on a previous occasion, in 1 Cor 16:1–9. There was more to Paul and the church's relationship than just the correspondence represented by 1–2 Corinthians.

That relationship was not smooth. An ambiguous explanation in 2 Cor 1:15–18 suggests that Paul did not keep a promise to visit the Corinthians at an anticipated time, or Paul's failure to meet the Corinthians' expectations for his visits apparently incited criticism from them. To add to the complexity, Paul also discusses his intentions of making a "third" visit to the Corinthian church (2 Cor 12:14, 13:1). If Paul ever went back to Corinth at a time after all the parts of 2 Corinthians had been written, no conclusive evidence of that visit remains.

Laying out all of these vague references to numerous letters, visits, and disappointments raises more questions than the references can answer, for Paul does not provide a precise timeline, and 2 Corinthians reveals only so much about why Paul wrote it. There may be a paucity of specific evidence offered in 1–2 Corinthians, but there is enough to reveal a complex and bustling relationship between an apostle and a church. The evidence establishes that frustration and discord arose and perhaps steadily increased between Paul and this community of Christ-followers. By keeping that backdrop in mind, interpreters gain insights into the rhetoric and foci of 2 Corinthians.

It is also helpful to keep 1 Corinthians in mind. The spiritual smugness Paul decries in 1 Corinthians appears to have persisted in Corinth despite Paul's admonitions, for in 2 Corinthians he makes frequent references to boasting. Paul criticizes those who boast in their spiritual experiences or in the indications of their personal strength; he chooses to boast instead in the Corinthians' faithfulness and the suffering he endures for the sake of the gospel. When 2 Corinthians speaks about the imperative to persist in ministry and describes the gospel as an act of reconciliation, Paul signals to his audience that he does not view their damaged relationship beyond repair, for it remains a priority to him and is rooted in what God has accomplished through Christ.

First Corinthians might not have healed the divisive atmosphere in Corinth, but the final chapters of 2 Corinthians suggest that Paul's audience had, however, recently coalesced around one common commitment: a disregard for Paul himself. He was not the kind of apostle they wanted, for in their minds he lacked the strength, accomplishment, and pizzazz they associated with spiritual power. Paul also indicates that the Corinthians did not come to disdain Paul entirely on their own, but others were actively discrediting him in his absence. Paul never identifies those people beyond his mocking epithets *false apostles* and *super-apostles*. They may have been other teachers who journeyed to Corinth from elsewhere or perhaps were members of churches in other parts of Achaia. In any case, Paul treats them with scorn when he defends himself against their attempts to malign him and against their conception of what makes for true spiritual vitality. By defending himself, Paul actually defends his understanding of the gospel as a display of divine power realized through the apparent weakness of a crucified Christ.

The Question of the Letter's Integrity

It is not difficult to imagine how some of the letters Paul wrote, whether to the Corinthians or to any other churches, became lost. If no one copied or disseminated a given piece of correspondence, it could soon cease to exist. Likewise, one easily imagines how multiple letters might have circulated together, if a person or community bundled a variety of noteworthy documents that eventually were reproduced and circulated as a collection. Many scholars propose that 2 Corinthians may be the result of the latter type of phenomenon. They contend the book is a composite document made up of several letters or letter fragments that Paul composed at various times and sent independently. Considering those proposals is helpful to interpreters as they try to make sense of a handful of jarring shifts in 2 Corinthians, places where the mood or focus changes without warning.

Theories about a composite document are not driven by evidence derived from any major inconsistences in the surviving ancient manuscripts. No such evidence exists; there are no surviving Greek manuscripts that include only 2 Corinthians 10–13, for example. Instead, the book's ambiguous and potentially inconsistent statements about Paul's other letters and visits to Corinth could indicate that different parts of the book were written at different times. In addition, the book's sudden shifts in tone and subject matter could suggest that certain parts of the book originally belonged to different letters and addressed different concerns. If 2 Corinthians is a composite document, that might explain why, for example, Paul devotes so much attention to reconciling with his audience in the first half of the book and then in the book's final chapters hurls acidic sarcasm toward those in Corinth who criticize him and his teachings.

The hypotheses about the origins of 2 Corinthians are occasionally intricate and cannot be explained or examined here in detail. At their simplest, they propose that 2 Corinthians 10–13 once was part of a separate letter. Additional hypotheses suggest, in addition, that the material in 2 Corinthians 8–9 originally belonged to yet an additional letter or even two letters. In their more specific and complex expressions, some hypotheses identify certain parts of 2 Corinthians, such as chapters 10–13, as parts of the anguished letter—or perhaps two separate letters—that Paul mentions in 2 Cor 2:4 and 7:8. A few interpreters even speculate that sections of 2 Corinthians might be pieces of a letter Paul wrote to Corinth sometime prior to 1 Corinthians, to which he refers in 1 Cor 5:9.

Unconvinced by the various hypotheses, other interpreters see no good reason to doubt the literary integrity of 2 Corinthians, meaning they consider it a single letter Paul and Timothy sent to Corinth sometime after the now-lost letter Paul composed in anguish and with tears, according to 2 Cor 2:4. Those interpreters insist that the letter's jarring transitions from one discussion to another might not be as dramatic or counterproductive as other interpreters contend. Furthermore, time might have passed between the writing of various sections of 2 Corinthians, as Paul and Timothy considered what to tell the Corinthians and investigated options for the letter's delivery.

Keeping track of the various theories and the evidence from which they draw proves confusing to many, especially when one is still getting oriented to what 2 Corinthians says in the first place and how Paul constructs his various theological arguments. The latter pursuit needs to take precedence over the former one. In other words, in no way should the debates about the document's literary integrity become people's starting point as they explore 2 Corinthians. Rather, reading the letter is the better place to begin. This brief overview of the issue has aimed only to draw attention to the fact that readers encounter a range of subject matter, moods, and rhetorical techniques in 2 Corinthians. The letter divides relatively easily into three distinct thematic movements (roughly speaking, chapters 1–7, 8–9, and 10–13), and those sections have their own distinctive concerns, no matter what the truth is concerning the book's compositional history, whether 2 Corinthians has always been one letter or it is a patchwork of two or more letters assembled soon after Paul wrote them. An interpreter can remain undecided or even unconcerned about the literary integrity of 2 Corinthians while still swimming in its deep waters; indeed, those interpreters who make up their mind about where the letter came from *before* taking time to plumb its depths have made their decision the wrong way.

Overview

Even if 2 Corinthians comprises multiple letters or fragments of letters composed independently but around the same general time in the history of Paul's relationship with the church in Corinth, the people who compiled the book nevertheless arranged its material more or less in conformity with the standard format of Paul's letters. Therefore, 2 Corinthians includes a single salutation and a single conclusion with a benediction. The document reads like a standard letter in between those formal bookends, as well, despite the occasional erratic transitions and a few ambiguous references about Paul's travels and his other correspondence.

Salutation and Blessing (2 Cor 1:1–7)

Even as the syntax and style of 2 Corinthians from start to finish, with the exception of 6:14–7:1, corresponds closely with the other letters Paul wrote, the letter claims to have two voices behind it. The opening verse names Timothy as a coauthor. One of Paul's closest associates, Timothy, played a key role in Paul and his team's ongoing efforts to provide encouragement and leadership to the Corinthian Christ-followers. According to 2 Cor 1:19, Timothy and Silvanus were with Paul when they first introduced the gospel to the Corinthians (cf. Acts 18:5). Paul refers to a return visit Timothy made to the city in 1 Cor 4:17, and in 1 Cor 16:10 he mentions the possibility that Timothy would travel there yet again. That latter visit might have resulted in Timothy bringing a report to Paul that prompted the apostle to write the anguished and tearful letter to which he refers in 2 Cor 2:4. The occasional use of a first-person plural voice in 2 Corinthians reminds readers that Timothy also stands behind this letter, even though the letter's prose and frequent use of a first-person singular address indicates Paul was the primary author and the dominant, if not sole, source of the letter's rhetoric.

With the exception of Galatians, all the other letters Paul wrote offer a thanksgiving to God immediately after the salutation. In 2 Corinthians, however, Paul offers a slightly different sort of prayer in which he magnifies God's blessedness, calling particular attention to God's ability to provide comfort in the midst of afflictions. Right away, Paul characterizes suffering and struggle as part of a believer's life and not as aberrations. In the midst of difficulties, a person has the opportunity to experience God's consolation. Paul thereby sets the stage for what follows in this letter, which will urge the Corinthians to reconcile with Paul as an expression of the reconciliation God accomplishes and which will exalt the ways God demonstrates power through weakness. The blessing Paul offers to initiate the correspondence essentially fulfills the same roles as the formal thanksgivings he includes at the beginnings of other letters. Eventually, in 2 Cor 2:14–17, Paul offers express thanks to God; in that instance it is for the triumph God achieves and the ways in which knowledge of God radiates from Christ-followers.

Defense of Paul's Conduct (2 Cor 1:8–2:13)

The opening blessing transitions smoothly into Paul and Timothy's description of their recent experiences and Paul's explanation of why he had not lately visited Corinth. No more details are available about the specific "affliction [Paul and Timothy] experienced in Asia," but they attribute their deliverance to God, offering the ordeal as a concrete example of the consolation God provides. In emphasizing at the letter's outset the suffering they endure for the sake of the gospel, the authors call attention to their willingness to endure hardship in their work on Christ's behalf. Beginning the letter in such a way could elicit trust as well as sympathy from the Corinthians. Paul and Timothy do not boast in their ability to endure hardship; they boast explicitly in their conscience, claiming to have been enabled by God's grace to carry out their ministry with sincerity and integrity. In time, boasting will emerge as a major theme in 2 Corinthians, as it is in 1 Corinthians. Paul rebukes those who boast in themselves and their own accomplishments or abilities, yet he approves of boasting in God and boasting about how God works in the lives of others.

Paul and Timothy's appeal to how they "have behaved in the world" puts accent on their single-mindedness and their pure devotion to God and to the Corinthians. That emphasis holds the whole of 2 Corinthians together, for Paul offers his faithful integrity as a token of God's power at work in him and Timothy. That integrity, as well as confidence in God's presence, leads Paul to commend a relationship of reciprocal boasting between him and the Corinthians, a boasting that will continue until "the day of the Lord Jesus." To boast in Paul means the Corinthians should put their confidence in him, or in God at work in him, just as he puts his confidence in them. Paul thereby sets the stage for seeking reconciliation with the Corinthians, even as he also appeals to reasons why they should accept his guidance and authority and therefore reject other teachers who set themselves against Paul.

Paul recognizes that recent events and disappointments might call into question his claims about his sincerity and integrity. He refers therefore to his failure to visit Corinth when he promised he would, his decision to send an anguished letter to Corinth, and conflict concerning an unnamed person in Corinth who might have been causing trouble after being disciplined according to Paul's instructions (cf. 2 Cor 7:12 and possibly 1 Cor 5:1–5). In all those cases, Paul insists he was trying to act in ways faithful to God and for the good of the Corinthian church. Because he assumed the Corinthians know the wider contexts around all the issues, Paul includes few details. Evidently Paul also believed the Corinthians were familiar with the weighty theological claims he offers in this section, for he does not elaborate on what it means, for example, to assert that in Jesus "every one of God's promises is a 'Yes'" or that God has "anointed" and sealed believers with God's Spirit "as a first installment."

Confidence in the New Covenant (2 Cor 2:14–4:6)

Despite all the suffering and conflict that come Paul and Timothy's way in their efforts to perform ministry, they rejoice in their work. This section of the letter extols Christian ministry as something permeated by hope and glory. Paul understands authentic ministry as living a life infused with divine power experienced in weakness, a life conformed to Christ's humiliating crucifixion and powerful resurrection. Paul's embrace of weakness in this ministry does not amount to a stifled or concealed expression of the gospel, as some of his hyper-charismatic critics in Corinth may have charged, according to chapters 10–13. Rather, his lifestyle of embracing hardship allows people to encounter nothing short of the glory of the Lord as it is reflected in their own experiences.

The authors begin this section by characterizing their ministry, including their relationship with the Corinthians, as participation in God's triumphs. The afflictions they suffer do not represent a departure from those triumphs. Furthermore, their ministry offers a view of God's glory because they focus on "a new covenant" (see Jer 31:31; cf. Luke 22:20; 1 Cor 11:25; Heb 8:13, 9:15), which they characterize as superior to the covenant associated with Moses, the giving of torah. The particular manner in which Paul and Timothy contend for the new covenant's superiority was familiar to Paul from contemporary Jewish biblical interpretation, an argument holding that if a lesser element is true or powerful, then a comparable greater element must be even more so. Therefore Paul and Timothy build on the strength or reliability of the covenant associated with Moses to declare the greater glory on display in the new covenant, the gospel of Jesus Christ. The authors do not imply that the gospel somehow replaces or invalidates the earlier Mosaic covenant (cf. Heb 8:13, 10:9); instead, the gospel magnifies what that earlier covenant promised about allowing people to encounter God's glory. According to the authors, what the initial covenant did, the gospel does even more so.

A vital theme in the comparison between the covenants derives from the veil Moses wears in Exod 34:29–35. In that story, whenever Moses emerges from speaking with God, his face shines as a reflection of the divine glory. He wears a veil when circulating among the people, shielding them from the glory he manifests, and removes it when relaying to them things the Lord has told him. Paul and Timothy alter the scriptural image to make a veil a metaphor for ignorance, like a shroud that covers people's minds. The veil disappears when people turn to Christ, allowing them to find true freedom and to behold the Lord's glory. Believers see that glory "as though reflected in a mirror" (2 Cor 3:18), something there but not yet in its fullest clarity.

The authors persist in employing veiling as a metaphor when they assert that their own ministry consists of open and bold proclamations of the gospel. In doing so, they continue to offer a theological description of the gospel as an expression of God's glory even as they also defend themselves from criticisms that they act in untrustworthy ways or that they conceal the true power of the gospel when they embrace hardships and repudiate ostentatious displays of spiritual power. They renounce cunning and falsehood, for those tactics would keep "those who are perishing" veiled and unable to see "the light of the gospel of the glory of Christ, who is the image of God" (2 Cor 4:4). Paul and Timothy imply that people naturally suffer from a kind of spiritual blindness because Satan, "the god of this world," exercises his power to such an end. Those who "proclaim Jesus Christ as Lord," however, bring people to the light of truth and divine glory, even as they also participate in the overthrow of Satan, whom God disarms through the gospel.

Affliction, Reconciliation, and the Authors' Appeal
(2 Cor 4:7–7:16)

The authors continue to defend their ministry and articulate their confidence in God as they simultaneously and subtly pursue reconciliation with the Corinthians. Lest the preceding discussion about the new covenant as an encounter with God's glory give the impression that divine glory makes life easy, the letter's attention next turns to afflictions and fragility. No one should mistake assurances of glory and power as justifications for boasting or for exalting fellow Christ-followers. Divine glory and strength remain God's possessions and are manifestations of God's presence, while believers resemble easy-to-break earthenware jars. The outward appearances of the hardships and resistance that dog Paul and Timothy's ministry hardly resemble a glorious life. The authors recognize that the Corinthians might assume that such travails make this life meaningless or worth escaping from, but Paul and Timothy quickly correct such an impression. They characterize their ordeals and the ministry that continues nevertheless as "preparing [them] for an eternal weight of glory beyond all measure" (2 Cor 4:17).

Paul and Timothy compare current life to dwelling in a tent while awaiting a promised house, indicating that believers' ultimate transformations (cf. 2 Cor 3:18) remain in the future, perhaps recalling a theme from a previous letter about the resurrection of the body resulting in a transformed, spiritual body (1 Cor 15:42–57). Decay, affliction, and longing remain inescapable realities for all who currently live in a mortal tent, but Paul and Timothy live with hope and confidence for the newness to come, spurred on by the Spirit given by God "as a guarantee" (2 Cor 5:5). Such hope urges the authors to serve others. For even though believers all die alongside Christ in his crucifixion (cf. Rom 6:5–6; Gal 2:20), they do not then hate this life or deny its difficulties. They devote themselves to persisting in making God's glory known to others.

Jesus' crucifixion and resurrection affect how Paul and Timothy view life and also how they regard others. Through Jesus' experience of death and rebirth, God has created everything new. The "new creation" (cf. Gal 6:15) now in existence marks the transition from an old era to a new era, from an old world and its systems to new ones. This divine act, this apocalyptic interruption and metamorphosis, occurs through the reality of people's participation in Christ's death and their new existence as people who dwell "in Christ." With a breathtaking declaration in 2 Cor 5:21, Paul and Timothy declare that God's saving activity—"the righteousness of God"—envelops humanity, allowing people to participate in God's care and presence so fully that they "become" God's care and presence. Even though the letters to the Corinthians do not refer to God's "righteousness" as frequently as Romans and Galatians do (e.g., 2 Cor 3:9; 6:7, 14), in this case the expression stands for the sum of God's commitment and power to reclaim the world for God's purposes. God's dramatic and effective display of righteousness through Christ compels the letter's authors to regard people in a brand-new light: as beings treasured by God. That insight provides a prime motivation for their ministry to others despite the difficulties that come.

Paul and Timothy's labor is a labor meant to bring others into the sphere of God's reconciling work. Because the letter characterizes God's salvation as reconciliation, bringing a sinful and estranged world back into its right relation to God, the letter's theological rhetoric implicitly buttresses Paul and Timothy's efforts to be reconciled with the Corinthians. A Christian "ministry of reconciliation" announces and embodies God's active commitment to reconcile the world to God's own self, through Christ, even as that ministry also promotes reconciliation among people as a consequence of their participation in God's transformative righteousness.

Finally, after multiple chapters in which Paul and Timothy have explained their ministry as an expression of what God demonstrates and accomplishes through Jesus' crucifixion and resurrection, they make a direct appeal to their audience. The appeal begins in 2 Cor 6:11–13 and resumes in 7:2–4, asking the Corinthians to open their hearts to Paul and Timothy. The letter has made its case for the authors' trustworthiness and also for their affection for the Corinthians. It has named the theological warrant for pursuing reconciliation. Now it forthrightly asks the Corinthians to respond. Paul and Timothy believe that reconciliation will offer new possibilities for their future relationship with the Corinthians. Reconciliation does not amount to denying or papering over past grievances. Reconciliation will mend old wounds and equip the relationship to endure future trials. Later in chapter 7, the letter's focus returns to other recent experiences and points of strife between Paul and the Corinthian church. When Paul there contends that afflictions, strife, and grief can be worthwhile if they lead to repentance and renewal, he suggests that reconciliation with the Corinthians will soothe the distress already caused by the fractures in their relationship. Reconciliation represents the way forward for all of them; it manifests the deep unity that they share as people united in heart and as people who have been reconciled to God.

The verses that sit between the letter's two-part appeal, 2 Cor 6:14–7:1, attract attention because they seem to interrupt and thus distract from what looks like a coherent plea in 2 Cor 6:11–13 and 7:2–4. In addition, the interrupting verses appear to contradict things Paul says elsewhere. For a general example, the verses' strong sectarian tone exceeds Paul's usual remarks about how a church distinguishes itself as a holy community. A specific point of contradiction stems from the command against believers being "mismatched" (literally, "unevenly yoked") with unbelievers. That command appears at odds with 1 Cor 7:12–16, which speaks approvingly of marriages between believers and unbelievers, and also with 1 Cor 14:22–25, which implies that unbelievers are welcome in the church's worship services. Some interpreters contend that 2 Cor 6:14–7:1 consists of material that was an original part of the letter and that it means to encourage the Corinthians to separate themselves from other teachers Paul considered rivals (see 2 Cor 10–13). More likely, however, the verses are the result of an interpolation. In other words, they come from either another Pauline writing or another document altogether that a scribe or compiler inserted at this point in the midst of Paul and Timothy's appeal. The debate over the verses in question plays a part in larger discussions about the overall literary integrity of 2 Corinthians, as discussed earlier.

Grace and Generosity (2 Cor 8–9)

This section begins with a sharp shift in the letter's focus, leading some interpreters to propose that the material in 2 Corinthians 8–9 originally circulated as part of a separate letter or even as parts of two separate letters. Even though the change in subject matter is jarring, chapter 7 nevertheless ends with a sense of closure when Paul discusses Titus' positive report about the Corinthians. Had 2 Corinthians not referred elsewhere to the existence of additional letters from Paul to Corinth, it is unlikely that interpreters would question whether chapters 8–9 originally belonged with 2 Corinthians 1–7. That is to say, the transition to the new subject matter beginning in chapter 8 may be abrupt, but it hardly represents a tectonic shift.

Paul and Timothy encourage the Corinthians to give generously to a financial offering Paul is collecting. The authors provide few specific details here, but passages in other letters indicate that the Corinthians would have been familiar with Paul's intention to bring a gift to the impoverished church in Jerusalem (e.g., Gal 2:10; 1 Cor 16:1–4; Rom 15:25–28). After all, the Corinthians already started to give generously "last year," and Paul was actively motivating the churches in Macedonia and the churches in Achaia by relaying reports to them about each of the other region's generosity.

These two chapters explain what should be the basis for the Corinthians' financial benevolence. Paul also takes care to reassure the letter's audience of his trustworthiness as the collection's steward when he mentions a delegation of Titus and two anonymous "brothers" who will visit Corinth to check on the progress of the church's charity. By involving a larger delegation of known and trusted people, Paul distinguishes himself from any appearance of being a traveling teacher determined to fleece a gullible group of disciples.

As Paul discusses why the Corinthians should give, he refuses to command them, preferring instead to characterize their contributions as a gift, a free statement of generosity, partnership, and love. Ten times in these two chapters the letter uses the Greek word meaning "grace" (*charis*), although English translations mask the concentrated use of the term when they render it variously as "privilege," "generous undertaking," "generous act," "thanks," "blessing," and "gift." The implication of the term and its frequent appearance is that financial generosity arises from and imitates the "generous act" or grace of Christ, for through Christ's humiliating death, God bestowed spiritual riches on others. The charity Paul seeks from the Corinthians is an opportunity for them to imitate and even participate in the divine grace made theirs because of Christ.

Like any good fund-raiser, Paul encourages the Corinthians to give as generously as they can. He speaks of God's ability to provide for their needs in abundance. Paul does not promise that God will pay back every gift the Corinthians give. Rather, he reminds them that God is the source of all good gifts and the ground of generosity in the first place. Along with prodding them toward more generous giving, Paul also emphasizes that the Corinthians' eagerness matters more than the amount of their gifts. After all, Paul aims for the offering not only to relieve suffering in Jerusalem but also to make a statement of "sharing" and eager partnership between the Corinthians and the saints in Jerusalem. Paul knows that a generous gift to the Jerusalem church might incline the believers there to view his ministry and the emergence of new, mostly gentile churches more favorably. Yet he also intends the gift to make a theological statement to everyone involved. The church in Jerusalem and the churches Paul encouraged in Macedonia and Achaia had sizable cultural, ethnic, and geographical distances separating them, yet Paul insists they all share a common identity in Christ—an identity celebrated and proclaimed by an opportunity to send financial support across the miles. None of those Christian communities can understand itself as independent from the others, because all of them share an identity situated in Christ. Generosity expresses that inescapable theological reality, a corporate identity that is the product of divine grace.

Power through Weakness, Both in the Cross and in Paul's Ministry (2 Cor 10–12)

In this section Paul offers a testy and sustained defense of his ministry and his authority as an apostle. He does so in response to people in Corinth who have criticized him for a variety of reasons, including his unimpressive personal presence and his willingness to embrace suffering and deprivation as evidence of spiritual vitality and not indications of failure. Repeatedly Paul contrasts weakness and power, both to characterize the hardships he has endured in ministry as corresponding to Jesus' humiliations (cf. 1 Cor 1:18–2:16) and to rebut any in his audience who equate mature spirituality with displays of personal power or extravagant religious experiences. Paul celebrates weakness and identifies it as a hallmark of apostolic ministry, for in weakness one discovers the power of God as the gospel of Christ manifests it.

Paul's opening salvo involves speaking boldly and promising to act boldly when he returns to Corinth to combat the teachings and teachers that he considers opposed to Christ. References to weapons and waging war demonstrate how seriously he takes the issue and his commission to do what is necessary. He eschews the opportunity to protect his reputation at all costs or to humiliate his adversaries. Instead, he declares his and Timothy's primary goal is "building up" the Corinthians.

Paul and Timothy also remind their audience that they were "the first to come all the way to [Corinth] with the good news of Christ" (2 Cor 10:14). With that reminder the authors present themselves as people who legitimately want to increase their influence among the believers there. The argument reassures the church in Corinth of Paul and Timothy's trustworthiness even as it reasserts the gospel as their standard for what it means to provide leadership to churches. Paul and Timothy will not abandon the church or allow it to damage itself by its own mistakes or by the poisonous teachings of unreliable leaders. Paul and Timothy imply that they are obliged to continue fostering the spiritual well-being of a church they have founded, for they understand their ultimate commission as an impulse to "proclaim the good news in lands beyond [Corinth]" (2 Cor 10:16; cf. Rom 15:20, 23–24). Although they set their eyes on an expansive ministry, no one would trust them to conduct such a thing if they simultaneously neglected or denigrated churches they already established. If they cannot appropriately boast about the positive and successful work God had already performed through their labors among the Corinthians, they have little warrant for founding new churches.

Paul says very little about the teachers in Corinth whom he considers his rivals, other than identifying them as "false apostles" and, with tongue in cheek, as "super-apostles." Paul has reason to believe that they have made personal attacks against him (e.g., 2 Cor 10:10). With respect to the teachings he thinks they promote, Paul says they proclaim "another Jesus" and depict "a different gospel." Like Paul, they are Jews, for he calls them "Hebrews," "Israelites," and "descendants of Abraham." Given that the Mosaic law does not appear to be an issue in these chapters, there is no good basis for simply equating the "false apostles" and their teachings with the teachers Paul criticizes in Galatians in that book's discussion of the role of the law. Instead, based on Paul's words in 2 Corinthians 11–12, the "false apostles" evidently promoted a more robust form of spiritual expression than Paul desired; perhaps they focused on flamboyant displays of spiritual gifts or modes of religious experience. They could have expressed disdain for embodied aspects of Christian living in favor of supposedly higher forms of spiritual existence. Any of those possibilities could have appealed to the Corinthians in light of the spiritual smugness and hyperinflated embrace of spiritual freedom that Paul criticizes in 1 Corinthians.

Paul denounces the other teachers as interlopers. Employing a metaphor that modern readers find problematic, Paul characterizes himself as a father trying to preserve his virginal daughter, the church, for her marriage to Christ while the "false apostles" aim to seduce her or otherwise lead her astray. Paul confesses that he lacks the rhetorical skill of those other teachers, but he insists he does not trail them in knowledge. Likewise, the Corinthians can trust Paul's guidance because he has not asked them to provide him financial support for his ministry, as apparently the other so-called apostles have. He insists he cares for the Corinthians more than the others do, for he characterizes the "false apostles" as eager to humiliate and take advantage of the Corinthians.

By all appearances, Paul's rivals led the Corinthians to regard him as a weak man and a fool, someone determined to diminish their ability to relish all the benefits and power they can claim in Christ. Paul accepts those condescending labels and exploits them in a sarcastic speech in which he glories in his apparent foolishness and his sufferings. Although Paul frequently decries boasting in this letter, here he boasts that his hardships show him to be a more authentic minister of Christ than the "super-apostles." Paul boasts about the experiences that most people in his culture would have associated with failure and shame: incarceration, beatings, shipwreck, hunger, thirst, deprivation, and even being forced to flee from imperial authorities by concealing himself in a large basket. Paul offers a long catalog of sufferings to show what it means to enjoy the benefits Christ provides: the gospel means participating in Christ's sufferings, discovering the power of God amid the experience of weakness and humiliation inflicted by others.

Paul continues his unique brand of boasting by talking about "visions and revelations" in 2 Cor 12:1–10. Against those in Corinth who celebrated spiritual excess or pursued religious experiences resembling what modern people call altered states of consciousness or transcendental phenomena, Paul boasts that he can match his rivals' claims. He understands visions differently than they do, however, for his experiences taught him deeper reliance on God instead of fostering spiritual elitism. Paul speaks about himself elliptically, as "a person," persisting in speaking like a fool and highlighting that his mystical insights into "the third heaven," the highest level of heaven according to some Jewish traditions, were beyond his own control. The revelatory experience did not elevate Paul's status or inflate his ego, for it left him with an affliction, one whose precise nature remains indecipherable from Paul's obscure references to "a thorn in the flesh" and "a messenger of Satan." Paul's lasting irritant, whatever it was, provided him with what he considered an incurable reminder of both the extraordinary revelatory experience and the consistent grace of God that has given him strength to persevere in any situation. Paul thereby uses his description of a captivating experience to show that knowledge and spirituality do not sustain a person; rather, God's grace provides all that is necessary.

On the whole, Paul's vigorous attempts to reiterate his own weakness and dependence obviously constitute an attempt to elevate him over his rivals in the eyes of the Corinthians. Truly Paul laments the threat of being spurned by the Corinthians and wants to reestablish himself as influential among them. At the same time, he consistently points to himself and his experiences as manifestations of the gospel and therefore indications of *God's* supremacy and not his own. Paul urges the Corinthians to look at his life and to see the gospel on display there insofar as they can detect "the power of Christ" dwelling in Paul in his weaknesses. It is a power Paul does not keep for himself. He yearns for the Corinthians to share in the power, for he reassures them of his love for them, his intention to build them up, and his commitment to see them leave behind their behaviors that damage their ability to function as a healthy community.

As mentioned, some interpreters suspect that most if not all of the material in 2 Corinthians 10–13 originally was written and sent to Corinth separately from the material in 2 Corinthians 1–9, for Paul's sarcastic and critical tone in these chapters sounds out of harmony with the rest of the letter's emphasis on reconciliation and generosity. The argument and mockery in these chapters have the capacity to anger an audience, and Paul does refer in 2 Cor 7:8 to another letter from him that grieved the Corinthians. Some therefore wonder whether the material in this section might have been from that letter. The sheer existence of various hypotheses helps interpreters appreciate the ways that 2 Corinthians 10–13 appears to clash with 2 Corinthians 1–9. At the same time, because all of the chapters now circulate together as a single biblical book, it is also valuable for interpreters to consider how the message and theological emphases of 2 Corinthians 10–13 might complicate or resonate with other parts of 2 Corinthians.

Future Plans, Closing Exhortations, and Benediction (2 Cor 13)

Even as the book starts to turn toward its final exhortations, its references to Paul's travel plans continue the focus from the preceding chapters on God's power on display through Christ's weakness. Paul reprises the bold threats he delivered at the beginning of chapter 10 while still reassuring his audience that his ultimate goal is to have them live with Christ and not to see them torn down. Recalling a central theological theme from 1 Corinthians, Paul tells his audience "Jesus Christ is in you," understanding the "you" collectively, in a plural form (2 Cor 13:5; cf. 1 Cor 6:15, 19; 12:12–27). Despite the reassurances, the rhetoric in Paul's exhortations remains urgent and arresting: he is concerned that some in the Corinthian church may discover themselves to be apart from Christ.

In Paul's final sentences, appearing in 2 Cor 13:11–13, the words he chooses recall the reconciliation he seeks—reconciliation between himself and the Corinthians and reconciliation among the contentious believers in Corinth themselves. Such reconciliation will not occur on its own as an act of the church's moral courage; God promotes it. Paul therefore speaks of "the God of love and peace" as well as the grace, love, and communion that stem from God. The letter thus concludes with a brief description of God as one who promotes harmony through God's close engagement with people. That harmony comes about through the good news Paul teaches.

The Letter's Themes and Theological Emphases

Second Corinthians offers an especially choice example of how Paul's theological convictions emerge through his letters' attempts to offer pastoral leadership to specific Christian communities in particular circumstances. This letter contains a number of profound theological statements that do not present themselves as products of abstract theological reflections but as critical foundations in Paul's very practical and personal efforts to rehabilitate himself in the eyes of the Corinthians and to dissuade them from following the misguided teachings of those he considers interlopers. Paul and Timothy pursue a primary goal of reestablishing a relationship that they believe is in the Corinthians' best interests. Their main avenue toward reaching this goal involves advocating for the gospel and confessing their unwavering confidence in God. The way the authors articulate the gospel in the document, with a keen focus on reconciliation and with repeated attention to God's ability to bring life from death and manifest power in weakness, resonates directly with the kind of leadership Paul promises to provide the Corinthians.

When the letter declares, for example, that the Spirit is God's "guarantee" of a promise to provide immortality (2 Cor 5:4–5), Paul hardly intends to offer a full account of his beliefs about the Holy Spirit. The larger point at work in the passage consists of clarifying, among other things, that God fuels Paul and Timothy's determination to persist in ministry, despite the afflictions they suffer, so God's glory can be known by others. The letter's context and the authors' purposes do not render the comment about the Spirit as a divine guarantee less meaningful or less important than if it had appeared in a different kind of document. Taking account of the letter's overall aims helps illuminate why Paul considered his beliefs about the Spirit to be meaningful specifically for discussions about Christian living and his ministry. The letter compels interpreters to consider the reasons why Paul gives attention to certain theological themes, and it invites interpreters to see how Paul expresses his pastoral guidance and his theology as an integrated whole, mutually informing each other.

God's Glory, New Creation, and Paul's Ministry

Paul and Timothy devote the majority of this letter, especially the material in 2 Corinthians 1–7, to substantiating their central appeal to their audience, laboring to regain the Corinthians' trust and openness toward them and their ministry. Given all the effort they made to reestablish their credentials and bona fides for leadership, it may appear at first glance that jealousy or bruised egos motivate the authors to write to the Corinthians. But the letter tells a bigger story. A current of envy or personal disappointment may flow through 2 Corinthians, but Paul and Timothy consistently characterize their leadership in theological terms, suggesting that their greatest ambition is to see the Corinthians rightly take hold of and embody the gospel of Jesus Christ. The gospel, as the authors understand it, provides the basis for understanding other people's inherent value, a pattern for human conduct, and the ground for future hope that exists alongside the obvious severity of life's current difficulties.

As in other letters from Paul, in 2 Corinthians the death and resurrection of Jesus Christ constitute the core of the Christian gospel. Those two decisive events demonstrate people's value, as well as the value of this current life, because Jesus "died for all" and thus created the possibility that "those who live might live no longer for themselves, but for him who died and was raised for them" (2 Cor 5:14–15). That new way of living creates a new perspective that utterly changes how Paul and Timothy—and, they hope, the Corinthians—view other people. Jesus' crucifixion and resurrection create the opportunity for reconciliation, in which people live together as full participants in God's "righteousness" (2 Cor 5:16–21; cf. 1:3–7). Corporately, people exist as more than beneficiaries of God's commitment to save and restore humanity; they also become a living extension of that active commitment.

Paul and his coauthor's understanding of the church's conduct also springs from Christ. God's grace, as manifested through Christ, creates the church's common identity and motivates the church to share its resources (2 Cor 8–9) and to rejoice in one another's faith (2 Cor 1:12–14; 7:4). The authors' exhortations about how to live emerge from their outlook on God's character. God's gracious character and the promise of God's judgment add urgency to the church's view of life, even as Christ-followers can draw confidence from the promise of its transformation through the power of God (e.g., 2 Cor 3:18; 5:1–10; 6:1–2).

God is also the source of the hope to which Paul and Timothy appeal in this letter, for God "raised the Lord Jesus" (2 Cor 4:14) and gave "the Spirit as a guarantee" (2 Cor 5:5; cf. 1:22; Rom 8:11, 23). As churches navigate the interim time, between Jesus' resurrection and the eternal dwelling God prepares for people (2 Cor 5:1–4), they live not with despair or an impulse to ignore life's struggles and limitations but with a desire to please the Lord (2 Cor 5:6–10; cf. Rom 8:18–27).

That a Pauline letter focuses so intently on Jesus' crucifixion and resurrection is no surprise. What makes 2 Corinthians, as a particular statement of Paul's understanding of the gospel, most distinctive from other books is its theological rhetoric. That rhetoric expands certain themes or yokes them to Paul's specific efforts to nurture the Corinthians' theological understanding. For example, other letters also speak of the gospel as a manifestation of God's "glory," but 2 Corinthians does so in particular ways, especially when it compares the gospel as a "new covenant" to Moses' covenant and its connections to God's glory. To take another example, in Romans Paul associates God's salvation with "reconciliation" (Rom 5:10–11), but 2 Corinthians offers Paul's clearest and most memorable account of what it means to be reconciled to God and others. Even though 2 Corinthians uses little explicit language about divine "revelations," still it describes one's participation in the gospel as nothing less than a direct encounter with the glory of God (cf. Rom 5:2), an encounter that transforms people (e.g., 2 Cor 3:18). Likewise, Paul also talks about "new creation" in Gal 6:15, but in 2 Corinthians the expression supports the claim that God has brought an entirely new state of affairs into being through Jesus' death and resurrection (2 Cor 5:17). A key piece of 2 Corinthians is its authors' express desire to help their audience live appropriately in the new creation. The letter urges its readers to understand the transformative power of the gospel not just as a future promise but as something that affects one's life and purpose right now.

Victories and Victims, Strength and Weakness

Nowhere else does Paul call attention to the suffering he and his coworkers regularly endured in the course of their ministry more than in 2 Corinthians, both in a general sense (e.g., 2 Cor 1:3–11, 4:7–10; cf. 1 Cor 4:9–13; 1 Thess 2:2) and with résumés of specific hardships (e.g., 2 Cor 6:3–10, 11:23–28). While Paul does not urge the Corinthians to seek out ways to participate in similar trials, as if he considered the endurance of pain a requisite part of Christian discipleship, still he presents those experiences as confirmations of his own faithfulness and his ministry as an apostle. When Paul and Timothy speak positively about their adversities as examples of "carrying in the body the death of Jesus" (2 Cor 4:10; cf. Phil 3:11), and when they classify those bodily pains as merely a "slight momentary affliction" (2 Cor 4:17), they raise the question of whether Christian disciples should celebrate suffering or otherwise embrace victimhood. This is a vital question, especially when interpreters use passages like those to make suffering into a virtue or when those passages are made to tell whole groups of people to endure their abuse, despondency, oppression, and social disadvantages for the sake of a promise about a greater good to come.

As always, context adds more nuance to the conversation. In 2 Cor 6:3–10 and 11:23–28, the overarching point aims to establish Paul and Timothy as faithful in their ministry. If the Corinthians have criticized Paul for being excessively timid or a swindler, the apostle's willingness to endure and re-endure various adversities could be an effective rebuttal, maybe especially so in Paul's age, when efforts to distance oneself from dishonorable or manipulative frauds were common rhetoric among teachers and preachers. Moreover, the theological emphases of the entire letter and Paul's relentless focus on Jesus' death and resurrection might speak against anyone who would interpret Paul's positive references to hardships as excuses for minimizing abuse or turning a blind eye to the dehumanizing potential of suffering. Not all suffering is the same, after all, and suffering may arise from very different types of causes. Paul's focus in 2 Corinthians is very particular: he calls attention to suffering he endures as one trying to preach the gospel with limited resources over a large geographical area in the face of frequent opposition. He claims that *those* hardships, arising from his sometimes contentious work as an apostle, resemble what Jesus endured in his ostensibly ignominious death (e.g., 2 Cor 1:5; 4:7–11; 13:4). Although Christ's suffering was horrific, new life sprang from it. Paul suggests that the same dynamic can be at work in Christian ministry, especially in adversarial cultural environments, and therefore he contends that his particular hardships possess no ability to shame or discredit him (cf. 2 Cor 2:14). Because Paul's mention of his ordeals contributes specifically to his sparring with the super-apostles over his credentials for ministry, the letter's strong accent on his hardships appears appropriate to the particular situation. Paul basically insists that he shares in all of Christ's experiences, just as he benefits from all the gospel's blessings. His participation with Christ is all encompassing.

At the same time, Paul's willingness to "boast of the things that show [his] weakness" (2 Cor 11:30) could have backfired on him in his cultural setting. His society had little sympathy for powerlessness. Weakness was widely scorned in Greco-Roman culture. Many of his contemporaries would have considered a man who eagerly boasted about his fragilities not a true man at all. Paul's efforts to celebrate his vulnerability as a reflection of Christ's weakness stood in contrast to ancient norms about masculinity and power, which equated true virtue with agency and control. Manhood and strength meant mastery over circumstances, others, and even oneself. Yet Paul celebrates weakness—his own and Christ's—and he urges people to submit to one another. He said similar things to the Corinthians previously (1 Cor 1:18–2:5) in his attempts to correct their spiritual elitism. Repeatedly in his letters he calls for a way of living that benefits one's neighbor instead of seeking to dominate others (e.g., Rom 14:1–15:13; 1 Cor 10:23–33, 11:17–34; Gal 5:13–26; Phil 2:1–8; 1 Thess 5:14). On one hand, then, Paul depicts the gospel in stark contrast to widespread assumptions about honor and masculine strength.

On the other hand, however, Paul still holds up strength—divine strength—as something desirable. He does not laud weakness in and of itself, for the weakness he sees in Christ serves as the means by which God expresses power and by which Paul taps into that power (e.g., 2 Cor 12:9–10). Convictions about a powerful God are important in the apocalyptic drama that informs so much of Paul's theology, for God must be strong to defeat such ruthless cosmic adversaries as sin and death. Nevertheless, Paul's creative juxtaposition of strength and weakness, manifested in the work of God through Christ and in Paul's own adversities, raises the question of how Paul can both subvert conventional values about power and rely on them to speak about the nature of God's work in the world. The nature of God's work is especially important when one considers, as has been discussed, that Paul roots his instructions about the Christian life in his understanding of who God is and how God operates through the death and resurrection of Jesus Christ. Accordingly, some Christians have claimed Paul's teachings about divine power discovered in powerlessness as incredibly useful for affirming human dignity, insofar as Paul names and celebrates *God's* presence among and within people who experience degradation and oppression. Still other interpreters have found Paul's ideas to be obstacles in the Christian church's ability to speak plainly about suffering's corrosive effects on human beings and their societies. The challenge, it seems, for Paul and his modern interpreters, is to extol a God who will not remain distanced from suffering while simultaneously avoiding the insinuation that the gospel romanticizes suffering in all its forms.

Religious Experience

Because Paul's letters offer so few glimpses into his life story and his ministry, beyond some of his teachings and assorted accounts of his travels, passages such as the one where he describes a vision of "the third heaven" (2 Cor 12:1–10) distinguish themselves. Paul refers to the vision he had as something that happened to "a person," allowing him another opportunity to mock those who boast about their spiritual insights as personal accolades. Paul nevertheless says little about this privileged revelation, other than that it occurred "fourteen years ago" and that he cannot divulge what he saw. In the same passage, he also describes "a thorn," or a persistent annoyance that torments him and prevents him "from being too elated." He does not say if the "thorn" is a physical or mental ailment, some kind of spiritual torment, a vocation as an apostle that subjects him to near-constant antagonism from opponents, or something else. Although it is impossible to identify the "thorn," this has not prevented interpreters from proposing a myriad of options.

The mysteries around this somewhat arcane passage about a visit to heaven elude interpreters' desires to decipher them, for the only person who could have offered details did not do so. The uncertainty reminds interpreters of how much about Paul remains out of view. Nevertheless, Paul's relative silence about his life and his spiritual experiences allows one to see the priority he placed, at least in his letters to churches, on things besides religious experience. Paul appears disinclined to impress his readers with details about his mystical encounters, preferring instead to emphasize a more foundational reality: *that* believers—all believers—participate in Jesus Christ's death, resurrection, new life, and body. For Paul, that emphasis takes priority over explanations of *how* participation with Christ happens and over meticulous descriptions of what that participation must look like in a person's daily life and religious activities.

Paul recalls his revelatory trip to the highest heavenly places to show he can match the super-apostles in any claims they might make about impressive spiritual experiences. But he also refers to the vision to make the point that the ultimate purpose of such an event is to increase one's dependence on God. Again, weakness provides access to divine strength. True spirituality, Paul insists, involves an acknowledgment of God's power and centrality; it does not consist of self-sufficiency. From Paul's perspective, the nature of authentic spirituality should caution the Corinthians against heeding the super-apostles in their midst; instead, they should affiliate themselves again with Paul and his ministry. In a modern setting, Christians might read 2 Cor 12:1–10 and ask what a dependence on divine power means for their attempts to articulate the gospel in their distinctive cultural settings. Paul would undoubtedly insist that, whatever strategies a church embraces, Christians can be agents of grace and change in the world only when they know their power to do so comes from God and not from the privileges their churches enjoy as a result of their cultural standing, nor from believers' own enthusiasm, gifts, rhetoric, or resources.

6

The Letter of Paul to the Galatians

No letter showcases Paul's rhetorical tenacity and theological fervor quite like Galatians. Paul wrote this letter to a collection of churches he had founded, urging groups of gentile Christ-followers not to listen to other missionaries who were telling them they had to follow the law of Moses. Paul considers the situation a crisis with incredibly high stakes, for he accuses the other teachers who have come to Galatia of utterly distorting and misrepresenting the gospel of Jesus Christ. Paul warns the Galatians that their obedience to those teachers would be tantamount to deserting the God who has already redeemed them. To equip the Galatians to resist the threat he perceives, Paul in effect repreaches the gospel to them. He insists that God alone, not the law, has the power to set people free from their spiritual captivity and make them God's children and thus full sharers in God's righteousness. Paul insists that the Mosaic law plays no role in how God makes people righteous, or "justifies" them; rather, only faith can accomplish that. As a result of God's power, both Jews and gentiles share equal standing as members of the family of God, a reality Paul describes as true freedom and the fulfillment of God's original pledges to Abraham.

Paul's letter adheres to a single-minded focus as it marshals a variety of short arguments to reconfirm its fundamental theological point: "a person is justified not by the works of the law but through faith" (Gal 2:16). The justification God provides through Christ results in freedom—freedom from the forces that imprison and enslave people, such as sin

135

and other spiritual powers aligned against God. Paul also says—in a shocking claim for a first-century Jew to make—that Christ sets people free even from the law of Moses itself. He tells the gentile believers in Galatia that for them to take up law observance would therefore be not only unnecessary but even counter to the gospel. Paul warns them that they risk trading in their newfound freedom for what are really new forms of slavery. In other words, if the gentile Christ-followers in Galatia rely on the law to make them full members of God's family, they risk forfeiting the justification they have already received in full.

Galatians has garnered fame for being an archetypal and forceful expression of Christian liberty. The letter's renown is deserved, but like all of Paul's writings, Galatians does not make its theological pronouncements in a vacuum. To understand what drives Paul's presentation, what fuels this letter's palpable passion, and why Paul characterizes justification and the law as he does, it is vitally important to investigate and to keep in mind the occasion that prompted Paul to write to the Galatian churches in the first place.

The Letter's Origins and Ancient Audience

The letter reveals considerable information about why Paul wrote it and what his audience was experiencing. His comments indicate that he wrote to people he had visited previously and with whom he shared an affectionate rapport (Gal 4:13–16). The total audience comprised more than a single community of believers (Gal 1:2), but Paul does not disclose how many churches or how large they were. From the mention of the Galatians' previous worship of other gods (Gal 4:8) and the letter's attention to the question of whether men in the churches should elect to be circumcised (Gal 5:12; 6:12–13), an interpreter can easily infer that Paul wrote the letter to gentile Christ-followers.

Galatia, the home of those churches, was not a city but a region. More accurately, it was a province created by the Roman Empire in the center of modern Turkey. The province included an area in the north that comprised such cities as Ancyra, Tavium, and Pessinus. The southern part of the province housed the cities of Pisidian Antioch, Derbe, Lystra, and Iconium, which were slightly more cosmopolitan population centers than those in the northern area. Considerable debate swirls around the question of whether Paul wrote this letter to churches in Galatia's southern region, whose cities serve as settings in parts of Acts that describe Paul's ministry, or to those in the northern region, which is where an ethnic group named "the Galatians" resided. Since Paul refers to his readers as "Galatians," and not "residents of Galatia," in Gal 3:1, it is rather plausible that he meant for the letter to circulate in the slightly more isolated area in the north of the province.

The debate over where in Galatia Paul's audience resided defies an easy solution, although it means almost nothing for understanding the letter and its impassioned argument. The issue matters mostly for determining when Paul could have written Galatians, based on how the book might align with what Acts says about Paul's travels in the province. Most likely, Paul wrote Galatians in the mid-50s CE. If indeed Paul wrote this letter to churches in northern Galatia, the letter itself provides the only known descriptions of his previous encounters with his audience. According to what Paul wrote, when he first visited them and proclaimed the gospel in their region, some of the Galatians received the Holy Spirit and began to experience "miracles" among them (Gal 3:2–5). Paul writes as if he has never lacked certainty about the authenticity and completeness of the Galatians' initial conversions. However, his letter indicates that other Christian missionaries subsequently came to those communities and sowed doubt about whether the Galatians' spiritual transformations were indeed complete.

Because Paul never names the other missionaries or fully describes their message, it remains difficult to know the specific teachings they promulgated and thus what teachings Galatians aims to combat. Paul describes their position as an altogether "different gospel" (Gal 1:6) that has begun to influence the Galatians' behavior (Gal 4:10–11). What appears to make the rival gospel different is its stipulation that gentile believers should observe the demands of torah, including circumcision. Evidently the teachers whom Paul opposed did not deny the possibility that God includes gentiles in the scope of salvation through Jesus Christ, but they asserted certain conditions by which gentiles enjoy the benefits of this salvation. To put it simplistically, the other teachers demanded that gentiles effectively live in accordance with Jewish expectations by committing themselves to torah observance.

In contrast, Paul's fiery rebuttal contends that God's salvation belongs to gentiles *as* gentiles, not because they take on Jewish practices or rely in any way on the law as a vehicle of God's blessing. He insists that there is no distinction between Jews and gentiles in the family of God, for neither can claim an advantage or superiority over the other.

Paul even goes a step further and declares there is no qualitative distinction between any two members of God's family, for all "are one in Christ Jesus" (Gal 3:28).

The Galatians, then, essentially found themselves in the middle of a theological dispute between Paul and a group of unidentified teachers. Paul addresses his letter precisely to the Galatians and not to his theological opponents: the letter consistently refers to the Galatians as "you" (plural) and the other missionaries as "them." Paul's elusive ways of speaking about that other group make it challenging to find a fitting word to describe the others, but "missionaries" and "teachers" provide decent generalizations.

Paul speaks about his opponents—the teachers—as people who identify with Christ. Paul never comments in Galatians about the validity of Judaism, nor does he imply a difference between Judaism and the new Christian movement as separate religions. He never addresses the issue of whether Jewish Christ-followers should or can practice law observance without violating the principles of the gospel. It is vital that interpreters keep those distinctions in mind, especially given the ways in which Galatians has been misused over the centuries. The misuse has involved disparagement of Judaism when interpreters imply that the letter's message forges a contrast between Christianity as a religion of freedom or grace and Judaism as a religion of slavery or legalism. Instead, what Paul directly criticizes in Galatians is not Judaism but the proposition that gentiles benefit from embracing law observance as a condition of their full participation in the gospel of Jesus Christ and its blessings. Paul does not say that Judaism is equivalent to slavery, but he does say that it is tantamount to slavery to require gentile Christ-followers to observe the law as Jews do.

It is difficult to tell whether the letter's rhetorical intensity owes itself to Paul's deep concern for the Galatians or to a ferocious desire to discredit the teachers who have come to the region sometime after Paul left. Both motives probably played a role. Even as the letter speaks pointedly to a very specific concern, it does not say much about other subjects. For example, Galatians discloses next to nothing about its original audience's social context. Paul does not refer to any of his readers by name. He does not provide insight into whether the Galatian churches were networked or what kind of leadership structure they used. Paul's occasional references to circumcision as a critical expression of a person's reliance on torah raises questions about whether he even considered how women in the Galatian churches might have experienced the letter and its urgent tone.

In addition, the book reveals few details about the teachers who came to Galatia after Paul. While Paul devotes much energy toward assailing their motives as duplicitous, they may have seen themselves as sincere advocates for a particular way of expressing Christian identity. Since no other New Testament document makes clear reference to this letter or to the precise situation it addressed, there is no way of knowing for sure what happened after the Galatians received it. They might have been convinced by Paul, followed the teachers' instructions instead of Paul's, or chosen altogether different options. It is impossible to say, then, whether Paul's argument convinced his audience. Nevertheless, Galatians continues to speak, attempting to persuade new readers to rely on God's activity through Jesus Christ and nothing else as the sure basis for their inheritance of God's blessings, the blessings first promised to Abraham.

Overview

Even though, for convenience's sake, an overview of Galatians must divide the letter's body (Gal 1:6–5:26) into discrete parts, it does not follow that Galatians moves back and forth among a variety of theological issues. Instead, Paul employs a variety of arguments throughout the letter to drive home various dimensions and implications of his basic understanding of the gospel. Galatians offers a number of ways for contending for a central point. Paul believes that the gospel is good news about God's power to fulfill old pledges to bless the world. God fulfills those pledges by bringing people to share completely in Jesus Christ's death, resurrection, and enduring status as a beloved child of God.

Salutation (Gal 1:1–5)

Paul addresses "the churches of Galatia" as a spokesperson for a larger group residing behind the composition of the letter. He refers to companions with him merely as "the brothers" ("the members of God's family," as the NRSV renders it) who are his associates without identifying any of them by name. The opening verses have important connections to the rest of the letter. Paul mentions the divine origins of his apostolic calling, contrasting it to expressions of human authority. He also describes Jesus as the one who provides freedom "from the present evil age." Accordingly, later in the letter, Paul will characterize the good news as a new reality created solely by God's action—action that sets people free from enslavements and initiates what Paul at the end of the letter calls "a new creation" (6:15).

Departing from conventional form, Galatians lacks a statement of thanksgiving after its salutation. By withholding a thanksgiving, Paul underlines the gravity of the situation he will address and makes clear his disappointment with the Galatians' apparent willingness to listen to the teachers. It is as if Paul can hardly wait to begin chastising his audience for veering astray. The issue is too urgent.

The Origins and Authority of the Gospel Paul Preaches (Gal 1:6–2:14)

Paul's intense disappointment with the Galatian believers goes hand in hand with his refusal to seek compromise about what the gospel is all about. Right away he sets unyielding terms for how the discussion will proceed: there is no other gospel except for "the gospel of Christ." Paul understands that gospel as the one he preaches; it is good news about what Christ has done and good news that originates in Christ himself. Anyone who proclaims a message that diverges from that one gospel corrupts and utterly deforms the gospel's most essential element: the true gospel describes an act of God, a divine event or achievement accomplished through Jesus Christ. Paul reiterates this key dimension of divine activity when he refers to his own personal introduction to the gospel as an utter surprise and a divinely initiated act. It was, for Paul, an encounter with God that occurred apart from human mediation. He includes autobiographical details in this section of the letter less as an attempt to contend for his own special authority as an apostle and more as an illustration of the gospel as a new, divinely wrought reality that reconfigures human identities, loyalties, and values. Paul's own history confirms that the gospel declares news about what God does. To speak of the gospel is to speak of God's initiative and God's power in action.

The information Paul recounts about his life calls attention to the distance between him and the church in Jerusalem, where Jesus' other apostles all began their ministries after his resurrection. Paul did not learn about the gospel from those people, for he had previously devoted himself to persecuting them. Instead, Paul discovered the gospel directly through a "revelation" (Greek, *apokalupsis*), specifically "through a revelation of Jesus Christ." Although elsewhere Paul says that the risen Christ appeared to him (1 Cor 9:1, 15:8; cf. Acts 9:3–7, 22:6–9, 26:12–16), in Galatians he does not explain whether he saw Christ, had a mystical experience, or gradually encountered Jesus over a period of time. Paul makes no reference to his own spiritual meditations or studies, or to information conveyed to him by other Christ-followers. He "learned" the gospel differently: through direct encounter with Christ and not by having other people relay a body of information or traditions to him. Why he stayed away from Jerusalem for so long after his revelation, he does not say, but his brief fifteen-day visit with Cephas (the Aramaic equivalent of "Peter") and James was enough for him to establish a connection to those apostles and their ministries without implying that they somehow contributed something new to Paul's understanding of the gospel.

Paul's next visit to Jerusalem came "in response to a revelation" and involved a meeting with Titus, Barnabas, and other "acknowledged leaders." What Paul describes sounds like the conference described in Acts 15:1–29, an event that confirmed that gentile Christ-followers in Syrian Antioch and elsewhere need not observe torah to complete their salvation. Paul's account in Galatians, however, characterizes the meeting as more disquieted in comparison to the narrative in Acts. The lack of deference he recalls himself showing to "those who were supposed to be acknowledged leaders" also affirms the presence of tensions between Paul and many Christ-followers in Jerusalem. Nevertheless, despite the bad feelings or the air of distrust, the meeting concluded with an expression of unity. The Jerusalem church and its leaders—the apostles James, Cephas, and John—resolved to continue preaching the gospel among "the circumcised," meaning Jews, while Paul and his companions would evangelize among gentiles. Paul implies that both groups share in one and the same gospel yet recognize a difference in their particular callings to certain audiences. Their theologies match, but they pursue their ministries among different groups of people.

This agreed-upon unity found itself imperiled, however, when Cephas subsequently visited the church in Antioch, a community comprised mostly of gentiles, and through his behavior drew and reinforced distinctions between gentiles and Jews in the church. Sensing the peril, Paul rebuked Cephas for hypocrisy. Paul implies that Cephas diminished gentile Christ-followers in Antioch for no apparent reason other than their lack of obedience to torah. Why exactly Cephas did so remains unclear, although for some reason he aimed to placate a group of Christ-followers who had traveled to Antioch from Jerusalem.

Justification, Blessing, Inheritance, Freedom, and Adoption (Gal 2:15–4:11)

Paul's description of the time he rebuked Cephas brings the letter to state implicitly yet squarely the primary theological question it seeks to answer: Does a qualitative difference exist between Jewish and gentile Christ-followers in God's eyes because one group's identity, practices, and embrace of torah provide it with an inherent superiority or advantage over the other? Paul answers this question with an unequivocal no. Both groups can rest assured in the effectiveness and completeness of their salvation because they know, just as Cephas knew even though his actions denied it, that "a person is justified not by the works of the law but through faith in Jesus Christ" (Gal 2:16). Therefore anything, such as Cephas' inhospitable behavior in Antioch, that would imply that gentiles are not completely justified and not already full members of God's family constitutes "hypocrisy" or a denial of the one true gospel.

As is also the case in Romans, by the expression *faith in Jesus Christ* Paul means Christ's own faithfulness as one who trusted God's promises and met death as an expression of his obedience (e.g., Gal 2:16, 20b; 3:22; Rom 3:22, 26; Phil 3:9b). Christ's followers live likewise by "faith," for they have been made coparticipants in Christ's faithful death and subsequent resurrection, two events through which God creates a new identity and existence for all who unite with Christ. Paul sets this faith in contrast with "the works of the law" both explicitly and implicitly throughout much of Galatians 3–4.

Why it is, exactly, that the effective "faith" of Jesus Christ diverges so completely from the ineffective "works of the law" remains a significant point of debate among those who analyze Galatians. The rest of the letter, mainly Galatians 3–6, sheds light on the question. Paul disparages "works of the law" as he does because they play no role in justification, for Paul locates God's justifying activity and the creation of something new solely in Christ's death and resurrection. Those pivotal events exposed the law's ineffectiveness when it comes to mediating God's blessings to people. As Paul sees it, an old understanding of salvation has yielded to God's dramatic revelation of grace in Jesus Christ. That revelation overturns old understandings concerning torah's effectiveness and role in God's intentions for the world. That revelation also brings about the transformation of the world, insofar as God discloses a new means—or a newly rediscovered means—of salvation. The all-encompassing new realities that God has engineered through Christ make salvation fully available to gentiles. Nothing about the law illuminated those new realities for Paul; instead, he came to see them through a new light generated by God's activity in Jesus Christ.

In Gal 3:1–4:11, Paul describes what he believes God has accomplished through Christ. He also illustrates and buttresses his claim about justification's exclusive link to faith apart from "the works of the law." He does not offer a variety of arguments to *verify* that claim; rather, Paul's arguments unpack and give substance to the claim. He has already stated his conclusion in Gal 2:16, and he assumes that the conclusion enjoys wide support among Christ-followers in general. From that point forward, Galatians proceeds more like a series of illustrations and demonstrations of the conclusion than like a logical proof. Paul reminds the Galatians of what they already know—or are supposed to know—and what they have already experienced.

Paul begins his rhetorical unpacking project by recalling the Galatians' experiences of the Holy Spirit. They received the Holy Spirit when they first heard the gospel, before they made any attempts to embrace, or even to dabble in, the Mosaic law. Because of the Spirit's presence in them, they can be sure that faith, and nothing else, made their salvation complete. Because the source of the Spirit and wondrous deeds associated with the Spirit is none other than God, the Galatians fully belong to God (cf. Rom 8:9–11; Gal 4:6; Acts 10:44–48, 11:16–17). Paul implies they need nothing else from this point forward.

Two appeals to Jewish Scriptures come next. The first quotes Gen 15:6 in the Septuagint and recalls Abraham, who "believed," or "had faith in," God, which resulted in his "righteousness," or "justification" (cf. Rom 4:1–12). In Abraham Paul discerns an essential link between faith and God's justifying activity. Paul extrapolates from this link that God's promise to bless all the gentles, or "nations," will also be accomplished through faith. True descendants of Abraham and true beneficiaries of God's promise to him are therefore "those who believe," or people who are aligned with "faith." Paul does not mention that Abraham himself was circumcised (Gen 17:9–14, 23–27) because his point derives strength from showing that *justification* language in the narrative about Abraham in Genesis is never associated with any "works of the law" Abraham might have performed. In Genesis, Abraham's justification connects explicitly only to Abraham's self-sacrificial response of "faith." In believing God Abraham put his life in God's hands, venturing forth with trust in God's gracious pledge to provide future blessings.

Paul's next appeal to Scripture compares and contrasts a number of passages that refer to either torah ("law") or faith. The comparisons do not mean to pose a question about the respective effects of *believing* and of *doing*, as if Paul is contrasting two modes of being religious, such as trusting God versus performing good works. Rather, the primary issue behind the comparisons is to illustrate that law and faith constitute two different systems or spheres of existence that purport to govern or define a way of life. An important theological distinction lies beneath the comparisons: according to Paul, the matter for the gentiles pivots on the question of what *God* does via faith and what *God* does via torah. Interpreting Scripture by connecting passages with similar vocabulary, Paul characterizes the law's role as ultimately a means of cursing people instead of blessing them. Christ suffers the brunt of the law's function, in that he received a curse pronounced by the law as a result of his public, shameful crucifixion. Yet Paul also knows Christ to be the source of the Holy Spirit, which has brought blessing even to gentiles, as Paul knows from what he has seen in his ministry among the Galatians and elsewhere. In contrasting the blessing associated with Abraham's promise with the cursing power of the law, Paul sees something new occurring in the Messiah's death and resurrection: Jesus, the one who should have been labeled cursed, instead becomes the vehicle through whom God unleashes blessing. As a result, through Christ's death and resurrection, the Holy Spirit has come even to gentiles, confirming them as heirs of God's ancient pledge to Abraham—a pledge that promised blessings would come to "all the Gentiles" (Gal 3:8; cf. Gen 12:3, 18:18, 22:18). The law did not contribute to the realization of this promise. Christ, the one whose faithfulness mirrored Abraham's, did. God therefore is active through Christ, justifying people through faith and not through the law, which could only view Christ in his death as a cursed man.

The next argument, beginning in Gal 3:15, continues to focus on Abraham's story as the prototypical demonstration of how God justifies people. Paul says that just as no one can alter a person's legal will

(Greek, *diathēkē*) except for that will's creator, God's original covenant (also *diathēkē*) with Abraham also remains unchanged by the coming of the Mosaic law 430 years after Abraham (according to Paul's interpretation of Exod 12:40–41). Believers therefore receive their expected inheritance—namely, their reception of the blessing God promised to Abraham—only because of Abraham and Christ, not because of anything about the torah that came long after the original pledge. Because it is through Christ that God pours out the blessings once promised to Abraham, Paul describes Jesus as Abraham's offspring. The point of the connection is not primarily biological; rather, both Abraham and Jesus expressed a faithfulness that caused them to participate in God's righteousness. Paul's implication is that, because of Abraham and Jesus, that same participation also becomes available to others. As Paul will say later, in Gal 3:29, anyone who "belong[s] to Christ" is also "Abraham's offspring." The blessings of God have come to gentiles through Christ, and the law played no role in unleashing those blessings.

Realizing he has characterized torah as useless with regard to what allows his audience to share in God's righteousness, Paul asks the obvious question: "Why then the law?" (Gal 3:19). He does not clearly answer the question other than to say that the law had a temporary role until the advent of "faith," by which he means God's action in Jesus Christ. The law's role, Paul insists, had all the effects of an imprisonment, as if the law was a severe "disciplinarian," a word referring to household slaves who zealously oversaw the moral and intellectual development of children in the Greco-Roman world. Now that Christ has come, however, the law's custodial function has become obsolete. That function was never contrary to God's purposes, but the gift of God in Christ now trumps it. Christ brings people from a period—previously governed by the law—of waiting for a promise to the point of arriving into a whole new period. That new period brings a new status that is available right away: freedom. Freedom means leaving slavery and enjoying adoption into God's family, an adoption that begins immediately, as the Holy Spirit attests by indwelling people of faith and calling God "Abba," the Aramaic word for "Father."

In the middle of Paul's discussion of torah, freedom, and adoption, he briefly mentions the unity shared by everyone who is "in Christ." In Gal 3:27–29, Paul insists there are no distinctions of value or status among those who are God's children through faith. The reference to baptism suggests Paul quotes material from an ancient baptismal liturgy at this point in the letter. Saying "there is no longer Jew or Greek, there is no longer slave or free, there is no longer male and female," Paul means that one's participation with Christ is so pervasive and elemental that Christ, and only Christ, comes to define a person's identity. Individual people remain Jewish and gentile, male and female, but neither those nor any other identifiers carry any inherent advantages or disadvantages in God's perspective. In Christ, no hierarchies or social stratifications make someone more prominent or a more valued adoptee than another. Paul offers that assertion as welcome news to gentiles in Galatia who are hearing teachers tell them that observing the torah will make their salvation complete.

Paul's statement about unity in Christ (Gal 3:27–29) has had significant influence beyond his specific argument to the Galatians about torah observance. His words have spoken to many additional audiences at countless points in history. The statement provides a powerful theological foundation for establishing the full worth and dignity of all people, no matter their ethnicity, social status, gender, or other characteristics. The statement has provided liberating news and a powerful theological resource to many who have suffered under and resisted slavery, patriarchies, bigotry, and other forms of dehumanization and oppression.

This theologically rich section of the letter concludes in Gal 4:8–11 with Paul wondering why the Galatians would opt for slavery instead of freedom. Those verses anticipate an appeal coming in Gal 5:1, when Paul offers two imperatives: "stand firm" and "do not submit again to a yoke of slavery." If the letter's audience heeds the teachers and takes up law obedience as a means of perfecting or completing the salvation God has already provided in full, the Galatians will find themselves enslaved. Even if the Galatians, being gentiles, were not themselves once enslaved by the torah and its inability to provide justification, they know what slavery looks like, Paul says, because they too were once enslaved. Paul refers to their enslavers as "elemental spirits" of the cosmos. Although the expression *elemental spirits* is enigmatic, Paul likely means it to refer to supernatural forces that, according to ancient assumptions, controlled people's lives. Given the influence that Jewish apocalyptic ideas exercised on Paul's ways of thinking, he might have had sin and Satan in mind as examples of those spirits. In any case, Paul warns the Galatians that choosing law observance would effectively replace their former condition of slavery or their previous reliance on now-vanquished cosmic powers with another form of enslavement—this time, slavery to the law and its powerlessness to provide justification.

Two Additional Appeals (Gal 4:12–5:1)

This section continues the letter's effort to persuade the Galatians about the certainty of their justification apart from performing works of the law. It diverges from the previous section in two significant ways: Paul refers to the other missionaries who are present in Galatia by highlighting the danger they pose, and his syntax begins to employ imperatives to instruct the Galatians how they should respond to his letter in their current circumstances. He directs two very different appeals to his audience.

The first appeal reminds the Galatians of the friendship they share with Paul. The letter foregrounds Paul's earnestness for the Galatians' well-being and their genuine concern for him, which they expressed when he was first present among them. Paul accentuates his pure motives in part by contrasting them with the teachers', whose motives he depicts as deceptive and hypocritical. Paul accuses the other missionaries of being unconcerned about the Galatians' freedom; he says, rather, that they will finally treat the Galatians as subordinates, perhaps because the teachers are Jewish Christ-followers who Paul thinks will claim some kind of original priority over gentiles, even gentiles who become torah-observant Christ-followers. When Paul implores his Galatian friends to become as he is, he means they should regard themselves as free and not under the law. They should see themselves as participants in the new creation God is bringing into being, a new reality Paul describes with child-birthing metaphors that recall imagery common in Jewish apocalyptic literature.

The other appeal comes wrapped in an allegorical interpretation of the scriptural story of the mothers of Abraham's sons, Hagar and Sarah, told in Gen 16–17 and 21:1–14 but retold by Paul in a cleverly creative way that identifies these two women as emblematic of slavery and freedom, respectively. Paul does not refer to the Genesis narrative because he intends to retell the story or to reflect on the distressing abuse Hagar and Ishmael endure; any comparison between this passage from Galatians and the original Genesis account quickly reveals that Paul is up to something quite different. By announcing his description as an allegory, Paul signals that he means to forge an imaginative, yet quite serious, contrast between the teachers' ministry and his own.

With his allegorical rereading, Paul implies that the teachers who have materialized in Galatia resemble Hagar, Sarah's slave and Ishmael's mother, because their efforts to advocate law obedience among gentiles is actually "bearing children for slavery." By contrast, "our mother," Paul says, "is free," meaning that the gentile believers in Galatia truly are free "children of the promise, like Isaac" was. The slightly convoluted allegorical comparisons, which Paul constructs to underscore the distinction between Hagar's slavery and Sarah's freedom, provide the basis for Paul to quote Gen 21:10 as a direct imperative to the letter's audience: he commands the Galatians not only to ignore but also to "drive out" the teachers from their midst, just as in Genesis Sarah insists that Hagar and Ishmael be banished from her home lest they cause harm to her free child, Isaac. Paul's point is this: not only are the teachers wrong about the gospel, but their determination to lead the Galatians into slavery also makes them dangerous and therefore deserving of expulsion from the Galatian churches' fellowship.

The Life of Freedom, Lived in the Spirit (Gal 5:2–26)

Having declared in Gal 5:1, "For freedom Christ has set us free. Stand firm, therefore, and do not submit again to a yoke of slavery," Paul turns to say more about what would make law observance a form of slavery for the Galatians. For the first time in the letter, he mentions the prospect of gentile Galatians presenting themselves for circumcision. Paul warns that adopting that rite would entail an abandonment of Christ. Paul's language is severe. What sounds like a claim that circumcision represents some unforgiveable sin refers instead to torah's capacity to make a complete, all-inclusive demand on a person. Circumcision in the Galatians' situation would imply their reliance on torah as a whole. Just as earlier in the letter Paul characterized "faith" and "works of the law" as two different systems that each govern and define one's way of life and spiritual identity, for the Galatians to opt for law observance in their present circumstances would be tantamount to them saying that the new identity Christ has secured for them through faith is not enough. The severity in the way Paul construes the situation compels him to assail the teachers again. He calls them a corrupting influence and an obstacle to the Galatians' ability to live in the truth. Seething with spite, Paul longs for the other missionaries to castrate themselves.

Next, freedom receives additional attention, although Paul describes the Galatians' liberty in an apparently paradoxical way. Freedom resembles a form of slavery when Paul says, "through love become slaves to one another" (Gal 5:13). Paul's notion of freedom therefore does not equate to utter self-determination, for it involves a life infused by self-giving love. It fuels a way of living that corresponds to the heart of torah, which itself commends love of one's neighbor. God may not justify people through the law, but the law still commends praiseworthy ways for justified people to live.

The Spirit enables people to support one another as they express such love, but the Spirit does so while engaged in ongoing struggle with what Paul calls "the flesh." Corporeality, the reality of human bodies, is not the problem. Rather, "the flesh" refers to a way of living or a sinful nature that continues to wage war against Christ-followers and their ability to live according to their new identity as redeemed persons. "The present evil age" named in Gal 1:4 continues to have its effects among those who are in Christ, although Paul promises the Holy Spirit still produces "fruit" in their lives, equipping them to forswear and resist the desires of their old and persistent sinful nature.

Concluding Exhortations and Benediction (Gal 6)

The Holy Spirit may produce commendable "fruit," but this does not happen automatically in believers' lives, for Paul follows his catalog of "the fruit of the Spirit" with multiple exhortations to his audience. Much of what he says recalls the virtues named in that catalog. A final warning about the teachers insinuates that their emphasis on circumcision and law observance stems from their desire to avoid persecution. If the teachers were indeed Jewish Christ-followers who had come to Galatia from Jerusalem, Paul evidently concludes that they sought to compel gentiles to observe the law so that other Jews would not accuse the teachers of abandoning Jewish practices through the close associations they shared with gentiles in Christian fellowships.

As Paul brings the letter to a close, again he emphasizes the centrality of Jesus Christ and his death. Paul's claim that in Jesus' crucifixion he too has been crucified, as has the whole world, reasserts the apocalyptic tenor that hums throughout Paul's presentation: Jesus' death altered the shape of the entire cosmos, for through his death God brought something old to an end and inaugurated new, transformed realities.

Paul goes beyond bearing testimony about new, divinely wrought realities; he claims he participates in them, for he has become totally identified with Christ. One of the new realities, or the overarching reality, is "new creation." Paul does not give a full description of new creation. The manner in which he mentions it, however, implies that God's new creation ultimately renders old distinctions and former systems obsolete. The new creation changes everything. It does away with familiar boundary lines and qualitative judgments among people and their value. In the new creation, any kind of person can come to be known by God (cf. Gal 4:9) and will enjoy a fundamental unity with everyone else "in Christ" (cf. Gal 3:28).

The Letter's Themes and Theological Emphases

Jews and Gentiles, One in Christ

Galatians presents a fervid and tenacious case for understanding faith as the key to justification, claiming God always has and always will justify through faith. Paul's reasons for making an argument for faith extend beyond a desire for the Galatians to learn the right doctrines or to preserve an orthodox theology. Paul's letter indicates that his audience already knew this theological principle but did not grasp its full implications. Paul writes so the Galatians will discover, perhaps again, how foundational faith is for understanding God and discovering their own value in God's eyes. As Paul sees it, any theological teachings that deviate from the centrality of faith therefore prove to be illusory if not downright perilous.

Nothing in the letter suggests that the other teachers were telling the Christian communities in Galatia that salvation comes through the law or through a person's own efforts to earn God's favor. Rather, the teachers evidently urged the gentile Galatians to observe torah because then their salvation would be complete. Paul's response to that teaching is unequivocal: not only is relying on the law for completing one's salvation an unnecessary and counterproductive decision, but it also will have disastrous effects. For one thing, it contravenes the basic notion that justification comes through Christ. Additionally, Paul warns the Galatians that their law observance will contribute to the disintegration of Christian unity, for law observance will result in them finding themselves diminished or excluded by the teachers. Paul's concern may simply betray his distrust of the character of those particular teachers, whoever they were, for the letter occasionally attributes unscrupulous motives to them and their ministry's goals (e.g., Gal 3:1; 4:17; 5:7, 10; 6:12–13). But much of Galatians suggests that Paul finds himself compelled to combat what he regards as a more pernicious danger: wherever law-observant Christ-followers expect law-free Christ-followers to observe torah, divisions are liable to erupt and create a church culture in which one group understands itself as distinct from others. Perceived distinctions will lead to value judgments, which will prevent the church from displaying the unity in Christ that is the heart of the church's God-given identity.

Paul's high regard for Christian unity manifests itself when he tells of the time he rebuked Cephas (Peter). Since Paul does not delineate what Cephas did wrong when he was in Antioch, Galatians leaves it for readers to determine what was hypocritical about ceasing to share meals with gentiles to avoid offending law-observant Christ-followers, those who were associated with James (Gal 2:11–14). Cephas might have been trying to keep multiple groups happy in a sensitive social situation, but Paul accuses him of invalidating "the truth of the gospel" when he separates himself from the gentiles. Cephas erred because his behavior subtly issued a value judgment, one based on distinctions derived from people's commitments to observing torah. By withdrawing from the gentile believers, Cephas intimated that there was something inappropriate or reproachable about sharing fellowship with them, especially when Jewish believers might have been present too. Consequently, Cephas implied the gentiles were somehow inferior. But if the true gospel is the good news about God's actions to create a new human family in which Jews and gentiles share equal status as God's children (e.g., Gal 4:6–7), then the gatherings of those brothers and sisters in Antioch, gatherings comprising both Jewish and gentile Christ-followers, should have reflected that new theological reality. That would have been the case especially when a gathering involved the intimacy and mutuality forged by a shared meal. Paul insists that any lingering sense of distinction based on law observance occludes the church's true identity as a family united in Christ, because reinforcing those distinctions is, in effect, reasserting the old barriers and marks of identity that the cross has obliterated or forever relegated to secondary importance (Gal 3:28).

Paul tells the Galatians they already belong fully to the family of God. Their identity is lodged in Christ and nothing else. They risk being construed as second-class citizens in the church if they listen to the teachers and embrace other standards of evaluating or distinguishing themselves. This issue for Paul, then, is only partly about the power of the law and the power of faith. He writes to the Galatians also to address the ways in which humanity's desire to make qualitative distinctions among people inevitably leads to stratification in a community, a situation in which one group is considered subordinate to another. God's new creation, by contrast, represents an entirely new means of understanding one's identity and value (Gal 6:15). In the new system, people's distinctions do not disappear, for believers remain Jew, Greek, slave, free, male, and female. What becomes new, however, is those distinctions' inability to define anyone's identity or worth in God's family, for the foundational identification mark of that family is its existence "in Christ." Membership in the family of God does not eradicate difference and diversity; adoption into the family means freedom from any basis for making distinctions that reassert hierarchies among people.

The Apocalyptic Drama

Themes and theological assumptions common to Jewish apocalyptic writings emerge throughout Galatians. With those motifs Paul articulates his understanding of the salvation God provides through Christ. Even though Galatians does not refer explicitly to Christ's future return, still it describes Jesus' crucifixion and its effects as a dramatic in-breaking of a new state of affairs. God brings to completion long-standing promises to Abraham by indwelling gentiles and Jews through the Holy Spirit. Old enslavements to ungodly forces end, resulting in freedom that arises from the destruction of old categories in the new creation. Paul describes the gospel message as more than a second chance or an opportunity to restart; his language asserts that God has established a new identity for people of faith—an identity defined solely by Christ and the justification God provides through him.

Paul recognizes that the dawning of the new creation does not eradicate struggles from believers' lives. His discussion of the flesh and the Spirit in Gal 5:13–26 keeps the letter's theological convictions from veering into escapism. One's salvation may be already complete through faith, but life lived simultaneously in "the present evil age" (Gal 1:4) and in God's "new creation" (Gal 6:15; cf. 2 Cor 5:17) still involves hardship and divisions. Paul presents the gospel as a divine act that bestows and guarantees a new identity and a new existence defined by Christ, but that existence remains marked by travails and skirmishes with God's adversaries (e.g., Gal 5:11, 17; 6:12, 17).

Despite the difficulties that arise from essentially living in two different ages at the same time, believers share their existence with Christ. They are the Son of God's own sisters and brothers (e.g., Gal 4:4–7), and they coexist with him by participating fully in his freedom-granting death (e.g., Gal 2:19–20; 6:14; cf. Rom 6:3–11, 2 Cor 5:14–15, Phil 3:10–11). The "revelation of Jesus Christ" (Gal 1:12) that Paul once received continued throughout his life; Jesus never went away, for "it is Christ who lives" in Paul continually (Gal 2:20; cf. 4:6). The Galatians enjoy that same participation with Christ as well.

Paul and the Law

Jews in Paul's era did not believe that their obedience to torah earned them salvation or favor from God. Because God had chosen the people of Israel and pledged fidelity to them through covenants and promises recorded in the Scriptures, Jews understood themselves as recipients of God's good favor. The law of Moses was important to them, for it promoted a way of life lived in response to God's graciousness. The law delineated the values, practices, and forms of justice that allowed Jews to express and enjoy the relationship that God had already established with them. Paul's fellow Jews believed the law promotes the justice God desires and helps God's people resist the defiling and damaging aspects of human existence. It would have been stunning, then, for some of Paul's Jewish contemporaries to overhear what he wrote to the Galatians concerning torah's ability to enslave people.

Paul knows his statements come close to painting the law as contrary to God's intentions (e.g., Gal 3:19, 21; Rom 7:7, 13), but he refuses to call torah a mistake or the product of a devious God. The law is not defective in and of itself in Paul's view. Having encountered the crucified and resurrected Christ, however, Paul came to see the law differently than he previously did. In his own encounters with Christ and his experience of seeing the Holy Spirit come to indwell gentiles, Paul became convinced that the law has no role in bringing gentiles to participate in God's righteousness. Paul, and those to whom he preached the gospel, encountered righteousness in Christ (Phil 3:8–9). When Paul became a Christ-follower, not much changed about his understanding of God's character and trustworthiness. But his new experiences with God's righteousness greatly reordered his understanding of the specific role of the law in God's purposes.

The law is hardly a pervasive or central subject in the full corpus of Paul's letters. He addresses it most in Galatians and in Romans, plus some assorted places in 1 Corinthians and Philippians. Paul never states clearly whether he still commended law observance for *Jews*, either for Jews who followed Christ or for Jews who did not, although in some passages he voices support for believers who persist in observing torah (e.g., 1 Cor 7:17–20, 9:19–23) or who adhere to scruples that may have a basis in the law (e.g., Rom 14). When Paul turns to discuss the law in Gal 3:21–26, however, he does so as a piece of a presentation he makes specifically to *gentile* believers about the ground of their justification and the basis of their full and secure membership in God's family. Torah, Paul tells them, has played no part in that defining aspect of God's good news.

Paul's Appeals to Scripture

Paul relies on Jewish Scripture to help him convince his audience. In Galatians 3–4 he appeals to a variety of passages in different ways. Those chapters make Galatians a valuable source for observing how Paul interprets Scripture, especially his efforts to exploit the terminology used in the story of Abraham's justification (Gal 3:6–9), his manner of linking biblical texts (Gal 3:10–14), and his use of allegorical interpretation (Gal 4:21–31). To oversimplify the matter, Paul turns to revered texts not so much to prove his points but to give him language and illustrations for expressing those points more vividly and persuasively. The methods Paul employs to engage Scripture are not unique, for they resemble those seen in other Jewish writings from the period. Allegory was also a popular rhetorical tool for gentile authors, as it was for Jewish ones. Paul did not employ the same interpretive practices that most modern people do, but this does not necessarily invalidate either his methods or modern ones.

Paul's repeated references to Abraham in this letter suggest that his disagreement with the teachers in Galatia can be framed as a dispute about how rightly to understand Jewish traditions and Scriptures. It is entirely plausible that the teachers, too, made their appeals to the

Galatians by citing Abraham as an example. They could have emphasized, as Paul surely would have, that the God the gentile Galatians have encountered in Jesus Christ has a long history with the Hebrew people, stretching back to the call of Abraham. The teachers might then have continued, now departing from Paul's perspective, that Abraham, who along with the men of his household was the first in the Bible to be circumcised, participated in that rite to show his commitment to the promises God made to him, promises that one day would benefit "the nations," or gentiles. Therefore, the teachers' logic may have reasoned, the Galatian men should circumcise themselves and all the Galatians should embrace the law to bring themselves into full affiliation with Abraham and the pledge God made to him, a pledge that committed God to include the gentiles in God's redemptive intentions.

If the teachers indeed made an argument like that one, then Paul's attempt to make his case with such a strong focus on Abraham and Abraham's faith appears rather bold, for he likely ventured into the same biblical narrative his rivals had also employed. The difference lies in Paul's attempt to reorder that narrative from Genesis, to insist that faith and not circumcision provides the primary detail. Through faith, Abraham's justification was complete. Through faith, God's righteousness enveloped Abraham and his future. Paul's theological tussle with the teachers therefore involved, in part, a dispute about what the Scriptures testify concerning God's activity. Paul insists that the statement in Genesis about Abraham's justification essentially seals the deal, for it marks Abraham's certain participation in God's saving power and care. The letter's argument about Jesus and the sufficiency of faith finds support, Paul believes, in what Jewish Scripture has already revealed about God and God's determination to justify through faith.

The history of Christian theology has always involved looking to Scripture to illuminate the character of God and God's intentions. Paul's writings provide examples of a first-century church leader attempting to square his theological positions with the witness of Scripture. Christians persist in those same kinds of efforts even today, with debate and scriptural interpretation almost always at the center of discussions about how Christians rightly understand their identity in Christ. Studying Galatians provides a window into how those efforts once happened while also reminding modern believers about the need to look to Scripture in their own deliberations about which beliefs and practices accurately express "the truth of the gospel" (Gal 2:5, 14).

7

Disputed Authorship

s has already been noted in discussions about Paul's letters, both in general and with regard to specific letters, interpreting a letter requires reading between the lines. That is especially true when a letter is the only surviving correspondence between two parties. Interpreters look for clues about the author(s), the recipient(s), the rhetoric, and the subjects discussed, all with an eye toward better understanding the letter's contents, purposes, and possible connections to other documents, ideas, and historical circumstances. Sometimes the scrutiny of the story residing behind and inside a letter is an attempt to flesh out a specific historical situation, but it also is usually an important, if not essential, piece of understanding what the letter itself has to say and how it says it. That is certainly the case with the letters in the New Testament, since those documents themselves are the primary source of information for learning about their ancient authors and those authors' ideas.

When it comes to letters from Paul, questions arise from reading between the lines because of what some letters purport to reveal about Paul and his teachings. There are thirteen books in the New Testament that attribute their existence to Paul, identifying him as the sole author or primary coauthor. Of those thirteen, seven demonstrate remarkable consistency and cohesion with respect to their style, vocabulary, terminology, general theological outlook, and insights into the details of Paul's life and personality. The conspicuous similarities among those seven warrant the near-certain conclusion that the same person was responsible for composing all of them, doing so within a relatively compact span of time in the mid-first century CE. The seven letters are Romans, 1–2 Corinthians, Galatians, Philippians, 1 Thessalonians, and Philemon. Virtually no credible scholar who has studied those seven doubts that Paul was originally responsible for what they say, except that some interpreters express legitimate questions about the origins of a few brief passages, which could have been inserted into existing documents by someone else, perhaps a compiler or copyist (e.g., 1 Cor 14:33b–36, 2 Cor 6:14–7:1).

Each of the other six letters that bear Paul's name—Ephesians, Colossians, 2 Thessalonians, 1–2 Timothy, and Titus—does not exhibit the same cohesiveness that the group of seven shares. That general observation alone does not establish much, even though it reasonably prompts questions about what could explain the differences. A deeper analysis of each of the six letters, however, yields more nuanced observations about what distinguishes the letters' styles and points of view in contrast to the seven highly consistent letters. The analyses and the specific observations that fuel them cast serious doubt on the claim that Paul wrote each of those six letters. It is possible, and indeed likely, therefore, that people other than Paul composed some or all of those six letters yet exhibited them as documents originally authored by Paul.

Ongoing debates about whether Paul or other people wrote the six letters in question have led to the six being called "disputed letters" in contrast to the seven "undisputed letters" that Paul certainly wrote. The two labels, which call attention to ongoing disputes among interpreters, do not necessarily imply disagreements about the validity of the letters' theological claims or about their overall value or usefulness. Neither do the disputes, at their most basic level, usually involve deliberations about whether uncertainty regarding who wrote a book makes that book somehow deficient or undeserving in comparison to other biblical writings. Instead, to call the six documents "disputed letters" simply acknowledges a lack of consensus about authorship, the issue of who wrote them. The lack of consensus makes it necessary for introductory investigations of those six letters, like the investigations to come in subsequent chapters in this companion, to ponder what can be determined about when those letters were written, under what circumstances, to whom, and for what purposes. For most people who interpret the New Testament, answering those questions is not the primary goal; instead, those questions are helpful to the degree that they can help readers reach a different goal: to understand the writings themselves and to converse with them. Accordingly, this companion delves into those questions, not to suggest that they must be answered before anyone can properly understand a letter, but to explore how the questions are sometimes an integral part of considering what a letter says, why the letter might have said it to an ancient audience, and how the letter might continue to participate in the ongoing theological conversations generated by the New Testament as a whole.

Conducting introductory overviews of the six disputed letters can provide only rough sketches of the issues that generate debates surrounding a given letter's authorship. Before considering those individual sketches, interpreters benefit from a wider-angle view that identifies the basic kinds of evidence from the disputed letters that cast doubt on the supposition that Paul wrote them. Those who interpret the disputed letters also need to take account of ancient literary conventions concerning the existence and circulation of documents written in the names of people who had already died. Finally, interpreters do well to consider a handful of implications that the disputes about authorship pose for the study of Paul, for understanding other New Testament documents, and for interpreting of all those books as pieces of Christian Scripture.

Evidence from the Letters

Debates about the authorship of the six disputed letters proceed differently depending on the letter in question. For example, a comparative analysis of literary style and vocabulary may matter more for investigating a letter like Titus than it does for 2 Thessalonians. The former document's style and vocabulary deviate substantially from the seven undisputed letters, while the latter's do not. Also, the theological claims in Colossians do not strike as great of a contrast with the undisputed letters as does the theological outlook offered in 1 Timothy. In addition, no one piece of evidence or a single argument can settle the question of whether Paul could have written a given letter or not. The cases interpreters build, whether they argue for Paul or for someone else as a document's author, must always be cumulative, drawing on a range of evidence and considering multiple possibilities about the circumstances behind a letter's creation. The evidence reviewed here is only representative of more detailed and intricate analyses.

Style and Vocabulary

The seven undisputed letters, although they vary widely in their length and tone, display remarkable congruity in their vocabulary and literary style. Even though Paul's transitions may occasionally be abrupt and his rhetoric may prove difficult to decipher by interpreters who reside two thousand years away from the letters' original contexts, still Paul's syntax generally maintains the same tendencies and level of sophistication. The seven undisputed letters also deploy certain theological terms in markedly consistent ways from letter to letter.

When interpreters compare the style and vocabulary of the six other documents to those seven, differences become evident. Ephesians, for example, includes several very long sentences that string together clauses and employ grammatical constructions in ways that are mostly absent from the undisputed letters (e.g., Eph 1:3–14). When Ephesians quotes Jewish Scriptures or other traditional material, it introduces quotations with the words *therefore it says* in contrast to the undisputed letters' use of the phrase *it is written* (e.g., Eph 4:8, 5:14; cf. Rom 9:13; 1 Cor 2:9; 2 Cor 8:15; Gal 3:10). As for the trio of letters often called the Pastoral Letters (namely, 1–2 Timothy and Titus), their syntax also exhibits a complexity that exceeds what appears in the undisputed letters, yet the Pastoral Letters' particular style does not duplicate what is on display in Ephesians, either. Moreover, the Pastoral Letters include several theological terms that do not appear in the undisputed letters, even as they also understand additional words, such as *faith*, in a divergent way. Additionally, the Pastoral Letters reflect particular inclinations in their general vocabulary: altogether, those three documents comprise nearly 850 different Greek words, not counting proper nouns. About one third of those words do not appear in the undisputed letters, and several of the unique words appear more commonly in Greek literature from the late first century and early second century—several decades after Paul's death. A different inventory of vocabulary might imply the work of a different author.

Theological Themes and Emphases

It would be a mistake to describe the seven undisputed letters as together expressing a theological perspective that is fully coherent, utterly consistent, comprehensively thorough, or somehow immutable.

As a small group of occasional documents, they do not give a full and final account of Paul's theology. In fact, they give evidence that some of Paul's views changed over time, including his expectation that Christ would return before Paul's death (cf. 1 Thess 4:14–17, Phil 1:20–24). Paul did not say the same thing to each and every audience. That fact makes it difficult to consider the seven as a fully reliable baseline for evaluating what ideas qualify as Paul's ideas.

At the same time, the seven undisputed letters do maintain a striking degree of consistency in several aspects of their theological outlook. The disputed letters, yet not all of them in the same manner, sometimes describe God's work in Christ and the proper shape of Christian living in ways that do not easily align with the vision articulated by the seven undisputed letters. Some examples illustrate certain differences. When 2 Thessalonians describes the future judgment of wrongdoers as a time of vengeance, motivating ancient readers to take comfort in the promise of God punishing their opponents (2 Thess 1:5–10), the passage catches interpreters' attention because the undisputed letters never speak in this retaliatory vein about a future, eternal punishment. Also, when 1 Timothy describes the church as something like a well-ordered Greco-Roman household and commends behavior and leadership that would promote the church's respectable reputation in polite society, it sketches a portrait of Christian living that appears to have been stripped of the radicalism expressed in the undisputed letters, a radicalism that casts the Christian life as a departure from many key cultural norms (e.g., 1 Cor 4:9–13, 2 Cor 11:16–33, Phil 3:17–20, 1 Thess 3:1–4). A similarly domesticated attitude presents itself when 2 Tim 4:7 and other passages in the Pastoral Letters speak of faith as an institutional mark or a summary of doctrine instead of as a means of uniting oneself with Christ in his death and resurrection.

Some of the disputed letters also give indications that Paul's theological ideas had undergone adaptation or assumed a more settled and foundational status among Christian groups. Ephesians and Colossians provide the best illustrations of those kinds of developments. Even though they are two disputed letters whose theological views do not diverge too far from those in the seven undisputed letters, still Ephesians and Colossians manifest subtle yet definitive differences from the seven. Ephesians, for example, lauds the apostles, even going so far as to call them "holy" (Eph 3:5) and pieces of the church's foundation (Eph 2:19–20). The undisputed letters never place the apostles in such an estimable light, however, for in those writings Paul never assigns a greater share of holiness to apostles, and he considers Jesus the church's sole foundation (1 Cor 3:10–11). Interpreters therefore wonder whether Paul would really have elevated his own importance as Ephesians does or whether those words represent the opinions of one of Paul's admirers.

Additionally, Ephesians avers that Christ "abolished the law" (Eph 2:15), a claim that Romans and Galatians come close to making but explicitly refuse to make in the end. Also, Ephesians does not speak about Christ's expected return but discusses future blessings in a broad and general sense, and even as realities that believers possess in the present. For example, the letter asserts that Christ-followers participate in God's ultimate blessings now, claiming that God has already "raised us up with [Christ] and seated us with him in the heavenly places" (Eph 2:6). Colossians makes similar claims about Christ-followers having already experienced resurrection (Col 2:11–13; 3:1). The claims in those two books strike sharp contrasts with Paul's statements in the undisputed letters (e.g., Rom 8:22–25; 1 Cor 15:50–55; 2 Cor 5:1–10; Phil 2:12–13; 3:12–14, 20–21), for those letters look forward to a future transformation and describe believers' current life as a continual striving toward the ends that God has promised but not yet fully bestowed on God's people. Ephesians and Colossians reflect a different point of view, speaking as if Christ-followers have in some way already arrived. If Paul wrote those books, it is striking that he does not explain whether or why his perspective changed.

Historical Circumstances and the Timeline of Paul's Career

Some of the six disputed letters describe circumstances in Paul's life that appear impossible to align with other evidence that exists concerning Paul's activities, his travels, and the churches he nurtured. For example, many interpreters find it very difficult to determine how 2 Thessalonians could have been written to the church in Thessalonica anytime near the writing of 1 Thessalonians, since the two letters describe very different kinds of crises occurring among the believers in that city. The discontinuities in the assumptions the two letters make concerning the conditions in Thessalonica cause the letters to seem geared toward two very different audiences. In addition, several references to Paul's travels in the Pastoral Letters (e.g., 2 Tim 4:9–15, Titus 3:12–13) do not fit neatly within the general itineraries that can be reconstructed from data in the undisputed letters and in Acts. It is difficult to imagine how Paul could have had time to travel to so many destinations and conduct ministry in them during the relatively short window of time available to him in the 50s and early 60s. As a result, the references in the Pastoral Letters appear dubious to some interpreters; perhaps an ancient author included those references to add color to those letters' general portrait of Paul as an active traveler and tireless pastor.

Even more striking, the organizational structure that 1 Timothy and Titus commend for churches, involving the offices of bishop, elder, and deacon, has no parallel in the undisputed letters, save for a single mention of bishops and deacons in Phil 1:1, a verse in what is probably the latest of the seven undisputed letters. The Pastoral Letters, with their sense of a well-formed structure of church leadership and respective offices, could therefore reflect a time, probably several decades after Paul's ministry had ended, when churches had instituted clear or perhaps more standardized leadership roles and authority structures. In contrast, the undisputed letters indicate a more fluid or shared form of communal leadership in most Christian communities during the years when Paul was alive and corresponding with churches. It seems very unlikely that so much institutional development could have transpired in the limited span of time that contained Paul's public ministry, and therefore perhaps the Pastoral Letters belong to a later period, after Paul had died.

Possible Explanations

The preceding overview of evidence proves nothing on its own; it only identifies some of the issues that arise from the letters themselves and prompt disputes about whether Paul could have authored certain writings, given the limits of his life span and his relatively consistent perspectives in the seven undisputed letters. There is nothing especially controversial about observing that there are distinctive elements in the literary style and theological perspective of any of the six disputed letters when considering a given letter in comparison to the seven undisputed letters. The debates turn, rather, on analyses of the specific kinds of differences and on whether the overall *degree* of difference is enough to call into doubt Paul's authorship of a letter. Interpreters do not always agree about, for example, how strict of a standard of consistency is created by the seven undisputed letters and their commonalities. Nor do they agree about the reasonable degree to which Paul's writing style might have evolved over time and whether he might have changed or expanded his mind on particular theological points. The debates about authorship prove to be useless if they deal only in general observations about groups of letters and unspecific proposals about Paul's career and his intellectual processes. Any discussion about the disputed letters needs to focus on each one of them, one at a time, as a specific document with specific tendencies and claims. The way a debate unfolds about one disputed letter will not necessarily match the way a debate about another one will.

Various explanations that interpreters propose to account for letters' similarities and differences pay particular attention to aspects of how Paul composed letters and also to the literary conventions of his time. For one thing, even speaking of Paul as an "author" requires nuance. Paul had help in writing all of his letters. Occasionally the undisputed letters reveal that Paul, like many of his ancient literary contemporaries, employed an amanuensis, a secretary, when composing letters. Near the end of Romans, a certain Tertius introduces himself as "the writer of this letter" and expresses his greetings alongside a series of additional greetings that Paul conveys to his audience (Rom 16:22). A mention of "what large letters I make when I am writing in my own hand" in Gal 6:11 suggests Paul temporarily released his amanuensis from his duties in order to finish the letter to the Galatians himself and thus increase the emphasis and intimacy of the document's parting words. Interpreters wonder whether Paul could have given his amanuensis considerable rhetorical freedom in composing his letters after Paul explained the basic substance and structure he had in mind for a given piece of correspondence. If that were so, the noticeable differences in style and theological perspective found in one or more of the disputed letters might owe themselves to the idiosyncrasies of a new secretary, someone other than the creative hand behind the seven undisputed letters. Theories about a different amanuensis struggle to gain traction, however, because there is no definitive evidence to demonstrate that amanuenses in the Greco-Roman world were typically given creative license to insert their own perspectives and arguments into documents. If Paul gave his secretary such freedom and responsibility, it would have been a very unusual practice.

Additional proposals about the letters explore the possibility of another ancient literary convention at work: other people may have written them in Paul's name, entirely separately from Paul, probably without Paul's knowledge, and in some cases many years after his death. Those proposals contend that Paul's influence and popularity in certain Christian circles spawned a desire to keep his legacy visible and active after his final arrest and death. Pauline disciples, perhaps including some who once knew him well, might have composed letters in his name as attempts to promote his teachings and bring his theological convictions to bear on new circumstances or new challenges facing Christian communities. Letters written in those kinds of situations could have been attempts to ask and answer the question, What would our beloved Paul have said about this situation, and how would he have instructed us to serve and represent the gospel in faithful ways, according to what we remember about his example and commitment?

Paul clearly remained influential among Christ-followers after his death. Documents from the second century CE, from church leaders such as Ignatius of Antioch and Polycarp of Smyrna, testify to Paul's ongoing importance as one who inspired Christ-followers to persevere with boldness. Perhaps Paul had other followers and admirers who expressed their high regard for his contributions by contemporizing his ideas for new times, new audiences, and new locations. By writing letters in his name, they might have sought to extend his authority. Those letters could have allowed Paul's voice to continue speaking. By including various details and composing documents as if they were actual letters from Paul to specific audiences—such as, by employing references to specific associates of Paul and certain travel destinations—those new literary vehicles for disseminating Pauline ideas could infuse their rhetoric with verisimilitude, all to make Paul appear even more present and therefore still relevant to Christian communities in need of guidance and nourishment.

It may sound far-fetched, strange, or ethically indefensible for Paul's ancient admirers to have composed letters that creatively, but falsely, claimed to have been written by Paul. But people in the Greco-Roman world might have perceived the matter very differently. It was not so unusual in that setting. Other groups during that time, including Jews and gentiles, produced obviously pseudepigraphic writings—meaning writings that bear a false or inaccurate epigraph or that attribute themselves to someone other than their actual author. Christ-followers undeniably did the same during the second through fourth centuries. The disputed letters may establish that Christ-followers composed pseudepigraphic documents also in the first century or soon after.

Many ancient pseudepigraphic writings were produced centuries after their purported authors' deaths, making the fictional character of the documents' origins fairly apparent to their original and subsequent audiences. For example, a Jewish writing called 4 Ezra was created in the first century CE, about five centuries after its attributed author, Ezra the scribe, had died. If the disputed letters in the New Testament are indeed pseudepigraphic, then their creation *so soon* after Paul's death could have made them unusual since a pseudepigraphic writing composed while its purported author was still alive or only recently deceased would more likely be deprecated as a forgery instead of being honored as a way of remembering and saluting an influential figure. If Paul did not write 2 Thessalonians, for example, then the possibility remains that that letter's author might have written it to deceive audiences. But the letter instead could have been offered to an audience in nondeceptive ways. It could have been presented to readers ingenuously and frankly as a document meant to honor and remember a Paul who everyone knew fully well was dead and gone and therefore not the actual author.

Clearly some pseudepigraphic documents in the ancient world provided tools for frauds and deceptions. At the same time, others of those writings served as legitimate and creative means of honoring an important figure from the past, for they attempted to give voice to how that person's ideas or reputation might address new generations or a new situation. Much would depend on what a pseudepigraphic letter said and how it was presented to audiences. A document written in Paul's name could speak meaningfully to new audiences who knew very well that Paul did not write it. Even though a letter might have fashioned itself around a fictional premise, such as Paul writing to a trusted associate in ministry (e.g., 1–2 Tim, Titus), still the document's message and evocation of Paul's character could be quite meaningful and profound. Its rhetorical appeal would depend, in part, on its imaginative application of Paul's teachings and persona, arranged for a new and different audience to hear, even if the document's true author remained unknown or just uninterested in taking credit. The letter's value could be construed to reside in how well it brought memories of Paul's insight and legacy to bear on the question of how to live faithfully in new times and circumstances. The fact that other pseudepigraphic writings were circulating in the ancient world could make a letter written in Paul's name after his death appear less peculiar and its motives not necessarily disingenuous. Again, much would have depended on how the letter was presented to audiences by its actual author and its disseminators.

The possibility that other people created pseudepigraphic letters to perpetuate and expand Paul's ideas and influence does not answer the question of whether the six disputed letters' authors intentionally tried to deceive their ancient audiences into thinking they were reading words Paul himself wrote or dictated. If a given letter is pseudepigraphic, its unknown author's motives and original circumstances remain beyond any modern interpreter's ability to reconstruct, although it remains important to stipulate again that many in the first century might have found it unusual to encounter an obviously pseudepigraphic document within only a few years or decades of Paul's death. Anyone in the ancient church who used a letter claiming Paul's authorship as a tool for manipulating an audience by perpetrating a contrived misunderstanding about the letter's origins probably deserves disdain, irrespective of what the letter itself teaches and any value that readers might assign to or withhold from those teachings. On the other hand, a transparently pseudonymous letter—a document whose creators and audiences openly acknowledged the pseudonymous fiction and clearly identified the letter as pseudepigraphic—might have propagated ongoing admiration for Paul without trying to fool anyone about the letter's true origins. One can easily imagine that a Christian community might have received, cherished, and circulated a pseudepigraphic letter with full awareness that Paul had not written it. Equally imaginable is how that awareness could have quickly faded within a few generations or as the letter became more widely distributed among additional congregations that did not know the document's history. A pseudepigraphic letter that grew increasingly dislocated from its earliest and more informed audiences could have gradually become widely mistaken as authentically from Paul, not through any fault of its own, its creators, or its earlier audiences. If that happened, future audiences would find themselves not fully "in" on the story of the letter's real history and might justifiably assume Paul was its original author, as it claims.

If the evidence in the six disputed letters provides strong indications that Paul did not write them, then the existence of other pseudepigraphic writings in the ancient world gives a plausible explanation for why someone else might have written a letter in Paul's name. At the same time, and as explorations of each disputed letter will reveal, not all six of them are pseudepigraphic in the same way. That is, they do not all reflect the same perspective, nor do they all come from the same time and place, nor does each one pursue the same purposes. All of the preceding general reflections about authors' motives and transparency concerning a document's origins mean to show that it is simplistic to speak about ancient pseudepigraphic letters—including the disputed letters—as either clear-cut forgeries or as a common form of literature. The distance between the current time and the creation of those letters is vast. Recapturing an ancient audience's specific *experience* of one of the disputed letters is not possible. Without being able to see clearly how a letter like 1 Timothy was originally circulated among an original audience, and then recirculated among new audiences, it is impossible to know for sure whether ancient people thought they were reading Paul's actual words or a writing meant to advance Paul's ideas in a new day. Interpretations of a possibly pseudepigraphic letter should therefore avoid excessive speculation on how an ancient audience might have been moved by the letter.

In sum, what the letters say matters more than exactly who wrote them. At least, that is usually the case when an interpreter is seeking to investigate the early growth of Christian ideas and seeking to understand how the Bible continues to inform Christian faith. This is not to say that the authorship question is totally incidental to understanding the books. Rather, exploring the question of who wrote the six disputed letters is properly a part of the process of investigating and evaluating what those books have to say.

Implications

Lively discussions drive the debates over the authorship of each disputed letter, and people of good faith representing different theological traditions end up embracing various positions and hypotheses within those debates. It grossly distorts the picture to presume that interpreters who think Paul wrote 2 Timothy blindly trust whatever the book says, while those who deny Paul wrote it are radical skeptics who think they know more than other interpreters have throughout the church's history. Moreover, the debates concerning each of the disputed letters remain ongoing, always considering new dimensions of the relevant issues. The best way for interpreters to approach the questions of who wrote each of the six letters and why it matters is to explore the various options, test each option's ability to make sense of what a given letter says, and remain open to allowing new evidence and arguments to change one's mind or otherwise refine one's opinion.

When people begin to study the New Testament in depth, some of them experience shock at discovering that Paul possibly did not write one or more of the letters attributed to him. The idea looks offensive in light of modern notions of intellectual property and copyrights, although ancient audiences would not have viewed the phenomenon with the same lenses. One must bear in mind, however, that concluding that a letter is probably pseudepigraphic is not equivalent to claiming that a document is lying, inherently flawed, or a bad-faith effort of some kind. Any book's authority or merit as Christian Scripture depends on much more than the question of who wrote it. A larger part of the issue is the question of what the book is trying to say—which itself requires an interpreter to ask what kind of writing it is and what kinds of purposes it might have been created to serve. Pseudepigraphic literature served particular purposes in ancient settings, just like any other kinds of writings served purposes. Simply because forms of pseudepigraphic writings might be disreputable today does not mean they always have been in all cultural contexts.

Ancient audiences might have encountered pseudepigraphic materials in other settings. Students may have learned to write persuasively by producing pseudepigraphic documents as school exercises. Because pseudepigraphic documents were not entirely rare phenomena in the ancient world, no one should be too quick to label the disputed letters as deviant or unusual. Pseudepigraphic writings might be considered an ancient literary genre in their own right, and so pseudepigraphic letters justifiably share space with the other genres of literature that are represented within the diverse collection of Scripture. Pseudepigraphic books could—and probably do—occupy a place alongside the patterned legal codes in Leviticus, the poetry of the Psalms, the legend of Jonah, the diverse biographical memories of the Gospels, Paul's seven authentic letters, a treatise like Hebrews, and the apocalyptic journey recounted in Revelation. By including such a wide diversity of genres, the Bible's own design implies that various kinds of literature can potentially fulfill the functions of canonical Scripture.

While some people find it startling to learn that Paul may not have written or been directly responsible for six letters that bear his name, others experience relief when they discover this. Several of the ways in which the disputed letters deviate from the undisputed letters have to do with how the documents describe the proper organization and conduct of Christian communities. Regarding those subjects, most of the disputed letters make statements that have proved to generate significant controversy, especially regarding proper family structures and the church's conciliatory embrace of conventional Greco-Roman social values and hierarchies. Viewing the disputed letters separately from the undisputed letters can release interpreters from the inclination to find ways to make all thirteen Pauline Letters agree or to make all their teachings coalesce in a single perspective associated with a single person, Paul. The debates about authorship compel interpreters to let each book speak for itself before turning to compare and contrast each letter with others. As a result, interpreters often discover the story of the early church, as relayed by the New Testament writings, was hardly a story of strictly uniform beliefs and practices. Not everyone in the early churches agreed with each other, and not every Christian community lived or adapted in the same way.

Members of the early church were always in the process of remembering, restating, and adapting their beliefs and traditions to make them sensible and memorable for new circumstances. The four Gospels themselves are evidence of that dynamic, as is any other New Testament writing. The authority ascribed to a document or a tradition was not necessarily dependent on its author—who first wrote or disseminated it. The early Christian movement was more interested in affirming the authority of teachings and ideas based on how well they expressed widely acknowledged Christian beliefs and fostered Christian faith. What a document said and its ability to nurture Christian communities were usually more important to consider than who wrote the document.

Even today, judgments about a biblical writing's authority or value are always more than judgments about a book's origins. The disputes about who authored six letters cannot replace rigorous analysis of each letter. Those who decide Paul wrote 2 Thessalonians must come to that judgment based on their interpretations of the entire book, not just what it says in the few verses that name Paul as the writer. In addition, engaging in abstract discussions about authorship and about the production process or possible motives behind pseudepigraphic writings in antiquity is hardly enough when it comes to interpreting a letter. Interpreters who conclude that Paul could not have written Ephesians still cannot determine the identity of the actual author. They still need to elaborate the letter itself and make sense of its message, considering how that message might have once served an unknown author's particular purposes. All told, the debates about who wrote the disputed letters force interpreters to acknowledge how little can be known about the author of *any* biblical book. First Peter and 2 Peter are almost certainly pseudepigraphic writings too. Some interpreters find reasons to suspect that James and Jude may be as well. The authors of Hebrews, the four Gospels, and Acts all kept silent about their identities. Interpreters can therefore confidently discern very few details about the lives and specific theological influences behind the creators of most biblical books, yet most modern Christians understand all of those writings as somehow valuable, instructive, and authoritative for describing Christian theology and life.

In the end, all thirteen letters attributed to Paul remain "Pauline," in one way or another. Paul may not have written all of them, yet all of them direct attention, in various ways, back to Paul. All of them, in various manners, owe their message and their sense of their own importance to Paul's ideas, prominence, and legacy. Some of the letters may do that more directly and in less objectionable ways than others. Yet each one of them nevertheless provokes interpreters to consider whether it legitimately or sensibly renders what might be consistent with or derived from Paul's perspective on an issue, whether the issue is a theological question, ecclesial dispute, or matter of Christian self-definition. Comparing and contrasting all thirteen letters allows interpreters to construct a better understanding of who Paul was and who he was not. But more important: in scrutinizing all the letters, interpreters learn about the changes, challenges, and debates that were part of ancient Christ-followers' efforts to understand who they were and to determine how exactly they should live in ways that conformed to the Christian gospel.

8

The Letter of Paul to the Ephesians

Just like the seven letters that certainly came from Paul himself—the so-called undisputed letters—Ephesians devotes much of its energy to instructing an audience about Christian identity. As the undisputed letters also do according to their own distinctive style and rhetoric, Ephesians describes believers as people situated "in Christ." Members of the church participate, in a fully experiential way, in the salvation made possible through Jesus Christ. Corporately, people share in Christ's life and status. They receive from God benefits and a new standing as adoptees whom God claims and loves. This new Christian identity brings with it a distinctive unity, forged entirely by God's gracious actions: together, believers enjoy a shared intimacy with God because of their collective coexistence with Christ.

Ephesians gives particular weight to the notion of a social and communal unity that springs from believers' intimacy with God, for the letter describes Christian unity in a particularly foundational way, saying that old distinctions among Jews and gentiles have given way to the formation of an altogether "new humanity" created in Christ himself (Eph 2:15). That elemental claim, along with other aspects of the letter's theological rhetoric, offers one of the New Testament's strongest declarations that God's salvation brings about a totally new understanding of human existence. In Christ, people constitute a single humanity, brought together by God into an essential union as an expression of God's power and as a fulfillment of God's purposes.

The basic notion of a new, equal standing shared by Jews and gentiles alike shows up frequently in Paul's writings and in other New Testament books. In Paul's undisputed letters, he occasionally focuses on one of the main consequences of Christian unity: the arrival of new social realities that do not align with many familiar cultural conventions and social hierarchies (e.g., Rom 12:4–5; 1 Cor 12:12–13; Gal 3:28; Phil 3:20; Phlm 15–16). Ephesians, however, expresses the implications of a newly unified humanity in different ways, especially when the letter issues instructions about the proper way to live in response to God's work in Christ. When Ephesians commands its audience about how to relate to one another, the letter reasserts assumptions about social hierarchies that reinforce distinctions among people. Paul's undisputed letters occasionally subject such hierarchical assumptions to criticism. Ephesians does not. At least, Ephesians does not understand the practical ramifications of Christian unity along the same lines.

On the whole, Ephesians offers a theological perspective that zealously builds on and adapts some of Paul's ideas but also appears to depart from others. When read alongside Paul's undisputed letters and also the rest of the New Testament, the letter provides yet another reminder that people in the early church did not all speak from the same script in their efforts to articulate the Christian message and to promote social practices that best correspond to that message. The development of Christian self-understanding was a diverse, wide-ranging, changing, and lively conversation. Similar discussions about what it means to be and live as Christians remain so today. Ephesians often finds its way into many of those discussions.

The Letter's Origins and Ancient Audience

Ephesians yields very few clues about its original audience. Unlike the seven undisputed letters, it makes no references to Paul's previous or anticipated travels to where the audience resided. The lack of such references seems peculiar for a letter ostensibly sent to Ephesus, given what other sources reveal about Paul's extended activity in that city (e.g., 1 Cor 15:32, 16:8; cf. Acts 19; 20:17–38). But the letter greets no members of the audience by name. It offers no clear mention of any distinctive controversies among its addressees. There are no specific concerns, for example, about faulty ways of celebrating the Lord's Supper (cf. 1 Cor 11:17–34), about false teachings in the audience's community (cf. 2 Cor 10–12; Galatians), or about hardship caused by persecution (cf. Phil 1:27–30; 1 Thess 1:6, 2:14). Apart from a very general reference to a report about the audience's vibrant faith and love (Eph 1:15), an exhortation to pray for Paul and his ministry (Eph 6:19–20), and a parting mention of the letter's deliverer, a companion of Paul's named Tychicus (Eph 6:21–22), the letter has a very generic sense about it. It reads like a treatise meant for broad distribution among many different audiences as opposed to a piece of correspondence directed to a particular set of circumstances. It therefore could have been composed to address a variety of communities or people relatively unknown to the author, whether that author was Paul or someone else.

If Ephesians was actually first sent to numerous groups, they might have resided in multiple locations, either in addition to Ephesus or not in Ephesus at all. The document's only mention of the city comes in its first verse, where the letter addresses itself, according to most published translations, "to the saints who are in Ephesus and are faithful in Christ Jesus." That translation reflects a longtime traditional view that the letter was originally written for congregations in Ephesus; however, the most reliable extant Greek manuscripts do not include the words *in Ephesus*. According to those manuscripts, the letter addresses itself simply and generally "to the saints who are also faithful in Christ Jesus." Moreover, reports from the ancient church say that Marcion and his disciples in the second century thought that this letter was addressed to Christ-followers in Laodicea, another city in western Asia Minor. Those pieces of evidence give further credence to the proposal that the letter known as Ephesians was originally an encyclical document meant for widespread distribution. Perhaps one copy went to Ephesus and included the words *in Ephesus* in its salutation, while another copy went to Laodicea with a different salutation, and others went elsewhere across Asia Minor.

Ephesus, a comparatively very large city, boasted about a quarter million residents in the first century. Rich in natural resources and situated on a coast, it was a wealthy center of commerce and banking. The letter speaks about family structures that include slaves, indicating at least some diversity in the social statuses of the document's intended audience. Those details do not necessarily matter for interpreting Ephesians, given the letter's overall lack of specificity about its audience and their circumstances. Nevertheless, the letter still provides plenty of reminders that its original audience, or audiences, dwelled in Hellenistic settings that pulsed with the cultural norms associated with Roman economic and social networks. The letter warns against idolatry and falsehood, things that might provide challenges for Christ-followers because of all the forms of religious expression they encountered in cosmopolitan contexts.

Repeatedly the letter addresses readers as gentiles and highlights Paul's distinctive ministry to gentiles. When the letter tells its audience that they "must no longer live as the Gentiles live" (Eph 4:17), it does not necessarily imply that some in the audience were Jews; rather, Ephesians tells gentile Christ-followers that their new identity as part of God's new humanity should influence their conduct, distinguishing them and their behavior from their former patterns of living as people who were at that time estranged from God. Although the letter occasionally quotes from the Septuagint, adapts language or imagery from Jewish Scriptures, and makes reference to circumcision, it is not clear how much Jewish tradition the letter assumes its audience would have known.

Ephesians addresses itself to gentiles to help them understand that they have received a new identity in Christ—an identity that they share with Jews. The letter may assume that Jews are also present among the audience of saints or are somehow eavesdropping on the conversation. Ephesians asserts that the unity created by that new Christian identity brings an end to hostilities and rivalries between Jews and gentiles. In fact, God has brought both groups into a common existence. If, for any reason, any gentile believers in the audience were thinking about separating themselves from Jewish believers, or vice versa, Ephesians might have dissuaded them through its strong emphasis on the unity God creates through Jesus Christ.

The Question of Authorship

Ephesians claims to have been written by Paul alone (Eph 1:1, 3:1), and for the vast majority of the last two thousand years, that claim has gone unchallenged. As the overview of the disputed letters noted, however, strong support exists for the proposal that someone else wrote this letter in Paul's name. Those reasons include more than the previously described character of the letter and its overtly generalized manner of addressing its audience, which no other known Pauline letter does. Even more noticeable, the style and theology of Ephesians diverge from the undisputed letters in significant ways. The question of the letter's authorship is therefore first a question of how to understand the letter's theological perspective and its original purposes.

Several of the stylistic peculiarities, especially the author's penchant for very long sentences, have already been noted, as have a couple of the theological characteristics of Ephesians. None of the letter's theological claims baldly contradict what Paul says in other writings, but they do manifest inconsistencies that become especially notable when one considers the remarkable stylistic, linguistic, and theological congruity of the seven undisputed letters. For example, when Ephesians speaks of the "church" to refer to a universal body composed of all believers, questions arise, for the undisputed letters use that word to refer to discrete congregations. When those other letters discuss sin, they usually refer to a power that enslaves humanity, while in Ephesians the lone mention of "sins" infers that they are trespasses or particular wrongs a person might commit (Eph 2:1). Ephesians commends marriage and describes a marital relationship as a reflection of Christ's relationship to the church, an opinion very different from 1 Cor 7:1–9, which concedes that believers can opt to marry if their lack of self-control makes celibacy unrealistic. Ephesians speaks of "forgiveness" (Eph 1:7, 4:32; cf. Col 1:14, 3:13), a word Paul never includes in the undisputed letters except in Rom 4:7, where it appears in a quotation of Ps 32:1. Ephesians mentions "the devil," a word absent from the undisputed letters, which speak instead of "Satan." This letter never mentions Christ's return. Ephesians speaks of Christ's enthronement over all things as if it has already been accomplished, a claim that effectively mitigates the importance or the urgency of Christ's return, an event Paul eagerly expects in the letters he wrote to other churches during the 50s CE. None of these examples plainly disconfirms what Paul says elsewhere, but they do reflect a difference in perspective. The differences add up.

The book's perspectives are not totally unique, however. Colossians and Ephesians share similarities in their form, themes, and phraseology. Most likely, whoever wrote Ephesians did so after Colossians had been written, and the author based Ephesians on Colossians, building on ideas from Colossians and expanding specific phrases found in that letter. If in fact Paul wrote both letters, perhaps around the same time near the end of his life, then that probably occurred in the early 60s CE. But the connections between Colossians and Ephesians could still be explained if Paul wrote Colossians and then someone else wrote Ephesians at a later date, using Colossians as a guide or inspiration. More likely, and as an analysis of Colossians helps to clarify, someone else, or multiple people, wrote both of the letters and claimed Paul as the author. Some interpreters argue that Paul could have directly commissioned another person to write Colossians and perhaps also Ephesians on his behalf, especially if he was indeed incarcerated (Col 4:3, 10; Eph 3:1; 4:1) and limited by overly taxing conditions. Even in that case, the contrast that both Ephesians and Colossians strike in comparison to the theological perspectives and rhetoric of the seven undisputed letters remains remarkable.

The prominence and pervasiveness of the differences throughout both Ephesians and Colossians become clearer as one studies the letters. The kinds of claims they make and the behaviors they commend for Christian living further set them apart from the undisputed letters. When all the debates are considered, the cumulative evidence makes a satisfactory case for concluding that Colossians and Ephesians were composed after Paul died. The high regard Ephesians expresses for the apostles and for Paul's ministry provides an additional hint that one of Paul's admirers or former associates wrote it after Paul's death and at a time when pressures to compel gentile believers to observe torah had subsided. If indeed Ephesians is a pseudepigraphic letter composed after Paul's death, most likely it was written between 75 and 90 CE. In that case, the letter articulates the efforts of some in the early church to develop Paul's ideas and perpetuate Paul's legacy so his voice could influence congregations in a new generation. In those decades after Paul's death, the threat of disunity remained a concern. The ways of understanding Christian hope and God's promises were changing, perhaps because Christ had not yet returned as expected. The impulse for Christian communities to embrace conventional, stable social values may also have been increasingly strong among Christ-followers who wanted the church to set down deeper roots and thrive in certain cultural contexts, lest believers find themselves isolated and forever under suspicion from their neighbors.

Answers to questions about who wrote Ephesians and what relationship Ephesians has to Colossians are more detailed than this summary can describe. The task of understanding each letter must first involve reading it on its own terms and not reading it so as to make it fit or to make it contrast with other letters. Whether Paul wrote them or not, Ephesians and Colossians present a description of Christian identity and instructions for Christian living that obviously do not merely restate what Paul said in other documents to other audiences. Interpreting and evaluating each letter involves understanding what the letter says and then pondering what might account for the differences as well as the similarities.

The resemblances shared by Ephesians and Colossians can make it beneficial to investigate both documents at the same time. Those who read the current chapter in tandem with chapter 10 in this same volume will find that both chapters together provide a fuller orientation to the two books.

Overview

Salutation, Blessing, Thanksgiving, and Prayer (Eph 1)

Following a sparing and nondescript salutation, Ephesians launches an extended prayer that blesses God. In delaying its statement of thanksgiving until later in the opening chapter, the letter resembles 2 Corinthians. The blessings, here and in 2 Cor 1:3–7, resemble numerous exclamations and prayers in the Old Testament prefaced with "Blessed be the LORD." Ephesians begins with a wide theological vision, for the blessing introduces numerous themes that will return later in the letter, including election, adoption, knowledge, forgiveness, inheritance, and the Holy Spirit. The syntax of the initial blessing has a sprawling, interconnected style that reinforces the theological heart of all its nearly hyperbolic theological claims. The claims, as well as the syntax, revolve around God as the acting subject: *God* is the source of all the benefits, having made them fully available now "in Christ." References to God choosing, destining, and ordering things through "a plan" reflect a worldview that understands God as the primary influence behind all of the world's history and the one who aims to guide history to its meaningful goal. While some Bible readers still take statements like those as indicators that God predetermines each event of human history, the more basic theological claim in view throughout the letter's extended blessing is that in Christ God demonstrates an active and unrelenting commitment to accomplishing salvation.

The letter's soaring theological perspective continues when it mentions Paul's thankfulness to God for the audience's faith in Christ and love for one another. The basic statement of gratitude opens up into a larger prayer that asks God to provide enlightenment and knowledge, so the audience can truly comprehend what God has accomplished and will yet accomplish. The prayer strongly affirms God's power, a power demonstrated not explicitly through suffering or weakness of any kind but in the resurrection and exaltation of Christ. The imagery depicts Christ as a transcendent ruler who holds authority over all that is, including all other cosmic powers, whether angelic or demonic. God has made everything else subject to Christ, placing it all "under his feet" (recalling Ps 8:6, 110:1). God also "has made him the head over all things" (cf. Col 2:10, 19), employing an image of headship that will occur again later in the letter.

Salvation and Belonging, Accomplished through Christ (Eph 2)

Having completed the prayers, the letter pivots to describe the audience, using the plural form of "you," and connecting those readers to a wider, collective "us": the gentile audience, along with Jews like Paul, formerly lived in "trespasses and sins." Nevertheless, God, acting in mercy, love, and grace, "made us," both groups, "alive together with Christ." The emphasis falls on the shared experiences of gentiles and Jews and on God as the agent who accomplishes salvation, with all of its past, present, and future aspects. God has saved. God will yet "in the ages to come . . . show the immeasurable riches of [God's] grace" (Eph 2:7). And even now, God has made believers to be what God intends them to be: people made truly alive and thus equipped to live a life of "good works."

The letter's distinction between "you" gentiles who once were "far off" (cf. Isa 57:19) and "we" Jews who have a history with God continues and gains clarity when Ephesians describes the audience as uncircumcised and thus at one time "aliens from the commonwealth of Israel" (Eph 2:12) and outside the reach of certain covenants God previously made with the ancient Hebrews and Israelites. Again, the change in status occurred through Christ. Effecting a new status that the letter signals with a dramatic "but now" (Eph 2:13), Christ's death—referred to indirectly as his "blood" and "flesh" (cf. Eph 5:2)—ended the gentiles' previous estrangement and made "both groups," gentiles and Jews, "into one." With a striking statement that asserts a radically new way of understanding humanity and its place in God's purposes, the letter says Christ abolished the law of Moses and created "in himself one new humanity in place of the two." The unity that other Pauline letters describe between Jews and gentiles thus becomes even more acutely elemental and existential in Ephesians.

This new humanity enjoys peace among itself as "one body"; former hostilities between gentiles and Jews have been put to death, for both corporately have been reconciled to God (cf. Col 1:20, 22). That reconciliation also means the two groups enjoy peace, belonging, and access to God together. The access comes through "one Spirit," which makes all believers into cocitizens and comembers of God's "household." The metaphors continue to pile on one another when the letter describes the household as a physical building that organically grows as a unit into a temple in which God dwells. Through Christ, walls of former divisions give way to buildings made of a new community of people in whom God dwells. God transforms death, alienation, dislocation, exclusion, hostility, and division into new life, belonging, citizenship, integration, peace, and unity.

Paul's Ministry and the Mystery of the Gospel (Eph 3)

The unity shared by Jews and gentiles and the new access to God's household that the gospel provides for gentiles open the door to a discussion of Paul's ministry. Paul's ministry expresses Paul's identity: he lives as a servant of the gospel. The good news Paul shares with others is news about God's grace—a grace described as a "mystery" that Paul discovered through a "revelation" (cf. Gal 1:12, 16; Col 1:26). The term *mystery* in the New Testament usually refers not to a puzzle or a secret but to something previously unknown that comes to be comprehended in time or through a divine disclosure. Therefore, those who have come to experience God and God's truth now have eyes to discern what they previously could not. In this case they can perceive a particular mystery: the reality that through Christ God makes gentiles into "fellow heirs" alongside Jews, "members of the same body, and sharers in the promise" (Eph 3:6). Commitment to those new realities was a defining aspect of Paul's theological understanding and his missionary efforts. When Ephesians speaks of Paul's ministry in this way, it characterizes the good news as something deeply embedded in God's "eternal purpose," not the plan-B effort of a God who has been stymied or who acts capriciously.

Paul's commitment to the gospel message may have resulted in his incarceration from time to time, but Ephesians indicates that any unpleasantness Paul suffered was worthwhile because it was nothing more than a minor side effect of Paul's zeal for proclaiming the divine mystery about the new realities God has accomplished through Christ. A fervent prayer and doxology reiterate that zeal, expressing a passionate desire for the letter's audience to comprehend what God has done for them and who they are as people enriched by the love of Christ. The prayer impels the letter toward one of its primary intentions: to instruct believers so they might understand the fullness of the gospel and know with certainty that Christ dwells in the hearts of gentile Christ-followers—gentiles whom God is generously willing to fill "with all the fullness of God" (Eph 3:19; cf. Col 1:19, 2:9).

Living as a New Person (Eph 4:1–5:20)

Doxology leads to commissioning when the letter exhorts its audience to "lead a life worthy" of the good news, which is news about what God has done and about the new fellowship believers share with God. A key theme in Ephesians, and a familiar emphasis in Paul's own letters, is unity. The letter commends maintaining unity through love, forbearance, and peace so Christ-followers' actions and attitudes may reflect the one new humanity God has made. Christian unity does not equate to uniformity, for the letter mentions different gifts and roles given to various people in order to equip the church to live out its purposes. Likewise, being filled with God's fullness does not mean a life without struggle and controversy, for the letter warns against deceitful teachings. The community of believers still needs to grow—like an interconnected body that must cooperate and mature. The body metaphor in this section resembles 1 Cor 12:12–27 and Rom 12:3–8, except Ephesians names Christ as the body's "head" (cf. Col 2:10, 19), as opposed to imagining the whole body collectively as the substance of Christ himself.

The letter sets the new behavior it commends in contrast to a "former way of life." Ephesians instructs its audience to clothe themselves with "the new self"—literally, "the new person" (Eph 4:22–24; cf. Col 3:9–11). As a result, they will cultivate virtues that promote interpersonal harmony (cf. Col 3:5–8, 16–17; 4:5). The author presents all those instructions not as a strategy for a community's survival or as an expression of abstract kindness but as a particular way of imitating God and expressing the love Christ displayed in his sacrificial death. Members of the church have no real choice when it comes to caring for one another, for they exist as "members of one another."

Light and darkness also contrast two different ways of life. Those are familiar images from biblical writings and other ancient Jewish texts, including apocalyptic literature and much of the extrabiblical literature found among the Dead Sea Scrolls. Wisdom and foolishness also appear as a pair in this section. The dualistic imagery characterizes life as a struggle fraught with danger. The earlier chapters of Ephesians may resound with glorious claims of divine power and with celebrations of the new existence given to believers, but the letter's subsequent discussions of daily life in this section refuse to allow the letter to lose sight of the challenges created by the current state of the world.

An Orderly Household (Eph 5:21–6:9)

This section does not divert from the focus established in the previous one, for it continues to describe certain ways of living that the letter's author deems appropriate for believers. It begins with a simple exhortation meant to promote mutual support and the desire for believers to assist others when it says "be subject to one another" (cf. Gal 5:13).

Things grow more complicated when the instructions turn to name the specific forms of subjecting to one another in familial settings and households. The commands appear to create not a model of mutual subjection, however, as much as a system of involuntary submissiveness that classifies relationships and power corresponding to a hierarchy defined by gender, legal privilege, and identity. Wives are subject to husbands. Children are subject to parents. Slaves are subject to their masters. Unmarried adults receive no mention. The author appears not to consider whether slavery may be inherently dehumanizing or whether it might be worth considering that ancient mores generally condoned physical and sexual violence perpetrated against slaves by their owners.

The letter's specific instructions are hardly unique to Ephesians. Several other New Testament writings say very similar things (Col 3:18–4:1; 1 Pet 2:13–3:7; cf. 1 Tim 6:1–2; Titus 2:1–10). Neither is this material and the rationale that likely supported it unique to the New Testament. Ancient Greco-Roman moralists and Hellenistic Jewish authors expressed approval for similar ways of assigning rights and responsibilities, promoting a vision for well-ordered households that were capable of mirroring and fostering a well-ordered society. Many considered households as microcosms of the imperial ideal in which each person played his or her appropriate part to promote a supposed greater good. The Pastoral Letters also endorse that moral vision but in an even more prominent and far-reaching way. Investigations of those letters will help illuminate why their author, and perhaps also the authors of Ephesians and other New Testament writings, might have found the vision appropriate for organizing Christian communities and households according to familiar hierarchical structures.

The author of Ephesians offers explicitly Christian justifications for the instructions about submission (cf. 1 Cor 11:3, 7–9), and the author also exhorts believers at the top of the hierarchies—husbands, fathers, and slave masters—to love deeply those who are subordinate to them or to renounce their right to abuse others. The instructions to those who are presumed to be the more powerful individual in a particular interpersonal relationship set this section of Ephesians apart from some similar codes composed by ancient moralistic philosophers. At the same time, however, the assumptions about status and power in this "household code" appear out of step with the letter's earlier claims about the "one new humanity" God has created. They also can be taken as colliding with Paul's claim in Gal 3:28, which asserts that distinctions among persons have no power to make qualitative statements about a person's value. The author of Ephesians here promotes a vision of Christian community that corresponds more closely to ancient social conventions. Possibly he wanted Christian communities and families to blend into their social settings and therefore not to appear contrary to conventional moral structures. If so, then this part of Ephesians represents a domestication, if not a perversion, of theological foundations Paul once set forth, especially in letters like 1 Corinthians and Galatians. It also commends an accommodation to cultural norms. Yet it does so without specifying why such accommodations do not make the church complicit in the "ignorance" and futile practices that the letter elsewhere says infect the wider world of "the gentiles" (Eph 4:17–19).

Those throughout history who have found in these verses license to devalue and oppress women, wives, children, and slaves because of the supposed superiority of men, husbands, parents, and slave owners have done considerable damage to people's lives. They did so, in part, because the author of Ephesians evidently affixed dubious theological rationales to conventional Greco-Roman social hierarchies.

Closing Exhortations and Benediction (Eph 6:10–24)

Recalling familiar images of wearing one's salvation and divine protection as pieces of armor (e.g., Isa 59:17; Wis 5:17–18), Ephesians exhorts its audience to put on armor God provides to shield themselves in their combat against cosmic powers. Christ may rule over all things (Eph 1:20–23; cf. 3:10), but Christ's supremacy does not mean that believers have nothing to fear from the devil, "the evil one." Spiritual forces that advance evil, along with political or social constellations of power that cause harm, remain viable threats, but God provides the defenses necessary to endure life in an existence likened to a battlefield. "The word of God" also operates like a sword in the hands of the Spirit, promising an offensive weapon in this spiritual battle as well.

At the end of the letter, exhortations asking for prayers on Paul's behalf and comments concerning Tychicus contribute to debates about the origins of Ephesians. The references to Tychicus and his efforts nearly duplicate Col 4:7–8. If Paul commissioned someone else, perhaps even Tychicus, to write Ephesians for him while he still was alive, that could explain why the letter concludes with such a clear echo of Colossians. Yet these verses hardly prove that Paul was living when Ephesians was written. Instead, they represent a means by which the pseudepigraphic letter embellishes itself with realistic details, as seen also in 2 Thessalonians and especially 1–2 Timothy and Titus. The details provide pieces of verisimilitude, either to deceive an ancient audience about the true source of Ephesians or to enhance the letter's quality as a sincere tribute to Paul, his teachings, and his indefatigable commitment to preach among gentiles despite obstacles.

The Letter's Themes and Theological Emphases

Discussions of Ephesians and its theological message sometimes pay so much attention to delineating how the letter differs from Paul's undisputed letters that it becomes easy to lose sight of how Ephesians conveys a theological perspective in its own right. Yet comparing and contrasting theological themes provides valuable insights when this comparative work can isolate and clarify the letter's distinctive emphases. This approach does not mean to belabor questions concerning the letter's authorship. The goal remains to discover what this ancient book reveals about early Christ-followers' efforts to think theologically—to understand who they were in light of what they believed God had done through Christ.

The Realization of God's Purposes

Fullness has arrived, according to Ephesians. Jesus has power, the letter declares, and he possesses that power now. Operating from a perspective similar to the one offered in Colossians, the letter describes Christ as a cosmic ruler whom God has installed in a position of authority over any other force in all creation (Eph 1:20–22; cf. Col 1:15–17; 2:10, 15; Phil 2:9–11). The perspective differs from those in the undisputed Pauline letters that anticipate a future time when Jesus will finally exercise his full authority (e.g., Rom 16:20; 1 Cor 15:24–28). In addition, Ephesians enthusiastically announces that believers already dwell with Christ, for they too have been "raised" along with him (Eph 2:6; cf. 1:3; Col 2:13). While other letters emphasize the gospel as a guarantee of future hopes (e.g., Rom 8:18–25, 1 Cor 15:20–23, 2 Cor 4:13–18, Phil 3:20–21, 1 Thess 5:9–10; cf. Eph 1:7, 13–14; 4:30), Ephesians portrays ultimate realities as accomplished and available now.

Grandiose claims about fulfilled spiritual realities might make Ephesians appear guilty of promulgating a theology that borders on a delusional flight from current existence were it not for other parts of the letter that describe life as a high-stakes struggle requiring strength and God's help. The letter acknowledges that its audience does not experience daily life as a tranquil paradise of bathing in power and glory alongside Christ. Believers find themselves still engaged in apocalyptic-themed warfare against the devil and other hostile forces (e.g., Eph 3:14–17, 4:14–19, 5:15–16, 6:10–17). The contrast between Jesus' power and ongoing spiritual strife in the world does not make Ephesians irredeemably contradictory. Nor does the contrast urge believers to discount the risks and pains of flesh-and-blood existence. In effect, the letter's claims concerning current spiritual threats and Jesus' power imaginatively blur distinctions among past, present, and future. The letter is so exuberant and excessive in its theological expressions that time and limits collapse in its theological rhetoric. God's purposes are so certain, it is as if they are able to be fully experienced and realized now. God's will is not only inscrutable, gracious, and magnificent, but believers can discern it in the present (e.g., Eph 1:8–10, 3:18–19), even though the present remains a time of conflict. The author appears uninterested in delineating a timeline or a sequence to explain such details of how, when, and where God's salvation manifests itself. Instead, the letter's hyperbole declares that in Christ believers come to find themselves included in the overarching compass of God's eternal purposes, for those purposes come to full fruition because of Jesus Christ. What matters less to the author is clarifying whether those purposes have already come into fruition, are coming into fruition, or will yet do so. Ephesians simply insists they are real.

Even as Ephesians accentuates the severe risks that confront believers in their struggles against the devil and other forces, the letter does not include specific references to persecution suffered by the audience. Ephesians does not explicitly attempt to instill resolve in an oppressed community as Philippians and 1 Thessalonians do. It does, however, nourish its audience's faith when it directs focus toward the magnificent power that is available to Christ-followers. Ephesians looks forward to "the day of redemption" (Eph 4:30), but it does not describe the day as a time of judgment, just as the letter includes no mention of Christ coming again at a future time. Ephesians motivates its audience not through any language about believers being united with Christ in his suffering and death (cf. Rom 6:3–8; 2 Cor 5:14–15; Gal 2:19) but in reminders of God's power displayed in Jesus' resurrection (e.g., Eph 1:20) and in reassurances about an "inheritance" received (e.g., Eph 1:11, 18; cf. 3:6; Col 1:12). The letter's rhetoric about divine power and already realized promises thus has a particular function: it gives a theological basis for an audience to persevere in their calling and to understand their place in God's purposes. That particular theological basis, with its focus on resurrection power, differs rather substantially from the more cross-focused theological rhetoric and pastoral strategies in writings that unquestionably come from Paul, yet it still assigns God the decisive role in humanity's prospects for experiencing the fullness of God's blessings.

Theology in a Doxological Key

Ephesians offers its grand theological assertions with an almost ethereal air. New theological realities are so certain and all-encompassing that they sound almost otherworldly, as if the letter transports its audience into heaven so they can see for themselves. Accordingly, Ephesians has a liturgical sense about it; its message veers into worship as it instructs and exhorts its readers. For example, at the document's outset, it extols God's blessedness and repeatedly praises God's "glory" (Eph 1:3–14). The letter commends worship and prayer (Eph 5:19–20, 6:18–20) while it also offers prayers (Eph 1:15–22, 3:13–21). Ephesians presents those prayers as Paul's intercessions to God on behalf of the audience, who represent the universal church that comprises all believers. The letter also brings God's majesty to earth. With similarity to Colossians, Ephesians associates God's glory with the grace and inheritance God has given to people (Eph 1:6, 18; Col 1:12; 3:24; cf. Rom 5:2; 1 Thess 2:12). The church manifests divine glory in its existence and activity on earth (Eph 3:21; cf. Col 3:4).

The letter's soaring and almost excessive eloquence therefore appropriately accompanies the letter's lofty theological message. Not only does the letter talk about Christ's glorious existence, it seeks to have its audience experience God's presence. Ephesians occasionally dissolves the boundaries between earth and what the author calls "the heavenly places." Just as time collapses in parts of the letter, space sometimes does the same. In the theology of Ephesians, divine glory hardly resides far away.

A Distinctive and Perhaps Totalizing Perspective on Unity

Unity occupies a critical place in this letter's efforts to describe God's salvation and the kind of power God has displayed through Christ. Unity refers to more than a cooperative and friendly community of believers in Ephesians. The letter speaks about an all-inclusive sense of unity as a "mystery" that has now become known through Christ. That mystery consists in God's plan to bring all things together into one, "to gather up all things in [Christ], things in heaven and things on earth" (Eph 1:9–11). In the letter's view, "all things" achieve a kind of fundamental union not only because they belong to Christ but also because they are ruled over and contained by Christ, who is the "head" or "source" (which is another possible translation) of "all things" (Eph 1:22; cf. 4:15). Those claims of a new, elemental union in which Christ encompasses all things are clearly far-reaching. They encompass the totality of creation and human experience. Whether the claims constitute liberative news or oppressive news depends on who wields them and for what purposes.

Ephesians presents its notion of comprehensive unity as an outgrowth of Paul's particular emphasis on the unity that Jews and gentiles share because of the gospel (Eph 3:1–10; cf. Col 1:26–27, Rom 3:21–31, Gal 3:25–4:7). Both parties become heirs of God's promises and enjoy membership in the one "household of God." The incorporation of gentiles into the long legacy of God's fidelity touches on all aspects of their identity (Eph 2:11–22), giving them a home and also fashioning them into a home for God to inhabit. The sense of intimacy and belonging is profound.

Even the imagery Ephesians uses to describe the unity that gentiles and Jews share in Christ appears extravagant in relation to other New Testament writings. The claim that Christ "has abolished the law" (Eph 2:15) conflicts with Jesus' statements to the contrary (Matt 5:17, Luke 16:17) and with Paul's teachings about torah's ongoing value (e.g., Rom 3:31, 7:12; Gal 3:21). Other writings depict gentiles as people summoned to *share* in God's saving purposes, purposes that reach their fulfillment through Christ (e.g., Acts 11:17–18; 15:13–21; Rom 9–11; Gal 3:9, 14). The rhetoric in Ephesians, however, promotes unity while in the process intensifying the notion of unity nearly to the point of erasing vestiges of Judaism from the description of salvation through Christ. In other words, Ephesians comes close to obliterating any lasting sense or value of Jewish particularity. This dimension of Ephesians represents an extreme perspective in comparison to the rest of the New Testament. It makes the theology of Ephesians a minority position. Given all of the theological and political malfeasance that has historically followed from the Christian church's amnesia about its Jewish foundations and about God's covenantal fidelity, many interpreters rightly emphasize the importance of stipulating that Ephesians does not represent the only way that one might rearticulate or expand on Paul's theological convictions about the unity shared by Jews and gentiles. A conception of unity that totally discounts certain distinctions among its members, especially distinctions related to the Jewish heart of the gospel, threatens to promote a Christian theology that forgets who Jesus is and what the broader witness of Scripture recalls about God's history among and for the people of Israel.

The unity envisioned in Ephesians makes bold statements about how believers should understand their corporate identity as the church. The boldness of the letter's language contains a risk, insofar as this unity has such an absolute, all-encompassing flavor that it could threaten to nullify *any* sense of individuality or particularity among those who make up the unified whole. The idea of incorporating all beings into a single entity, transforming scattered aliens into citizens of a single state or organism, can be heard as extoling the generosity, power, and benevolence of a far-reaching God as God expresses those qualities through Christ. At the same time, the language about conflating all things into one might also be taken as mimicry of the propaganda and ideals of the Roman Empire, which made similar promises about social centralization and cultural homogenization, casting those developments as expressions of a beneficial empire's virtue and might. The observation is not to say that Ephesians endorses the Roman Empire or sees the empire as a partner in the church's ongoing vitality. Indeed, the letter's teachings about the church call instead for believers to distinguish themselves from their imperial setting (e.g., Eph 2:1–3; 4:14, 17–22). Rather, the rhetoric and grandiose vision of a rudimentary unity comprising "all things" imitates a Roman political value of subsummation, in which members of a society lose their individuality or surrender it to become assimilated into a dominant yet imposed collective identity.

In short, the theological vision of Ephesians extols a unity that God creates by assimilating everything and everyone within Christ, thereby offering people peace and belonging that are guaranteed by divine strength. If a trustworthy God one day unambiguously creates a harmonious coexistence among the varieties of God's people, that may justify the letter's vision of oneness as something desirable. But the particular language and imagery of Ephesians must be handled with care by Christ-followers, for in a world that remains a venue for believers' dangerous struggles "against the rulers, against the authorities, against the cosmic powers of this present darkness" (Eph 6:12), power and unity can be alluring ideals for those who seek to speak and act for God. Rhetoric about irresistible power and elemental unity easily becomes a tool for malice in the hands of those who intend to control or subordinate others—including those who do so in the guise of Christian charitableness.

Exactly who mediates power that claims to be divine power makes all the difference for how this letter's theological claims might benefit and take shape in people's actual lives. If promises of unity secured through divine power serve as a Trojan horse for certain interpreters, leaders, cultural expressions, claims of ethnic supremacy, or narrowly defined religious traditions and ideologies bent on protecting their own dominance by dissolving away otherness, then the letter's theology has a disputable claim to being good news. Such an appropriation of the letter's theology—whether done intentionally or not—peddles sameness as a false substitute for oneness. It enslaves people to a uniformity that bogusly names itself as community. It promises fellowship but enforces assimilation. In such conditions of hegemonic conformity, the church comes to resemble empires and imperialistic icons who care only for their own glory, power, and longevity.

9

The Letter of Paul to the Philippians

Everything about Philippians indicates that Paul's relationship with the Christ-followers in Philippi brimmed with mutual love and regard. Paul wrote to the Philippians very near the end of his life, or during a time when he worried his demise was imminent, and his letter can hardly contain the joy he felt. Paul's joy comes across as a theological utterance as much as emotional warmth. The joy stems from all he shares with the Philippians, including friendship, ministry, and the confident hope that they, like all believers, will share in Christ's glory. With the exception of 1 Thessalonians, no other letter written by Paul comes close to the genial, tender, and encouraging tone that animates Philippians. The letter provides a permanent reminder that Paul wrote to churches sometimes for reasons other than conflict resolution and managing the logistics of his ministry. In this case his deep love and longing for his audience prompted him to write even as he acknowledges several problems and threats facing the Philippian believers. Popular caricatures of Paul as an unyielding and cold authority figure have a difficult time accounting for this letter's pathos-infused expressions of joy. Paul derived deep personal satisfaction from a life in Christ and the work of ministry as well as from the people with whom he shared that ministry.

Paul might have had an excuse to write a very different kind of letter, for he wrote Philippians during a time when he was held as a prisoner, detained in a location and for reasons he does not identify. Paul refuses to let his conditions dictate his outlook on his life and ministry, however. Instead of imposing limitations or shame on Paul, his incarceration allows him opportunities to advance the cause of the gospel he preaches. Paul describes his positive outlook on his situation as more than wishful thinking or an ability to find a cloud's silver lining. Paul's sense of security and well-being transcends any circumstances, for it is embedded in the gospel itself. The gospel, in Paul's view, is good news of confidence and true fellowship with Christ, not a message of upbeat optimism or compliant devotion. As Philippians presents it, the good news Paul preaches is also the gospel Paul lives out in his own experience, for it involves sharing intimately in Jesus' sufferings and humiliations so that believers can also share in Jesus' resurrection and exaltation. Custody ironically reminds Paul of his ultimate freedom as a believer. Being confined to one place cannot squelch either his earnest longing for his spiritual siblings in Philippi or his confidence in the full transformation that awaits him.

The Letter's Origins and Ancient Audience

As he writes, Paul tells his audience a few details about his circumstances, even though he expects the Philippians already know the full story about his incarceration. Paul expresses hope that he will gain his release, yet he also acknowledges that his situation is grave. He speaks of his looming death, which compels some interpreters to assume that Paul wrote this letter from Rome in the early 60s CE, soon before his execution there. Because Paul says nothing in the letter that must indicate his presence in Rome itself, however, it is perhaps more sensible to assume that Philippians comes from an earlier time, sometime prior to his final custody in Rome, probably around 58 CE. In either case, Philippians appears to be the latest of the seven letters in the New Testament that Paul undoubtedly wrote.

Philippi occupied a valuable position in the arrangement of the Roman Empire. The city's value came from its geographic and economic advantages, for Philippi's natural resources included prosperous farmlands, valuable minerals, and proximity to both the Aegean Sea and the Egnatian Way, a vital overland trade route. Politically speaking, Philippi was not just an ordinary city but a designated Roman colony, populated and actively managed by people with close ties to the Roman military and political apparatus. Philippi's official name during Paul's day—Colonia Iulia Augusta Philippensis—invokes the city's historical associations with Augustus, Rome's first emperor. Octavian, who became known as Augustus after his military victories that consolidated the empire in 27 BCE, settled many of his soldiers in and around Philippi, which was not far from where he had defeated Cassius and Brutus, two of Julius Caesar's killers, in 42 BCE. Augustus sent additional colonists to Philippi at a later date. Even when Paul came to Philippi well over a half a century after the city's colonization, still Philippi retained its formal status as a colony, meaning that Roman officials and the Roman citizens among the city's population cultivated a strong Roman ethos there. Although it was a modest-sized city of only about ten thousand residents, Philippi had a large Roman heart.

Paul's letter does not indicate much about exactly who his audience was or how large was the Christian community in Philippi. Negative comments about those who might compel the Philippians about circumcision and observing torah (Phil 3:2–3) echo Paul's argument in Galatians and may suggest the Philippian church was composed mostly if not entirely of gentiles. The letter yields only a few clues about those people's social status.

When Paul does make references to the social environment in Philippi, he does not make clear what familial or formal connections his audience might have had to Philippi's colonial history and social architecture. At the same time, Paul speaks openly about his incarceration and the role of imperial authorities in his custody (Phil 1:13). He writes as the empire's prisoner to believers in a region where the empire loomed large in the population's consciousness. Using language his readers would understand in distinctive ways in their particular setting, Paul refers to "citizenship" (Phil 3:20), to his audience's public and political conduct (Phil 1:27), and to other believers he knows who participate in some way in Rome's political and military structures (Phil 4:22). Paul therefore speaks about his and his audience's Christian witness in forms that acknowledge the political implications of their association with Christ. Christian faith might have attracted negative or suspicious attention in Philippi. Christian claims certainly had potential to clash with statements made in imperial propaganda. Paul's comment about the Philippians' "privilege" of suffering for Christ indicates that believers there may have already found themselves the targets of chastisement or defamation (Phil 1:28–30), just as Paul himself suffered some kind of mistreatment in Philippi many years earlier (see 1 Thess 2:2; Acts 16:11–40). Specific details remain concealed, nevertheless, and no evidence indicates for sure that the Philippians' hardships entailed physical violence.

The Christ-followers in Philippi enjoyed an affectionate relationship with Paul, according to the gratitude he expresses for their faithfulness and their material support (Phil 4:10–20). He longs to see them again and to continue to play a role in fostering their faith. He displays patience with them, as evidenced by his brief reference to a division or disagreement among some of them (Phil 4:2–3). Two women named Euodia and Syntyche, whom Paul identifies as his coworkers, were at odds over an unknown issue, yet Paul calmly asks an unnamed companion in the letter's audience to assist in mediating a peaceful resolution.

The Philippians evidently saw themselves as partners with Paul and active contributors to his ministry. Prior to the composition of this letter, the Philippians sent one of their own, a man named Epaphroditus, as an emissary to Paul. He brought Paul a gift and tended to Paul's needs during a period of incarceration before falling gravely ill and causing concern to his friends back in Philippi. Paul indicates that he sent Epaphroditus back to Philippi carrying the letter (Phil 2:25–30; 4:18). This man, about whom nothing else is known, represents for Paul the self-giving character of his audience. They make sacrifices to support Paul and his ministry.

Overview

A few sudden shifts in tone and subject matter lead some interpreters to wonder whether Philippians might be a composite document, like 2 Corinthians, and not originally one single letter. A relatively common hypothesis, but far from a consensus view, proposes that all or some of the material in Phil 3:1b–4:20 was once a separate letter. The letter's transitions, however, are hardly so disjointed as to reveal distinct seams between different pieces of correspondence. Philippians most likely preserves a single, coherent letter that Paul wrote or dictated. The letter proceeds in a relatively coherent fashion.

Salutation and Thanksgiving (Phil 1:1–11)

Like most of Paul's letters, Philippians includes mention of a coauthor: Timothy. The rest of the letter, however, speaks in the first-person singular and with a style that bears strong resemblance to the voice of the other six letters Paul certainly wrote. No one should therefore doubt that Paul bears sole or primary responsibility for the full letter.

Paul introduces both himself and Timothy as slaves of Christ Jesus (cf. Rom 1:1; 6:16, 19; 1 Cor 7:22; Gal 1:10) and refers to his audience as "saints" (cf. Rom 1:7; 1 Cor 1:2; 2 Cor 1:1; Phlm 5, 7). The mention of "bishops and deacons" among the audience in Philippi provokes the question of whether those people might have occupied specific and formal church offices, akin to what the titles indicate today. Elsewhere in his writings Paul uses the Greek word for "deacons" in a general sense, as indicated by its usual translation as "ministers" or "servants" (e.g., Rom 16:1; 1 Cor 3:5; 2 Cor 3:6, 6:4, 11:23; cf. 1 Tim 3:8–13). The term designates people who serve Christian communities and support churches' missions in real, useful, and usually public ways, yet in Paul's time the word does not appear to refer to an organized office. Likewise, the term *bishop*, meaning "overseer," would eventually refer to a recognized leadership office in later Christian documents (cf. 1 Tim 3:1–7; Titus 1:7–9). Here in Philippians it is not clear whether Paul means such a formal office or merely refers to church leaders in a general sense. In any case, his letter addresses "all" the saints, not just certain recognized leaders.

The letter's thanksgiving renders gratitude to God while also speaking about God to the audience. By opening the letter that way, Paul lays before readers most of the primary themes he will revisit later in the document. Most prominent in the thanksgiving is the notion of completion: God will finally bring to fruition God's "good work" among the Philippians when all of God's intentions reach their full realization at "the day of Jesus Christ," the time of Jesus' return, when Paul expects believers will find themselves rendered "pure and blameless" (Phil 1:6, 10). Paul also asks God to foster greater love and knowledge among the Philippians. He expresses joy and his longing for them, for Paul views them as people who share in the gospel with him. The Philippians are not the objects, targets, or market for Paul's ministry. Rather, the relationship they share is much more mutualistic. Paul shares solidarity and identity with the Philippians, for they are his coparticipants in the good news about the things God has accomplished through Jesus Christ.

Persisting toward Salvation (Phil 1:12–2:18)

If the Philippians were inclined to worry about Paul's well-being or disposition because of his incarceration, Paul quickly assuages any concerns. His circumstances, he claims, actually further the gospel. The officials who administer Paul's detention now know about the good news he preaches, and other believers speak the word of God "with greater boldness and without fear," evidently because Paul sets an example for them through his own courage. Paul underscores his determination to persevere because he values the ongoing proclamation of Christ, whether evangelism occurs through other people's pure or impure motives or through whatever Paul is permitted to do during his time in custody. Paul communicates with an urgent tone, as if his life currently hangs in the balance. Even as he rejoices in the spread of the gospel, he senses the limitations of his own time. Apparently, as he writes he awaits either a hearing or a ruling after a hearing. He could be released or he could be killed.

Paul describes his own incarcerated body as a source or instrument of exalting Christ. If Paul lives, he will continue to serve Christ with boldness and will return to Philippi in person to assist in those saints' "progress and joy in faith." If he dies, he will be with Christ, which means he will experience a bodily transformation to make his salvation complete (cf. Phil 3:11, 21; 1 Cor 15:50–55). No longer does Paul expect he will be alive when Christ returns, as he did when he wrote 1 Thess 4:16–17. He will continue in his ministry, or he will die; he sees either alternative as a means of participating in Christ's glory. Ministry provides additional opportunities to live out the gospel; death means the chance to experience the fullness of God's intentions.

Paul's confident expectation of experiencing the fullness of God's glory carries the letter toward a new focus when Paul instructs the Philippians about their own conduct. As believers who inhabit a Roman colony, they must carry out their obligations "in a manner worthy of the gospel," a gospel to which they owe their full allegiance. Despite the pressures that come with their social setting and its political expectations, they should seek unity and remain undaunted by their opponents. The Philippians' situation is not so unlike Paul's, and thus both parties should strive to remain faithful despite the struggles and limitations that beset them. They are partners in endurance.

Jesus Christ himself provides the motivation and the power for Paul and the Philippians to persevere, for Christ's own story holds forth the assurance that God will bring about believers' final and complete salvation. Christ also offers the basis for the Philippians to pursue unity based on each person's willingness to consider others as better than themselves. Paul explains this by quoting what was, judging from the poetry of the words' parallelisms and cadence, an early Christian hymn or liturgical statement (Phil 2:6–11). If the hymn was familiar to the Philippians, then evidently Paul cites it as an illustration and not because he wants to provide his audience with new teaching about who Christ is. The hymn nevertheless offers strong theological claims about Jesus Christ's willingness to refuse any advantage on account of who he is. Instead, Christ willingly took on "the form of a slave," surrendering all privilege and perhaps his own unique identity to suffer a shameful death. Because of Christ's obedience in this regard and his willingness to seek others' well-being even at the cost of his own honor and life, God "highly exalted him."

Paul presents the brief theological hymn about Jesus' identity, death, and resurrection as something much more than an ethical model or a motivational speech. The short rhythmic narrative describes God's willingness to resist the lure of seizing power over others at the same time as it describes God's ability to exalt those who serve others and those who suffer as a result of their religious obedience. Therefore, the Philippians can take confidence: the same God "is at work in [them]," enabling them to "work out" their salvation by persisting despite their obstacles and seeking to live in contrast to their "crooked and perverse" surroundings. Their salvation will one day become complete, while in the meantime they must hold fast to "the word of life" that Paul shares with them. Persistence will be the best gift the Philippians can give Paul. He knows he might die, reflecting on the prospect of his passing in slightly melodramatic fashion as "a libation," a drink offering poured out on an animal sacrifice. But even if Paul's death should come, everyone should rejoice because of what awaits all believers: their participation in the Messiah's exaltation.

Travel Plans (Phil 2:19–30)

The letter moves toward its conclusion in this section, although it will take some time before Paul finally concludes the document. Here, Paul announces his plans. He will send Timothy to assist the Philippians, as soon as he and Timothy learn what will be the outcome of Paul's juridical ordeal. Paul hopes he will be able to get to Philippi, assuming he gains his release. No one knows whether this ever happened since it remains unclear exactly where and when Paul wrote this letter and no sources reveal whether Paul was released from that particular custody. Paul also announces that he will send Epaphroditus back to Philippi, probably bearing the letter. Even though he recently fell deathly ill in the process, Epaphroditus served the Lord well, probably by offering material, emotional, and spiritual support to Paul as a representative of his friends in Philippi (cf. Phil 4:10–18). Paul would have needed that kind of support from a companion, depending on the conditions of his incarceration, for most prisoners in the Roman Empire had to provide their own means of survival. Maybe Epaphroditus brought clothing, food, skilled legal protection, or basic encouragement. Paul was probably held in a governmental building, a military barracks, or under house arrest, but depending on his location and his access to people who could support him, his physical conditions may have been trying.

Exhortations (Phil 3:1–4:9)

Not all of this section contains exhortations, strictly speaking. Although Paul's first exhortation begins with the word *finally*, actually he still will have much more to say before he ends the letter. For one thing, he warns the Philippians about dangerous influences, whether they be "dogs," "evil workers," or teachers who demand circumcision and perhaps also law obedience from gentile Christ-followers, like the teachers Paul refuted in Galatians. Because Paul offers his cautions in Philippians as "a safeguard," it remains unclear whether he has in mind certain groups that actually were influential among the Christ-followers in Philippi or whether he desires to equip his audience against the kinds of opponents he had struggled against in other places.

Paul counters misguided Christian teachings that call for gentiles' observance of torah by referring to himself, Timothy, and the Philippians as the true "circumcision," for they construe their salvation and their devotion solely in terms of their participation with Christ and not because of any adherence to laws or mandated rituals. They "boast in Christ Jesus" and do not put their "confidence in the flesh" (Phil 3:3; cf. Gal 2:15–21, 5:2–6, 6:12–15; 1 Cor 7:19; cf. Col 2:11).

The letter's explicit and implicit references to confidence and to works prescribed by the Mosaic law lead Paul into a tangential reflection on his own personal history, in which he lists his bona fides as a Jew who was once zealous for God's law. Paul expresses no shame about his history. Nor does he describe his experiences prior to meeting Christ as a time of dissatisfaction or guilt. Instead, when Paul came to know Christ Jesus as his Lord, all of the things that once defined his identity and gave him confidence about his standing in God's eyes suddenly proved utterly insignificant *in comparison*. Paul expresses the comparison in perhaps the most extreme rhetoric he can imagine. He now describes his previous commitments and privileges as "rubbish," or excrement, compared to "the surpassing value" of what he gains from Christ— God's righteousness "based on faith" that connects Paul to Christ himself (Phil 3:8–9; cf. Rom 1:17; 3:21–26; Gal 2:15–21, 3:6–9). Through that connection built on faith, Paul participates in Christ's death and will participate in Christ's resurrection (cf. Rom 6:5–11; Gal 2:20).

The confidence Paul expresses in the salvation God provides through Christ does not mean Paul understands his salvation as now entirely complete. He therefore reiterates a theme he treated earlier in the letter: perseverance. Just as the Philippians should "work out" their salvation by embracing humility while awaiting their future exaltation (Phil 2:12), so too they should emulate Paul and "press on" to reach the goal, which is their eventual resurrection or the "call of God in Christ Jesus" (Phil 3:14). Effort alone will not get the Philippians there; they persist and pursue the consummation of their salvation because "Christ Jesus has made [Paul and the Philippians] his own." Although Paul does not describe exactly what it looks like for believers to press on resolutely toward the full realization of their salvation, he does speak about it in terms of remaining aligned with Christ against opposing forces. Therefore he exhorts the Philippians to "stand firm in the Lord" and to remain resolved. Paul also names the end result of that perseverance: Jesus Christ "will transform the body of our humiliation that it may be conformed to the body of his glory." Such a transformation corresponds to God's ultimate victory over all the things that oppose and obstruct God's purposes. It will happen at the time when Christ finally makes "all things subject to himself" (Phil 3:21; cf. 1 Cor 15:28; Phil 2:9–11).

Paul returns to shorter exhortations when he urges Euodia and Syntyche "to be of the same mind in the Lord." Philippians provides the only known information about these two women, whom Paul calls "co-workers." Nothing else is known about their particular conflict. When Paul urges his unnamed "loyal companion" to "help these women," he affirms the value of unity in the church, a theme familiar in this letter (cf. Phil 1:27; 2:1–4) and in others Paul wrote (e.g., Rom 15:7–12; 1 Cor 1:10; 12:4–27; Gal 3:28; 5:13–15). The dispute between

Euodia and Syntyche was significant enough to attract Paul's concern, suggesting their strife touched on the work and identity of the Christian community in Philippi. Nevertheless, Paul appears unconcerned that the feuding parties were women, in particular. Paul does not ask his "loyal companion" to censure or silence Euodia and Syntyche, nor does he want them removed from positions of influence or leadership. Similar to many of the women Paul commends in Romans 16, those two Philippian women appear to have been people whose outspoken contributions to the church's work Paul valued. It was their disunity that concerned him.

This section of the letter concludes with encouraging words. Paul praises ways of living that reflect the generosity of the gospel. He reminds the audience of prayer's role in allaying worry, and he promises that God's peace will sustain them as they live in anticipation of the return of the Lord who is "near"—whether or not Paul remains alive to support them as they wait.

Effusive Gratitude, Greetings, and Benediction (Phil 4:10–23)

This letter functions, in part, as a thank-you note to the Philippians in response to gifts they sent the incarcerated Paul via Epaphroditus. Paul carefully avoids implying that the believers in Philippi had an obligation to support him, and he also declares his willingness to suffer hardship as a prisoner if necessary. He considers their material support as a superlative contribution to his ministry, as a statement of nothing less than their commitment to the gospel. Although Paul does not dwell on incarceration's potential for discrediting him and his ministry, or for branding him a threat to the empire's values, it appears he interpreted the Philippians' gifts to him as a strong assertion of their willingness to stand by him and his work without concern for any possible repercussions. He therefore likens their gift to a sacrifice meant to show devotion to God.

The greetings at the very end of the letter reaffirm the corporate and collaborative nature of Christian fellowship and ministry. Paul reminds the Philippians of others in his orbit who might continue to support him even after Epaphroditus departs. He also names "saints" who are part of "the emperor's household"—probably converts Paul knows who work or have responsibilities in the Roman Empire's widespread administrative apparatus. An audience living in a Roman colony alongside descendants of Augustus' loyal troops would have likely appreciated the reminder that they were not the only Christ-followers in the world who were trying to navigate their way in a pro-Roman environment while they awaited the victorious arrival of their true Lord and Savior from heaven (cf. Phil 3:20).

The Letter's Themes and Theological Emphases

The occasion that prompted Paul to write to the saints in Philippi appears simple enough: he wanted to thank them for their support and reassure them of his well-being and confidence as he endured an incarceration. In the process of communicating those things, the letter speaks as a theological document. Much of what Paul says derives from his understanding of God and the good news. Even Paul's statements of his love and affection for his friends in Philippi have theological resonance (e.g., Phil 1:8; 2:1–2; 4:1). The letter's palpable joy and longing express themselves not in instructions passed down from a leader to his followers but with a sense of commonality. Paul and the Philippians share an identity through Jesus Christ (e.g., Phil 1:5, 2:1), certainly, but they also share a mutual regard for one another and a mutual concern to foster the vitality of Christian ministry (e.g., Phil 1:7, 27; 4:14–15; cf. Philemon). Such an intimate sense of shared interaction, shared values, and shared possessions resided at the heart of Greco-Roman notions of true friendship. The understanding of friendship in terms of commonality was at least as old as Aristotle. The particular friendship Paul shared with the Philippians as beloved partners and confederates aligns with the virtues prized in the Greco-Roman world, therefore. But the quality of their friendship was based on a specifically theological foundation: in Philippians Paul describes a comparable kind of close communion at work in what God accomplished through Jesus Christ, for God shares God's own self with the world (Phil 2:6–8) and promises people that they will share in the Christ's new, resurrected life (Phil 3:10–11). Friendship among Paul and the Philippians finds its source and sustenance in a God who gives and shares.

The Christian "Mind" and Christian "Citizenship"

Paul makes frequent reference to how the Philippians should think and what kind of "mind" they should adopt on certain matters (e.g., Phil

2:2, 5; 3:15, 19; 4:2). The relevant Greek term in those passages is a verb related to the Greek noun *phronēsis*, which refers to a notion of wise practicality. Sometimes translated as "prudence" or "practical reason," the concept is hardly unique to this letter, for it appears in other Greek writings as well as in other Pauline letters (cf. Rom 8:5, 12:3, 15:5; 2 Cor 13:11). The prevalence of such language in Philippians offers another reminder of Paul's Hellenistic education and ways of thinking. More important for the current discussion is how the language serves as a part of Paul's characterization of Christian identity and Christian living, especially when he refers to a community's attitude or a Christ-follower's holistic disposition. Paul had little interest in transmitting knowledge or doctrine, as if he saw himself as a catechist dispensing intellectual formulas. Instead, Paul sought to shape believers' entire mind-sets and their ability to integrate their religious understanding into their lifestyle and practical values.

All of Paul's letters aim to reinforce a distinctively Christian identity among his audiences. Even though it is difficult to tell from this letter what specific challenges might have potentially impeded the Philippian Christ-followers' attempts to live in an appropriate manner, Paul's subtle references to their political identities suggest he was eager to help the Philippians discern the gospel's implications for these identities. When he asserts, "Our citizenship is in heaven" (Phil 3:20), he does not mean that heaven and not earth is a Christ-follower's true home. Nor does the statement express a desire to live in heaven instead of earth. Rather, the word the NRSV renders as "citizenship" refers to a person's loyalties; it calls to mind the social group and political organization to which one belongs. A believer's heaven-focused citizenship stands in contrast to the citizenship possessed by many residents of Philippi in their formal obligations and personal allegiances to the Roman Empire.

A citizenship anchored in the place where Christ currently resides, heaven, represents the new political realities that derive from the Messiah's identity as the Philippians' Lord and Savior. Believers' true Savior, Paul insists, dwells in heaven for now. But soon this Savior will come to reign on earth (cf. 1 Thess 4:16–17). The emperor in Rome is therefore not the one who truly saves humanity or ensures human flourishing (Phil 3:20). While statements like those would have made for provocative claims in the Philippians' context, Paul nevertheless falls far short of advocating a revolutionary or resistant posture against Roman authority. Christ will indeed "make all things subject to himself" (Phil

3:21; cf. 2:9–11; 1 Cor 15:27–28) but not until a future time. Until then, Paul counsels the Philippians to "live" in their Roman colony—using a Greek verb for "live" that refers in particular to one's political obligations and affairs—"in a manner worthy of the gospel" (Phil 1:27–30). Such a manner of life could very well attract opposition in a place like Philippi, for the life Paul commends is one that pledges full allegiance to Jesus (Phil 3:20). Certainly Paul does not entreat his audience to blend in with their surroundings or to court a reputation for respectability in their social circles. Paul's vision of practical living did not necessarily amount to acquiescent living.

Christ's Humiliation and God's Final Victory

One of the most memorable parts of the letter, the hymn Paul quotes in Phil 2:6–11, offers an important expression of who Jesus is and what God accomplished through his death and resurrection. Although the precise meanings of the hymn's expressions *in the form of God* and *found in human form* remain ambiguous, still the hymn claims that Jesus is more than an ordinary man. Although many interpreters probe the hymn to figure out exactly what Paul and other mid-first-century believers believed about Jesus' nature, the hymn nevertheless says more about Jesus' conduct than it does his identity or the quality of his divinity. The hymn summarizes his conduct as renunciation. Jesus refused to regard "equality with God" as something he could snatch, reserve, and use for his own benefit. Instead, he "emptied himself" and submitted to others, suffering an extremely contemptible form of death. Paul refers to the hymn at a specific point in the letter to advocate humility and to encourage his audience to seek the welfare of others as they await the opportunity to share in Christ's new life. The hymn alone does not reveal a nuanced understanding of how or why salvation occurs through Jesus' cross and resurrection, but it says much about characterizing Christ as one who willingly surrenders power and privilege to allow for the realization of a greater good.

The greater good, Paul implies elsewhere in the letter, involves sharing in the benefits of God's ultimate triumph. The hymn in Phil 2:6–11 suggests as much when it claims that "Jesus Christ is Lord" and expects the universal recognition of Christ's supremacy (cf. Isa 45:23). Paul's reasons for quoting the hymn therefore extend beyond extoling Christ as a fine example to follow. The hymn also allows Paul to reaffirm the power of God to exalt Christ—and, by extension, the power to exalt believers who participate in Christ's act of faithful obedience—over any other power or creature in the cosmos. As other Pauline letters also make clear, Paul understood the gospel as a declaration of divine actions that result in the defeat of God's enemies and the inauguration of a new age in which God's purposes come to fulfillment (cf. Phil 3:21). Themes of newness and transformation, familiar motifs related to God's regenerative activity as described in Jewish apocalyptic writings, inform Paul's outlook on what the gospel is all about. Jesus modeled the renunciation of power, but the Christian message is good news because God demonstrates power to set all of existence on a new course.

The newness Paul celebrates with the Philippians has begun to emerge, yet its full realization, which will correspond to God's final victory (cf. Rom 16:20; 1 Cor 15:24–28), remains in the future until "the day of Jesus Christ" arrives (Phil 1:6). Paul therefore balances a fervent and glorious hope with a realistic understanding of the struggles that life brings, especially those struggles that erupt when Christ-followers like him disrupt the imperial status quo. With that balanced perspective, Paul instructs the Philippians to persevere and remain steadfast in their commitment to Christ, emulating Christ's humility as a means of participating even now in his death and in the confident expectation of a future resurrection. Paul himself provides an additional model for that type of expectant and resolute posture, for he expresses a willingness to die and be with Christ as well as a willingness to continue in his labor on behalf of others (Phil 1:20–26). Despite the hardships that come his way, Paul does not despise his life, nor does he advocate escapism. But his patient, hopeful outlook would be only wishful thinking were it not for the complementary assurance that God remains ready and potent to transform and exalt God's people. Accordingly, Philippians remains a book that many people consult to foster their hopes when they sense the rapid approach of death or find themselves trapped in desperate or powerless circumstances. Without dismissing the real pain people might experience in the present, the letter cultivates a joyful outlook because of a future that God has already set in motion—a future that, Paul insists, God will finally realize.

10

The Letter of Paul to the Colossians

Colossians declares the utter sufficiency of Jesus Christ. The letter's most foundational and general claim asserts that, in Jesus Christ, humanity's reconciliation to God is complete. Christ is sufficient; those who live with him need no supplement. Even though the letter's ways of explaining the implications of that claim might differ from what Paul says in the seven undisputed letters, the letter's nearly singular attention to the sufficiency of Jesus' death and resurrection sings on key with the songs of Paul's theology.

With its fixation on Jesus, Colossians does not present itself as an abstract theological treatise about salvation and the nature of Christ. Rather, this letter aims first and foremost to help an audience—an audience whose identity and circumstances are difficult to determine from the letter—grow and persevere in their faith. Colossians lets believers know that they are on the right track, one that has allowed the gospel to bear fruit in their lives thus far and one that needs nothing added as a boost or catalyst. Because the letter means to reassure its readers, it therefore concentrates on who Jesus is and how he is uniquely suited to bring people to share in God's presence and glory. True spirituality exists in Jesus' own body, where believers encounter the fullness of God. Because Jesus himself occupies "first place" in the whole cosmic landscape (Col 1:18), other spiritual pursuits or ascetic practices offer no substitute for what he provides. Rather, those devotions correspond to the powers in the universe that God has subjugated to Christ. Keep focus instead, the letter says, on the supremacy of Christ, for the true power resides with him, and he already holds believers' lives firmly within himself.

The Letter's Origins and Ancient Audience

Since no other New Testament book even mentions the city of Colossae and its residents, the history of the Christian community there remains very difficult to decipher. Situated amid a series of river valleys in western Asia Minor, Colossae had little to distinguish itself culturally or economically during the mid-first century. Nearby Laodicea, to which this letter is also directed (Col 4:13–16; cf. 2:1), was much more prosperous and flourishing. Colossians mentions a special relationship between the believers in Colossae and a man named Epaphras (Col 1:7–8, 4:12–13; cf. Phlm 23). Evidently that otherwise unknown associate of Paul and Timothy founded the church there. The letter further implies that Paul had never been to Laodicea and Colossae (Col 2:1).

As was the case in the other urban settings of western Asia Minor, part of Colossae's population was Jewish. A reference to "the uncircumcision of your flesh" (Col 2:13) suggests that the church in Colossae, or the communities that were the actual intended recipients of this document when it was first distributed, was composed entirely or mostly of gentiles, however (e.g., Col 1:27). The almost complete absence of any other allusions to Jewish symbols and Jewish sacred texts could indicate that the letter's author did not expect the audience to recognize the Scriptures or their authority.

Sometime between 60 and 64 CE, one or more powerful earthquakes struck the region in which Colossae sat. It remains unknown whether the disaster destroyed the city or only damaged it to some degree. The letter makes no reference to the event. Either the letter originated prior to the earthquake, the author believed a community of Christ-followers was still functioning in Colossae after the disaster, or Colossians is a later document that presents itself as a letter that was created and sent before the earthquake.

Although its themes and language have much in common with Ephesians, Colossians manifests a greater specificity and familiarity in its manner of addressing its audience. Not only does this letter refer to Epaphras' ministry in Colossae and his ongoing labors to support the church there, but it also mentions several other people by name, including a few of Paul's associates identified also in Philemon (Col 4:7–17;

Phlm 2, 23–24). If Paul wrote Colossians, then those verses offer minute insights into some of the people who formed a wider pastoral network with him. If Colossians is a pseudepigraphic letter, then the author took care to include those details to supply touches of realism, perhaps by drawing from well-known knowledge about Paul's associates or by using Philemon as a source.

Colossians 2:8–23 cautions its readers about particular dangers they must guard against: "philosophy and empty deceit," expectations regarding diet and the observation of certain days or festivals, and people who advocate practices such as "self-abasement and worship of angels." According to that passage, one of the letter's primary goals is to steer its audience away from misleading doctrine or practices, although Colossians makes no real effort to identify the specific identity of any threats. Its warnings are firm but hardly dire. Perhaps Colossians meant to counter the influence of particular teachers among the church in Colossae or in another region altogether. Or possibly the letter aimed to contend against a viewpoint gathering momentum in Colossae or elsewhere that considered special obligations and pieties as necessary for believers to maintain their fellowship with God.

The letter's admonitions about harmful doctrines or practices do not necessarily require the conclusion that Colossians has narrowly specific religious ideas in mind. In other words, the book's intended audience need not have been incorporating elements of a *specific* Greco-Roman religion or particular mystical rituals into their ways of living out the gospel. Interpreters' efforts to identify the precise worldviews and practices that the letter opposes can gather a number of plausible options, yet Colossians remains silent about details that might yield more certainty. Whatever the exact cause of the author's concerns, Colossians reiterates the sufficiency and fullness of what Christ has done to accomplish the audience's forgiveness and to give them new life. The letter's remedy against the temptation to add additional religious practices or devotions to the gospel is to remind readers of the supremacy of Christ, the one who holds sway over their salvation and indeed over the entire universe, too.

The Question of Authorship

As an investigation of Ephesians also revealed, the theological similarities of Ephesians and Colossians make it helpful to explore the books' peculiarities as a pair. The family resemblance these books share, however, should not be overstated. Colossians has its distinctive qualities that require the letter to be considered on its own terms. For example, the language and style of Colossians are not different from the undisputed Pauline letters in exactly the same ways that the language and even more cumbersome style of Ephesians are different. Subtle discrepancies in the two books' theological perspectives and parallel phrases indicate that Colossians was written first and Ephesians came at a later date, using Colossians or its characteristic rhetoric as a source. Although the debates about whether Colossians is a pseudepigraphic letter are considerably more evenly contested than the generally more settled debates about the authorship of Ephesians and the Pastoral Letters, all the data, considered cumulatively, still makes a fair case that Paul did not write Colossians. Whoever wrote Colossians probably did not also write Ephesians, given the differences in style between the two books. The various options for answering the question of who wrote Colossians do not have an especially weighty influence on how an interpreter might understand the letter's message.

The theological outlook of Colossians coheres with Ephesians in several ways that distinguish both books from the seven undisputed letters. Reviewing those theological characteristics matters for determining whether the letters are pseudepigraphic, and it also illuminates the books' distinctive theological perspectives. According to both letters, forgiveness of sins occurs through Christ (Col 1:14; 2:13–14; 3:13; Eph 1:7, 4:32). The collapsing of time seen in Ephesians also occurs in Colossians, for the letters hold that believers have already been raised with Christ (Col 2:12, 3:1, Eph 2:6) and experienced deliverance (Col 1:13; 2:10, 15; Eph 2:5). No other New Testament books describe Christ as the church's "head" (Col 1:18; Eph 5:23; cf. 1 Cor 11:3), and Colossians and Ephesians alike emphasize God's glory and Christ's current authority over all other cosmic powers (Col 2:10; Eph 1:20–23). Finally, both books include a household code that enjoins believers to live according to patriarchal values that were widely considered socially respectable and a foundational piece of Roman imperial culture (Col 3:18–4:1, Eph 5:21–6:9).

As for notable differences between Ephesians and Colossians. while the former lacks references to Christ's return and a future judgment, Colossians mentions those subjects (e.g., Col 3:4, 24–25). Unlike Ephesians, Colossians notes the Pauline notion of believers' participation in

Christ's death (e.g., Col 2:12, 20; 3:3). Colossians refrains from making the kinds of statements Ephesians makes about God creating a cosmic, organic unity in Christ (e.g., Eph 1:10, 23). Also, this letter does not sanctify the work of the apostles as Ephesians does (e.g., Eph 2:20, 3:5), although Colossians does call attention to Paul's incarceration for the sake of his ministry and makes an odd statement about Paul's sufferings being a completion of what Christ's own afflictions lack (Col 1:24).

The naming of Timothy as the coauthor of Colossians, along with the letter's references to people supposedly known among the audience, raises the possibility that Timothy wrote the document, perhaps because Paul's incarceration was grievous enough to prevent him from doing so. Paul could have directly charged Timothy or someone else to write on his behalf. There is no way of confirming those hypotheses. Nevertheless, if they are accurate, it would mean that Colossians probably was written in the early 60s CE, in the final years of Paul's life. If, as the letter's theological peculiarities intimate, Colossians was penned at a later time and thus after Paul's death, which occurred sometime between 60 and 64 CE, then one of Paul's admirers or followers wrote it, probably between 65 and 75 CE. Supposing that Colossians is a pseudepigraphic letter written at that later date, there is no way of confirming that its author originally sent the document to anyone who might have lived in or near what remained of Colossae at that time. Perhaps the letter was circulated elsewhere and passed off either openly or deceitfully as a letter Paul had once sent to the believers in preearthquake Colossae or as a letter Paul could conceivably have sent them if only he were still alive and their city still fully intact. For simplicity's sake, it is helpful to follow the book's own rhetoric and refer to the letter's audience as "the Colossians," even though the actual audience that the document was originally created to address could very well have dwelled in other places.

Overview

Salutation, Thanksgiving, and Prayer (Col 1:1–12)

Following a concise salutation, the letter commends the Colossians for the ways their faith in Christ has manifested itself in their love for one another and in the "fruit" that the gospel bears in their lives. The introductory words affirm the reality of the gospel's power in the Colossians and assure the audience that they have "truly comprehended the grace of God." The expressions of confidence anticipate what will come later in the book, when the author will insist that the Colossians need to add nothing to supplement the gospel and its power. When the letter describes Paul and Timothy praying for the Colossians, their prayer's focus is that those believers might continue to "bear fruit in every good work" (cf. Eph 2:10; Rom 7:4; Gal 5:22–23) and grow stronger in their commitment.

God's Accomplishments through Christ (Col 1:13–3:4)

The exhortation embedded in the opening prayer transitions into an extended theological reflection on what God has done through Jesus Christ. Hardly a tangent, this reflection on Christ's grandeur underscores the certainty of the Colossians' salvation. They can be confident that their status as sharers in the gospel is secure, for they have already been "rescued . . . from the power of darkness and transferred . . . into the kingdom" of Christ. The confidence derives from Christ—who Christ is and the authority he possesses.

The most prominent piece of this section consists of a series of confessional statements in Col 1:15–20. Judging from the verbal patterns and the cadence of the material, the letter may quote an ancient hymn or liturgy from the early church. Even though there is no way to know for sure that these sentences represent a quotation of familiar material, the patterns and content indicate that they may have been composed for the ear and for memory, either by the letter's author or by someone else. More important than the words' origins and poetic structure are what they say. They describe Christ with lofty claims, calling him "the image of the invisible God" and assigning him a role in the creation of all things. The brief depiction resonates with how John 1:1–3 introduces Jesus as the incarnation of God and a divine Word and with the statement in Phil 2:6 that Jesus Christ "was in the form of God" (cf. Heb 1:3–4, Prov 8:22–31, Wis 7:22b–8:1). Nothing less than "the fullness of God" resides in Christ, implying that God's willingness to act through Christ has a particular reliability about it. Jesus Christ, by his very nature, assures the world not only that God is present but also that God is committed to act on the world's behalf. The Colossians can trust that through Christ they have full access to God and can appear "holy and blameless and irreproachable" before God.

In response to God's reliability and availability, the letter urges its audience to remain steadfast in "the faith" (Col 1:23, 2:7; cf. 1 Tim 3:9, 4:1, 5:8, 6:12). Their perseverance is important, and it connects to Paul's long-term ministry among gentiles. Paul toils in his ministry to those outside of Judaism's borders because ministry to them plays a part in making known the mystery of the gospel: God's intention to extend God's glory also to gentiles (cf. Eph 3:1–13). Therefore, Colossians asserts, Paul struggles and persists so that gentiles might know Christ himself, "in whom are hidden all the treasures of wisdom and knowledge" (Col 2:3). Because Christ is the source of all those treasures, there remains nothing more the Colossians need to know and nothing they need to add.

Other kinds of teachings and religious devotions are therefore foreign and unnecessary; they correspond not to Christ but to "the elemental spirits of the universe" (Col 2:8, 20; cf. Gal 4:3, 8–9), other cosmic powers that have been made subservient and thus inferior to Christ. The gentile Colossians' uncircumcision is no hindrance to their fellowship with God, for they have received another form of circumcision, one performed without hands, what the NRSV in Col 2:11 awkwardly calls "a spiritual circumcision." They have been marked as God's own through something other than a ritual: they have been buried and raised with Christ and forgiven.

Since the Colossians possess "fullness" in Jesus, the one in whom "the whole fullness of deity dwells bodily" (Col 2:9–10), they can rest assured that in their bodies they participate fully in God's glory. They need not practice asceticism to subdue their bodies. Nor do they need to surpass their corporeal existence by pursuing transcendent forms of spirituality, whether those practices involve directing worship toward angels to secure protection from other spiritual beings or seeking a religious experience that allows one to join the angels' pristine worship of God. Not only are supplementary spiritual pursuits no help in restraining sinful desires, but they actually belong to the realm of the world's "elemental spirits" and not to Christ. Instead, those who have been raised with Christ should "seek the things that are above"—not ethereal matters but those things that are associated with Christ. After all, in Christ is where the Colossians now reside; their lives, which they now live as fully embodied people, are "hidden with Christ in God" (Col 3:3). Divine glory certainly awaits them if they remain identified solely with Christ, who holds their lives within his own self.

Instructions for Living (Col 3:5–4:6)

When the letter turns to instruct its audience about what it entails for them, to borrow language from earlier in the letter, to "lead lives worthy of the Lord" (Col 1:10), not much in this section is distinctively Christian. In other words, the ethical ideals are not extraordinary; the author makes little effort to root certain behaviors in the nature of the gospel or in the character of Christ. A list of vices corresponds to an old way of life, one that incurs God's "wrath" (cf. Eph 2:3, Rom 1:18, 1 Thess 1:10). A list of predictable virtues follows, commending behavior that contributes to communal harmony. The letter does not do much to say why Christ might commend some activities and prohibit others. Comparable catalogs of virtues and vices, not exhaustive but representative lists, would have been familiar to the original audience insofar as those people knew writings of Greco-Roman moralists. Jewish writings and other New Testament documents include similar lists (e.g., Gal 5:19–23; 1 Cor 6:9–10; 2 Cor 6:6–7; Eph 5:3–5; 1 Tim 3:2–3; 2 Tim 2:22–25, 3:2–4; 2 Pet 1:5–7). As ethical exhortation goes, this material in Colossians serves up ordinary fare.

What is striking, especially when viewed in comparison to Paul's undisputed letters, is that the letter puts so much responsibility on the audience for cultivating their virtues. Colossians makes no mention of the Holy Spirit empowering this way of life (cf. Gal 5:16, 22, 25; cf. Phil 2:13; 1 Thess 3:12–13) and no clear and explicit reference to God transforming people, other than a vague comment about "the new self"—literally, "the new person"—that "is being renewed," evidently by God (Col 3:10). Subtle allusions to baptism, indicated by language about clothing (cf. Gal 3:27, Eph 4:24), nevertheless connect the wearing of love and other morals to the new identity one shares with Christ. The reference to baptism, even if it is oblique, makes the letter's exhortations slightly less about the Colossians' own personal moral fortitude and a little more about God's power. The letter nevertheless does not develop the idea of how God's power changes people's behavior. When the letter commends prayer and thanksgiving, it casts those activities more as virtuous dispositions rather than means of harnessing God's power for living praiseworthy lives.

A household code also appears, one that the author of Ephesians appears to have expanded and included in that letter. The tables of instructions in both Ephesians and Colossians, as discussed previously with respect to the material in Ephesians, correspond to contemporary Greco-Roman patriarchal values. While Ephesians attempts to provide a theological rationale for the assigned responsibilities and the associated hierarchy that supposedly justifies them, Colossians does little of that, except for its instructions to slaves, likening servitude to one's master to service rendered to God. By consecrating slavery as akin to a religious devotion, the author of Colossians reveals that he probably did not understand slavery and its potential for oppression and dehumanization from the perspective of the people who actually endured it. References to Epaphras (Col 1:7) and Tychicus (Col 4:7) as metaphorical slaves (not "servants," as the NRSV translates the term) in service to God could threaten to glamorize the realities of slavery in the Roman world. The letter's tacit approval of slavery also fails to see a way in which human society might somehow be changed to mirror the letter's vision of a renewed existence in which distinctions between "slave and free" have been discontinued (Col 3:11; cf. 1 Cor 12:13, Gal 3:28). Colossians assumes slavery as a given and essentially tells its audience to make the best of it. That perspective appears to some interpreters ill-suited to the high-flying theological outlook expressed in the letter's first two chapters.

Greetings and Benediction (Col 4:7–18)

As Ephesians also does, Colossians identifies Tychicus as the bearer of the letter. Other appearances of this name in the New Testament indicate his reputation as one of Paul's associates (Acts 20:4, 2 Tim 4:12, Titus 3:12). There is no way of knowing for sure whether the reference to Onesimus means to indicate the same man at the center of the controversy in Philemon, but that seems likely. The greetings conveyed in Colossians reassure the letter's stated audience that they are not alone in their attempts to remain steadfast in Christ. Others support them, and they also have colleagues in the Christ-followers who reside in nearby Laodicea, about a half-day's journey away by foot.

The letter's final verse describes Paul signing the original copy of the letter in his own handwriting (cf. 1 Cor 16:21, Gal 6:11). Since that original copy no longer exists, nor does any sample of Paul's handwriting, this verse on its own proves nothing. Someone might have forged Paul's hand on an original document, either to deceive an audience or to add a greater feel of authenticity to the pseudepigraphic letter as a means of celebrating Paul and identifying the correspondence more closely with Paul, his pastoral labors, and his teachings (cf. 2 Thess 3:17). The greater point about the concluding verse is that it depicts Paul as one who still suffers for the sake of his testimony. The gifts that are his through Christ do not completely deliver him from life's challenges.

The Letter's Themes and Theological Emphases

The Utter Preeminence of Jesus Christ, the Image of God

Colossians sings Christ's praises. The letter's christological exuberance has many effects. When Col 1:13–3:4 describes who Jesus is and what God accomplishes through him, the letter offers the theological assertions toward a specific effect: to reassure readers that Christ has the power to reconcile them to God, for in Christ's death God established peace between God and "all things" (Col 1:20). Christ holds authority over all other forces in the cosmos. Because of Christ's effectiveness, superiority, and primacy, the letter's audience has no need to seek additional means or avenues of communing with God and bolstering their spiritual vitality. As Colossians makes the argument, its specific claims about Christ, "the image of the invisible God, the firstborn of all creation" (Col 1:15), touch on the issue of exactly who Jesus is—an issue that has occupied a pivotal place in Christian theological discourse over the centuries.

As with the hymn Paul cites in Phil 2:6–11, the language of the confessional material in Col 1:15–20 has spawned multiple interpretations. That should be unsurprising, given the poetic and nonsystematic qualities of the statements in those verses. For example, where some see a promise of universal salvation in a declaration about God becoming reconciled with "all things," others see hyperbole. When it comes to what these verses say about Jesus Christ, certainly Colossians posits close associations between Christ and God—in their existence and their responsibility for creation—yet the letter does not explain what exactly it means for Christ to be "the image" of God (cf. 2 Cor 4:4, Gen 1:27) and the dwelling place of "all the fullness of God" (Col 1:15, 19). Yet Colossians does not absolutely equate or blend God and Jesus Christ, for the former remains distinct as "the Father" of the latter (Col 1:3), who himself is "the Son" (Col 1:13). Obviously these verses over time have contributed to more specific Christian doctrinal pronouncements about the incarnation and the Trinity.

What the letter's theological assertions lack in terms of specificity about Christ's essence they make up for in the soaring and evocative way they describe his centrality in all God's purposes on behalf of "all things." Christ relates to all creation—not merely humanity alone—in multiple ways. One statement identifies him as creation's "firstborn" (Col 1:15), probably because his resurrection has made him "firstborn from the dead" (Col 1:18) and therefore the paramount figure in the new realities God has fashioned through Jesus' death and resurrection. Overall, Christ is also the source, vehicle, and purpose of "all things," for he integrates all of creation's parts and powers into an integrated and unified whole (Col 1:16–20; 3:11, 14). The Christ of Colossians is truly cosmic; everything—all things spiritual, material, and ecological—participates in the fullness of God because of him. Since nothing is excluded from that fullness, nothing lacks value in God's eyes. Much like the personified Wisdom of Jewish tradition (e.g., Prov 8:22–31; Wis 7:22b–8:1; Sir 24:1–6), Jesus Christ is the full, manifest expression of God, God's creative activity, and God's purposes on behalf of the entire world. In Christ, God communes with all aspects of creation and therefore potentially blesses all of creation.

The letter's depiction of Christ also resonates with apocalyptic-theological themes about universal conflict and divine victory over evil. Through Christ, God delivers saints "from the power of darkness" (Col 1:13), representing malevolent forces that have been routed but still exist and seethe (cf. Col 2:15, 20). The cosmic Christ of Colossians holds authority over all powers. While the letter understands powers as discrete spiritual forces, its claims about Christ's authority extend to cover any way in which one might understand evil. Evil and corruption of any kind have their sources, but more accessible are their physical, social, and ideological manifestations. Presumably the letter's author would also assert Christ's power over all those manifestations, for they cannot take "first place" away from Christ, either (Col 1:18). In addition, angelic powers are in Christ rightly coordinated to serve God's purposes (Col 2:10). Also, and more or less in line with Paul's perspective in the seven undisputed letters, Colossians depicts the crucifixion as a key piece of God's decisive victory and the creation of a new cosmic order. Because of the cross, disarmed powers are humiliated powers. Since they suffer humiliation explicitly because a victim who died in a despised way on "a cross" actually exposed their pretense, their disgrace intensifies, making the strange irony of God's triumph all the more starkly visible (Col 2:14–15). Christ's accomplishment constitutes God's victory over all the other powers while also signaling the vindication of God's means of doing so through a crucifixion that ultimately shamed the ruling powers, not the intended victim.

The Body, Baptism, and Participation

Although Christ now resides "above," seated with God (Col 3:1), Colossians does not view him as a disembodied spirit on a heavenly throne, for in Christ "the whole fullness of deity dwells bodily" (Col 2:9). The letter also pays attention to believers' embodied existence, especially in the subtle allusions to circumcision and especially baptism. Even now, as believers await the fullness of God's glory to arrive, they participate in Christ's existence (Col 3:3–4). Bodies are no hindrance to that participation; indeed, they are the sites where the participation occurs.

Baptism confirms the importance that bodies possess in the letter's theological perspective. Numerous references to clothing and disrobing in Col 3:9–14 resonate with an earlier comment about baptism in Col 2:12 (cf. Col 2:20). The short liturgical statement in Col 3:11, which promises the end of distinctions based on ethnicity, law observance, or other identifiers, resembles Gal 3:27–28 and the statement Paul offers there: "As many of you as were baptized into Christ have clothed yourself with Christ" (cf. Rom 13:14). Baptism entails participation with Christ, and some in the early church associated that participation with the taking on of new clothes. Over time, but most likely not as early as when Colossians was written, Christian baptisms began to include practices in which a person would disrobe, be baptized, and be clothed, literally, in a new baptismal robe, all symbolizing the gift of new life and the reception of Christ's identity on one's own self.

Even before those practices of disrobing and robing developed, clothing's symbolic association with baptism was difficult to miss. Clothing, in Greco-Roman society, signified identity. People's clothing could indicate their profession and social class. Some types of clothing were reserved only for those with elite social status. Maybe the quickest way to determine where someone belonged in the social order was to draw conclusions from what that person wore in public. People who symbolically wear Christ on their bodies, like a garment, therefore take on his identity and status. They participate in his death and new life (e.g., Col 2:12–13, 20; 3:1–3), but baptism implies that they also take on Christ's own identity and image. They project that identity to the public at large, like a person wearing a uniform. Therefore, those who have been baptized are experiencing nothing less than a bodily renewal, bringing who they are as embodied beings into consistency with "the image" of their incarnate Christ (Col 3:10–11), who himself is "the image of the invisible God" (Col 1:15).

The material and tangible quality of baptism, as a practice involving a person's body and resulting in a person's identity now showcasing the identity of Jesus Christ, is important to keep in mind when other parts of Colossians appear to denigrate embodied living. When a believer sheds "the body of the flesh" in a new kind of circumcision associated with Christ (Col 2:11), Colossians does not necessarily declare corporeality to be evil. The symbol of circumcision implies a body, after all. Circumcision *changes* a body; it does not declare a body irrelevant. Instead, then, the "flesh" that is cut away, according to Col 2:11, refers to people's sinful disposition. The letter sometimes uses "flesh" as a reference to a human body (e.g., Col 1:22; cf. Gal 2:20; Phil 1:22–24), but Colossians also uses the term symbolically to indicate the seat of sinful proclivities (e.g., Col 2:23; cf. Rom 8:7–8, Gal 5:16–17). "The circumcision of Christ" in Colossians 2:11 excises the sinful dispositions that rule people apart from Christ. Colossians therefore calls believers to abandon destructive behaviors (Col 3:5–17) because those activities do not correspond to their new identity as people clothed in Christ. The point is not that the things bodies do or crave are necessarily evil. Rather, damaging behaviors are truly damaging; they injure people's flesh-and-blood, embodied existence.

Interpreters who have insisted on asserting a facile equation between human embodiment and ungodly, "carnal" desires have contributed to inestimable harm through the church's history. Those interpretations disregard the ways that Colossians and other New Testament writings affirm the importance of embodied existence as a location where Christ's presence can be experienced (e.g., Col 3:3) and where a person can know, at least to a degree, what it means to be kept secure from the grip of destructive powers (e.g., Col 1:13). The cosmic Christ remains as close to the people of God as one's own skin is close to one's self. The theology of Colossians therefore continues to instruct Christians to honor and celebrate embodied existence, to protect the inherent worth and dignity of all bodies, and to find the fullness of God dwelling in bodies still today.

11

The First Letter of Paul to the Thessalonians

All of Paul's letters display his conviction that the relatively young communities of Christ-followers in his orbit required ongoing encouragement and instruction. The churches Paul knew needed those things, not simply to strengthen the intensity of their commitment and to further their knowledge, but to impress on them what it means to be part of God's new future and how their faith in Christ should affect how they live and interact. In 1 Thessalonians Paul reminds a struggling yet persistently faithful community of believers that they have been called to express a distinctive Christian identity. What especially sets the letter apart among all of Paul's writings is the intensity of its encouragements; none of Paul's other surviving correspondence shows him so consistently affectionate and tender toward an audience.

The letter urges the Thessalonians to embody their theology—their understanding of God and what God accomplishes through Jesus Christ—in how they view and conduct themselves as a community called by God to cultivate holiness and to express faith, love, and hope. Their identity as people who "serve a living and true God" (1 Thess 1:9) should not, according to Paul and his coauthors, compel the Thessalonians to ignore or forsake the world but to live within it as a set-apart community, as a family that awaits Christ's return with hope and readiness.

Paul, along with his associates, instructs the Thessalonians as an expression of pastoral concern for them. The concern manifests itself in the letter's frequent statements of gratitude and care. Repeatedly the authors describe Christian community and their relationship to the Thessalonians with language and images that pertain to families and familial relationships. The authors aim to instill and reinforce the audience's identity as a family held together in love and solidarity.

Written sometime within the period of 51–52 CE, 1 Thessalonians may be the oldest document in the New Testament and is almost certainly the oldest of all of Paul's surviving letters. The letter could therefore be the oldest surviving piece of Christian literature. Whether it was the first pastoral letter of any kind that Paul wrote is impossible to determine, but it nevertheless endures as a monument to Paul's ardent desire to teach and impart pastoral care to others with written words, using a medium as common as a letter to nurture Christian identity and community, even when large distances separated him from an audience.

The Letter's Origins and Ancient Audience

Situated on the Aegean Sea and along a vital east-west trade route connecting the Adriatic Sea in the west to the Black Sea in the east, Thessalonica enjoyed general prosperity and renown. As the capital of the Roman province of Macedonia, the city maintained close political and commercial connections to Rome even as the population of Thessalonica preserved a longstanding legacy of Greek culture. Like most urban centers in the eastern part of the Roman Empire, the city's citizenry practiced a wide array of religious devotions, as evidenced by the many temples and religious sites there.

First Thessalonians indicates that believers in Thessalonica experienced difficulties after they joined the Christian movement, although the letter does not explain the source of the distress. Converting to a religion that demanded devotion to only one deity might have made the Thessalonians appear odd to their neighbors. Confessing the lordship of Jesus Christ in a population center like Thessalonica, with such tight political ties to Roman wealth and power and historical ties to Greek culture, might exacerbate tensions, especially if the notion of a crucified Savior gave offense to certain people. If the Thessalonian converts had understood their new beliefs as requiring them to withdraw from or brazenly criticize their city's dominant values and public life, those actions too could have provoked their neighbors to respond with harassment or exclusion. Violence was also possible, although no evidence confirms that the persecution mentioned in the letter reached such severity. What comes across most certainly from 1 Thessalonians is a sense that the Christian church there possessed a commitment strong enough to weather hardship yet was, in Paul's estimation, still learning how to live in light of the Christian message in an environment sometimes inflamed by frictions between the church and the wider society.

Paul and his associates had previously been in Thessalonica, for they preached the gospel and founded the Christian community there (e.g., 1 Thess 1:2–2:16). Neither 1 Thessalonians nor another Pauline letter recounts what exactly occurred during that initial visit and how much time had elapsed between that time and the sending of this letter. Paul, writing in partnership with Silvanus and Timothy but occasionally standing apart from the trio in the rare occasions where the letter uses a first-person singular form, says merely that some Thessalonians had warmly welcomed the missionaries and "turned to God from idols" (1 Thess 1:9; cf. 2:13). By contrast, the book of Acts includes a short account of Paul visiting Thessalonica along with Silas—which is how Acts renders Silvanus' name—before hostility forces them to flee the city (Acts 17:1–10). The story in Acts claims that Jews and gentiles— including "not a few of the leading women"—responded positively to Paul and Silas' message before a group of Jews stirred up public unrest. First Thessalonians paints a slightly different picture; it also speaks of persecution but implies the church in Thessalonica consists entirely or largely of gentiles (e.g., 1 Thess 1:9; 2:14–16). It is impossible to declare with certainty whether Acts and 1 Thessalonians might be taken to tell a consistent story. The two writings take very different perspectives and offer their respective stories for different reasons. Nevertheless, both books indicate that Paul and others first came to Thessalonica after a trying experience in nearby Philippi (1 Thess 2:2; Acts 16:11–40) and headed south when they left Thessalonica, eventually reaching Athens (1 Thess 3:1; Acts 17:10–15).

Paul and his companions wrote to the Thessalonians, the letter says, after Timothy had visited the congregation. That visit came after a time of some distress, because Paul and his friends had for some reason been unsuccessful in achieving their desire to return to Thessalonica (1 Thess 2:17–18). The letter offers hints of Paul's nagging concerns about the Thessalonians' welfare, which precipitated Timothy's journey from Athens to Thessalonica in the first place. The concerns stemmed from reports of persecution in Thessalonica (e.g., 1 Thess 3:3), for Paul says

Timothy visited "to find out about [the Thessalonians'] faith" (1 Thess 3:5)—to make sure the hardships had not led the Thessalonians to abandon their commitment to Christ. Paul, Silvanus, and Timothy's fears turned out to be mostly ill founded, however, for Timothy returned from his visit with news of the Thessalonians' "faith and love" (1 Thess 3:6–9). The three authors then wrote 1 Thessalonians to express gratitude for the Thessalonians' perseverance, to encourage them until an opportunity would arise to visit Thessalonica again, and to offer instruction about a handful of issues that were of concern to the Thessalonians and the letter's authors.

Overview

Salutation and Thanksgiving (1 Thess 1:1–10)

The letter gives thanks to God with language that connects specifically to the ways in which the Thessalonians have manifested the gospel in their own lives. Right away, the authors express gratitude for the Thessalonians' reputation and capacity for faith, love, and hope. Paul may have considered those three qualities, or certain ways of manifesting them, to be central aspects of Christian attitude and conduct, for he calls attention to them elsewhere, too, sometimes as a concentrated triad (e.g., 1 Cor 13:13). The letter will return to address the qualities again later.

The thanksgiving draws close associations between the Thessalonians' initial participation in the gospel and the letter-writers' previous experience among them. Paul, Silvanus, and Timothy remember those days from their initial visit to Thessalonica, recalling "power" and the manifestation of the Holy Spirit. The missionaries call attention to their own generous conduct not as an outlet for egotism but to emphasize the genuine connections they share with the Thessalonians. The converts did not simply believe what Paul and others urged them to believe; they shared in the same kinds of experience. The missionaries performed and lived out the gospel as much as they spoke it. When the letter praises the Thessalonians for imitating the authors, it draws on a common feature in Greek philosophical traditions about trustworthy teachers who are themselves worthy of emulation (cf. 1 Thess 2:14). The gospel Paul preached was about more than doctrine; it has experiential qualities, for it announces the new realities God has created. When Paul and the other two missionaries preached the gospel in Thessalonica, it created intimate, permanent relationships among them and this new church, for together all of them share an existential connection to Christ.

Celebration and Additional Thanksgivings
(1 Thess 2:1–3:13)

The authors keep their attention on the past when the letter turns to recall additional details of their previous encounters in Thessalonica, highlighting their frank determination to proclaim the gospel and the tenacity it required. Apparently Paul and his companions faced social or legal opposition at that time. Nevertheless, they persisted and refused to make demands on their converts or exploit any gratitude they may have received for their own material gain. Indeed, the description of those former days repeatedly employs language of familial relationships and virtuous concern, allowing the letter to paint a picture of exuberant, self-sacrificial determination and intimate connections. The authors insist they did not seek their own well-being but only the Thessalonians'. When they speak of their desire to share "not only the gospel of God but also [their] own selves" (1 Thess 2:8), they highlight more than affection or generosity as ethical merits. Rather, they characterize the gospel itself as a declaration of God's goodwill and commitment toward humanity. The missionaries' persistence underscores God's unwavering concern, which should motivate the Thessalonian church to persevere in its own faithfulness.

The wealth of familial imagery in this section of the letter attracts attention. At times the authors refer to themselves as a wet nurse caring not for her master's children but her own offspring (1 Thess 2:7), as the Thessalonians' brothers (1 Thess 2:9, 17), as the Thessalonians' father (1 Thess 2:11), and as orphans rendered heartbroken and very vulnerable by a separation from their parents (1 Thess 2:17). Obviously the letter does not insist on a single way of describing the relationship between the authors and audience according to a single model of a family structure. The wide range of poignant terms accentuates various dimensions of the relationship and consistently reiterates a sense of intimacy and mutual belonging.

Maybe the most surprising metaphor to characterize the authors' relationship with the Thessalonian believers reckons the authors' commitment to them as like a wet nurse, a lactating household slave charged with the duties of nourishing and caring for an owner's child with great intimacy and tenderness. Similar to when Paul compares himself to a mother giving birth in Gal 4:19, here the evocative language communicates a strong sense of devotion and shared existence. The imagery of breastfeeding also implies self-giving and sustenance. To refer to a wet nurse's attention to her own child intensifies the degree of care in the relationship. Identifying himself with feminine and maternal descriptors and roles might have brought scorn on Paul in some settings, given Roman values about honor, masculinity, impassibility, and exercising power over others. Paul appears unconcerned with such repercussions, however. He may have been willingly subverting those conventions by employing a feminine image. Even if that was not his express intention, still the rhetoric suggests that Paul did not understand the gospel as a license to assert dominance over others. In 1 Thessalonians he and his companions sometimes imagine their relationship to a church they have founded in ways that diverge from customary notions of prerogative and hierarchy.

When the authors rejoice over Timothy's positive report about the Thessalonians' well-being, their relief is palpable. Focusing now on the present tense, they say, "For we now live, if you continue to stand firm in the Lord" (1 Thess 3:8). Again, the close connections between authors and audience show themselves: the Thessalonians' faith affects Paul, Silvanus, and Timothy's own ability to live in faith. Careful readers may note alongside the celebration a slight hint of concern, however, since Timothy reported on the Thessalonians' "faith and love" (1 Thess 3:6) with no mention of hope. Later in the letter, the authors will explicitly return to the question of hope when they instruct their audience on a proper understanding of how to grieve with hope (1 Thess 4:13) in light of what believers should expect to transpire in the future, when Christ returns.

This section of the letter concludes with three verses structured as a prayer or benediction, beseeching God to allow the authors to see the Thessalonians again, to increase the young church's ability to express mutual love among its members, and to bring the Thessalonians toward greater holiness to prepare them for the time when Jesus will come again. The prayer reiterates the strong bonds that the authors share with their audience, bonds that the authors expect the Thessalonians to realize and maintain among themselves. The prayer's focus on God characterizes those bonds as more than good manners or a blueprint for a community's effective functioning. The bonds of mutual love express the gospel, which itself is a message of good news about the new realities created by God's love. Finally, the prayer's concluding focus on "holiness" leads to the letter's next section, which addresses other ways in which the gospel and the Thessalonians' common life connect to God's character and intentions.

A Life of Holiness (1 Thess 4:1–12)

The letter's focus changes in 1 Thess 4:1, signaled not only by the word *finally* but also as the communication becomes more instructional. The first item of business concerns how the Thessalonians conduct themselves. In 1 Thess 2:12 the authors described their fatherly role among the Thessalonians as "encouraging" them and "pleading" that they "lead a life worthy of God." The same Greek term translated "lead a life" appears again in 1 Thess 4:1 (rendered as "live" in the NRSV) and 1 Thess 4:12 (rendered as "behave"). The character of life Paul and his friends have in mind for their audience is one imbued with holiness, which is also sometimes translated as "sanctification" (1 Thess 4:3, 4, 7; cf. 3:13).

The subject given the most attention in the short discussion of sanctified life is "fornication," a wide-ranging word indicating sexual immorality of various kinds (e.g., Matt 19:9; 1 Cor 5:1; Col 3:5; Rev 9:21; 17:1–6). The term's specific referents in ancient literature depended on who was using the word and what a given author considered iniquitous. There was no clear catalog of exactly what actions fell into the category of "fornication." The authors of 1 Thessalonians do not elaborate on the term, since their point is more general. Their argument becomes difficult for interpreters to follow, however, because of ambiguity in another term: the specific thing the authors advocate controlling in order to avoid fornication is metaphorical in nature, and the word in 1 Thess 4:4 could refer to one's "body," or perhaps genitalia more specifically, or even to a man's wife (cf. 1 Cor 7:2). In any case, with their instructions Paul and the others clearly express concern for those who are exploited, harmed, or shamed by anyone's unrestrained transgressions of sexual norms. What the authors advocate, instead, is self-control and sexuality conducted "in holiness and honor" (1 Thess 4:4).

The letter writers expect the church in Thessalonica to act differently from the wider world, which they describe, using caricature and hyperbole familiar from many ancient Jewish characterizations of gentile societies, as unrestrained in its sexual appetites. The letter contrasts virtuous self-control with the behaviors of people who fall prey to sexual desires. The comparison would have been familiar to the letter's audience; many Greco-Roman moralists argued along similar lines. Paul and his coauthors, however, employ their hyperbole to help the Thessalonians understand themselves as differentiated from their wider culture, distinct from it in both their identity and how they behave. The rhetoric imagines the Thessalonians as a community set apart, but it constructs this distinction on a theological basis, for it locates the primary motivation for sexual propriety in God's calling. The calling comes from God, who makes self-control possible, insofar as God strengthens people in holiness. Holiness is a gift from God to make people blameless (1 Thess 3:13, 5:23), a gift connected to the Holy Spirit God provides (1 Thess 4:8; cf. 1:5–6).

When the letter turns to discuss briefly believers' love for one another and their behavior toward "outsiders," the authors emphasize the health and reputation of the Christian community. By viewing the authors' words about the community in connection with the preceding discussion of sexual morality, interpreters can see that Paul and his associates' admonitions about sexual ethics pertain not just to the practices of consenting individuals but also to the social health of an overall community. Paul does not want the community to suffer because of the wanton deeds of a few of its members. The holiness the letter has in view involves an entire community that treats its members with respect, honor, and love. A community that does that, the authors believe, will sustain itself and be free both from potentially corrupting dependence on the wider society and from confusion with the wider society and its values. The letter thus urges the Thessalonians to understand themselves as a community set apart in various ways—not to be withdrawn from or hostile toward the world around it but to be respectable, harmonious, and in some respects independent from those on the outside.

Jesus' Return and Christian Hope (1 Thess 4:13–5:11)

Probably no part of 1 Thessalonians attracts as much attention in Christian teaching and preaching than this section, due to its colorful teachings about "the coming of the Lord," Jesus Christ's future reappearance. While Paul makes frequent references to Jesus' return in his letters, here he has the most to say about the event as a time when Jesus will be physically (re)united with his followers.

Understanding the teachings about Jesus' coming and why they appear in this particular letter requires an interpreter to consider the context in which this passage appears. Paul and his coauthors begin the section by mentioning "those who have died"—literally, "those who have fallen asleep"—and encouraging the Thessalonians to avoid grieving without hope. As mentioned previously, Timothy may have returned from his visit to Thessalonica with persistent worries that the Thessalonians' hope was flagging. The two appearances of the word *hope* in this section of the letter, a section that describes what will happen to those who have died before Christ's return, may indicate that the Thessalonian church's sense of hope had been diminished by their worries about members of their community who had died. The focus of this section suggests that the Thessalonians feared that their dead brothers and sisters in the faith would be excluded or in some way disadvantaged when Christ returned. The authors insist, to the contrary, that "the dead in Christ will rise first" and will actually be present with Christ alongside those who are still living when he comes. The dead are in no way beyond God's reach but will share in God's promised future. This confidence aims not to eradicate the Thessalonians' grief about the loss of their loved ones but to infuse their grieving with hope.

The letter addresses the question of Christ's return in two parts (1 Thess 4:13–18 and 5:1–11). Each part culminates with an assurance about both the living and the dead being present "with" the Lord Jesus. Following the assurances are commands to "encourage one another" with the letter's teachings. Both parts describe the circumstances surrounding Jesus' return. The first speaks of angelic calls, trumpet peals, and clouds. The symbolic potential of those images has a history in Jewish Scriptures and other ancient Jewish writings: the sights and sounds indicate the divine presence and divine communication. The authors do not paint a literal picture of Christ's return; they merely emphasize that the event will be an unmistakable spectacle and will coincide with the resurrection of the dead. The second part focuses on preparing for Christ's return. It commends a life of readiness and anticipation as people await his coming. Presumably the two parts connect because of an implied premise: the promise of Jesus' return and the new reality it will create for the living and the dead should spur Christ-followers to live in the present not only with hope in God but also with actions inspired by an eager confidence.

The second part of this section also emphasizes the sudden and surprising character of Christ's return. In language familiar from Jewish apocalyptic literature, language also ascribed to Jesus in the Synoptic Gospels (e.g., Matt 24:42–44, Mark 13:33–37, Luke 12:35–48), the letter urges a posture of wakefulness. References to "times and seasons" and "the day of the Lord" associate Jesus' return with the occasion of divine judgment, about which numerous passages from Jewish Scriptures also speak.

When the letter's authors strike a contrast between a coming "destruction," presumably an effect of God's judgment, and hollow reassurances about "peace and security," they mock common themes in Roman imperial propaganda that would have been familiar in a very Roman-influenced city like Thessalonica. Rome's subjects repeatedly heard that the Roman emperors established and guaranteed peace and security for the empire and its people, but Christ's reappearance promises to minimize those claims by revealing them as empty in light of the true salvation, peace, and security he provides. Those who diligently await Christ's return as their source of true hope therefore also express an unwillingness to be taken in by imperial pretensions rooted in the illusions of enforced peace or unjust security. The distinctively Christian posture of hope the letter commends stands counter to the status quo that the empire peddles as its own form of good news. Christ's return will be a time of revealing all rival claims about good news, salvation, and power as imposters.

Exhortations about Daily Living (1 Thess 5:12–24)

As the letter moves toward its conclusion, an interest in mutual concern and care undergirds the authors' instructions. Even as the Thessalonian church awaits Christ's return, its members should remain where they are situated and foster a healthy Christian community. There is no need to flee civilization or abandon one's ordinary affairs. Many of the commands recall themes that appeared previously in the letter as they encourage the Thessalonians to promote harmony in their shared life. The letter commends rejoicing, thanksgiving, and careful discernment—the same kinds of things the authors expressed in the letter's first half. Lest the church fall victim to thinking its future survival depends entirely on everybody's ability to generate their own holiness, the letter offers another prayer or benediction to reassert that God is the one who sanctifies and keeps believers. That theological bedrock makes Christian community even possible in the first place.

Conclusion and Benediction (1 Thess 5:25–28)

The letter concludes with little fanfare, although the final verses reassert the importance of community. The authors ask for the Thessalonians' prayers and encourage the group to remain unified as "brothers and sisters" in the same family. When Paul enjoins the audience to read the letter aloud to the whole church, he seeks for the document to have its widest possible effect among each valued member of the fledgling Christian community. The letter's warm encouragement and instruction belonged, Paul believed, to everyone who could hear it, not just to the church's recognized leaders or to a literate few.

The Letter's Themes and Theological Emphases

At first glance, 1 Thessalonians appears to reveal more about Paul's relationship with the Thessalonians than about his theology, but it is shortsighted to consider that relationship as something separate from his theology. The warmth and encouragement on display in this letter have functions beyond communicating general pastoral support. Paul's expressions of love and nurture actually embody theological truth. In reiterating his and his coauthors' deep affection for the letter's audience, Paul depicts the gospel as a phenomenon, an act of God, that creates unity that can be experienced in the church's activities and its ethos of mutual concern.

Even though 1 Thessalonians never mentions justification or explicitly refers to God's justifying activity through Jesus Christ, still the letter proceeds from an understanding of Jesus Christ as the means by which God's salvation becomes possible (e.g., 1 Thess 5:9). The letter's efforts to nurture hope build on the firm conviction that God will prove faithful to bring God's intentions to their full realization. Even though 1 Thessalonians never quotes a passage from the Septuagint, still the letter reflects the influence that the Scriptures and related Jewish teachings had on Paul's ways of thinking about God and the gospel. One example of that influence resides in the letter's emphasis on

God as the source of holiness and God's desire for believers to embody or be transformed into holiness (1 Thess 3:13–4:3). Another example is the depiction of Christ's return as an epiphany or a divine appearance, associated with scriptural traditions about the coming day of the Lord (1 Thess 4:13–5:11).

The Church's Identity and Posture within Its Social Setting

Modern psychologists and sociologists might describe 1 Thessalonians as Paul, Silvanus, and Timothy's efforts toward fostering identity formation among a young Christian community. The letter reinforces the church's identity as a family that expresses faith, love, and hope while living in expectation of Jesus' return, and 1 Thessalonians seeks to build and ensure the community's cohesion for the long haul. The authors tell the audience that they constitute a distinctive community, liable to suffer persecution in their cultural context (1 Thess 3:3–4). God calls that community to practice morality and loving interdependence intended to set it apart from other communities (1 Thess 4:1–12). The community also has reason to possess hope concerning the impermanence of death and the true source of peace and security. Of course, the letter describes those realities as consistent with claims about God and the salvation God provides through Christ and not as expressions of purely sociological dynamics.

By calling attention to the various ways in which the church's conduct and attitudes should set believers apart from their surroundings, and without asking church members to abandon their positions in society, Paul and his associates occasionally draw thick lines around the church, imagining it as quite separate from other segments of the population (e.g., 1 Thess 2:14; 3:3–4; 4:5, 12, 13; 5:3–9). Yet when the authors finally describe how the Thessalonians should live, their instructions commend rather ordinary behavior, reinforcing common values of love, fairness, and respectability that many outside the church would also endorse (e.g., 1 Thess 4:4, 10–12; 5:12–15). The church's ethics are not extraordinary, but its identity is. What therefore looks like the letter's strong but perhaps exaggerated statement of the church's otherness could veer close to summoning Christ-followers to sectarian isolationism, as if the church needs to move toward existing as a living expression of apocalyptic dualism that divides the world into obvious camps of the saved and the doomed.

Other interpretations of the letter's emphasis on the church's otherness are possible, instead. The references to persecution in Thessalonica might offer a different explanation for the thick boundary lines around the church in 1 Thessalonians. All the familial imagery in the letter implies that the Christian community offers its members a new family system, perhaps to replace old ones that had been lost. If believers in Thessalonica were experiencing rejection, harassment, and expulsion from their own households and neighborhoods—whether they were courting that antagonism or not, and whether they had resources or social standing to resist it or not—then the letter could tell a story of a truly endangered and potentially demoralized community. Perhaps the authors' attempts to distinguish the Christian community and instill it with an inward confidence and sense of mutual support might have been necessary to provide Christ-followers with relief from the anguishes and hazards of persecution. As Paul and his coauthors saw it, the new family created through Christian fellowship provides its members refuge from alienation.

The Coming (Parousia) of the Lord

Four times throughout 1 Thessalonians the authors refer to Jesus' future coming, using the Greek word *parousia*, which also means "appearance" or "arrival" (1 Thess 2:19, 3:13, 4:15, 5:23). Paul uses the same word in connection to Jesus' return in no other of his undisputed letters except for 1 Corinthians (1 Cor 15:23; cf. 2 Thess 2:1, 8). In 1 Thessalonians the discussion of Jesus' *parousia* describes the climactic event as a foundation for Christian hope and an impetus for a life lived in alert expectation. The authors do not address the subject to give a clear or literal description of future events. The subject receives attention because for some unstated reasons the Thessalonians were distressed concerning the fate of their fellow Christ-followers who had died. Perhaps Paul and his associates' preaching on their initial visit had led the Thessalonians to conclude that Jesus' resurrection spelled the end of death for any who live in Christ. If so, then a single death of a church member could understandably cause a panic. That might explain the amount of attention the letter gives to Jesus' *parousia* and to specific details about how the Thessalonians should live in expectation of it.

The letter's main emphasis falls on confidence in God's gracious reliability. Not only will the *parousia* vindicate God's faithfulness, but it also aligns with a key theme in Paul's understanding of the gospel: the intimacy and participation that believers enjoy with Christ. Therefore, the letter talks about the *parousia* with an accent on togetherness and shared experience. The dead and living alike will meet Jesus at his return and together "will be with the Lord forever" (1 Thess 4:17). The vocabulary used to describe that future encounter and its communal character would have been familiar to the Thessalonians from other contexts. Certain terms depict Christ's arrival as resembling the appearance of an imperial dignitary. In the Greco-Roman setting, the word *parousia* could indicate the manifestation of a deity or the visit of an important official. Likewise, a separate word used to describe the moment when believers "meet the Lord in the air" (1 Thess 4:17) sometimes indicated a similar thing: the arrival of a military leader or honored imperial representative. When such visits occurred in Greco-Roman culture, typically the point of initial contact occurred outside of a city. Residents would go out to meet the celebrated person along a road and provide an escort or a corridor into the city. The description in 1 Thessalonians suggests that believers will welcome the returning Christ not on a highway but in the sky and then accompany him back to earth. Nothing in the passage indicates that Christ appears to take people away to another place. The popular notion of a "rapture," which was developed over roughly the last century and a half to describe a sudden transmigration of people from earth to heaven, has little if any basis in this part of 1 Thessalonians, based on the terminology and descriptions that the authors employ.

The authors of 1 Thessalonians told their audience that the *parousia* would happen soon. When they refer in 1 Thess 4:17 to "we who are alive, who are left," they indicate they expected to be alive when the *parousia* occurred. During the first few decades after Jesus' death and resurrection, it appears that his followers assumed his return was imminent (e.g., Mark 8:38–9:1; 13:30 and parallels; 1 John 2:28). Over time that expectation obviously changed. Late in his life, Paul talked about his upcoming death as the time when he would be with the Lord (Phil 1:21–23). By the time Paul wrote Philippians, then, he had altered his perspective. Other writings, produced after even more time had elapsed, express little overt discomfort with the fact that Jesus had not yet returned (e.g., John 21:22–23, Acts 1:6–7, 2 Peter 3:8–10). Even as the authors of 1 Thessalonians assumed that the *parousia*'s arrival was near, still they insisted its precise timing was unpredictable (1 Thess 5:2).

Because 1 Thessalonians identifies the *parousia* as the time of uniting with Jesus and entering into the fullness of God's salvation, the issue offers an additional illustration of Jewish apocalyptic theology's influence on Paul's ways of understanding and articulating the gospel. The letter's attention to angelic noises, trumpets, clouds, and childbirth resonates with Jewish apocalyptic texts that mention the same phenomena to indicate a divine appearance or the effort to bring forth newness out of a cosmic struggle. The dualism between day and night, sobriety and drunkenness, and wakefulness and slumber also relies on stock images (1 Thess 5:4–8). Attributing obstacles to satanic interference enhances the apocalyptic tenor in 1 Thessalonians as well (1 Thess 2:18). More telling, however, is the letter's focus on Jesus' coming as an ultimate act, one that will finally secure salvation for God's people (1 Thess 5:9) and preserve them from a time of wrath (1 Thess 1:10).

The letter turns to the *parousia* because the authors regard God and God's reliability as the keystone of hope. If God cannot be trusted, hope vanishes. As the culminating act of God, however, Jesus' *parousia* promises finally to embarrass other powers, such as imperial forces that purport to engineer a self-congratulatory sociopolitical climate of peace and security, and bring the divine drama to its awaited goal. Meanwhile, as they wait with hope, the people of God should take courage to persevere and remain confident in God's commitment to bring about the expected result. For the result ultimately must be, according to Paul and his coauthors, entirely an act of God, a God of grace from beginning to end, as emphasized by the appearance of the word *grace* in both the first verse and the final verse of 1 Thessalonians (1 Thess 1:1, 5:28).

12

The Second Letter of Paul to the Thessalonians

S econd Thessalonians speaks to an audience of believers who are
in crisis. Without elaborating on the specific nature of that crisis, the letter warns that persecution and misunderstanding have
the potential to fracture a Christian community. It therefore instructs
Christ-followers to "hold fast" to what they have already been taught as
they await Jesus' return. Speaking with a severe tone about the perils
at hand and the judgment to come, the book urges its audience to keep
themselves fixed on their purpose. That purpose is to live a life of faithfulness to God, whose ultimate victory over wickedness and rebelliousness remains certain.

The letter's specific teachings about the future, especially about the
final judgment and the return of Christ, have influenced imaginations
about coming events among interpreters in both ancient and modern
times. Second Thessalonians distinguishes itself for several reasons,
but perhaps the book's most noteworthy features are its contributions
to the New Testament's diverse and colorful conversation about what
Christian communities should expect regarding the future and how
believers should commit themselves to live faithfully and cooperatively
amid the difficulties that come their way in the meantime.

The Letter's Origins and Ancient Audience

Interpreters who scour 2 Thessalonians in search of clues to reveal the
context in which the book first spoke and the purposes of the book's

message have to sort through a considerable amount of information. For one thing, the letter certainly has an air of crisis and concern about it. It calls attention to and criticizes Christ-followers who have become caught up in alarmed speculation about when "the day of the Lord" and Christ's return (Greek, *parousia*) will occur (2 Thess 2:1–2). Some members of the letter's audience had stopped working, apparently because they believed the *parousia* was immediately imminent. Their decision, according to the letter, strained the church's ability to function as a community and departed from the example established by Paul, Silvanus, and Timothy. To redirect and correct an anxious Christian community, twice the letter points back to "traditions," earlier instructions from Paul and his associates about the *parousia* and the proper ways to live as an expectant Christian community (2 Thess 2:15, 3:6). By appealing to those traditions' authority, the letter may acknowledge an ongoing debate among the audience concerning what Paul and his coworkers originally taught them. The letter nevertheless urges people to "hold fast" to what they learned from the authors, "either by word of mouth or by [their] letter" (2 Thess 2:15). It warns against correspondence and teachings that falsely claim to originate from Paul, Silvanus, and Timothy (2 Thess 2:2) and against anyone who promulgates deceptive teachings (2 Thess 2:3). It even claims to bear the distinctive and therefore authenticating mark of Paul's own handwriting (2 Thess 3:17). Through it all, the book asserts that it offers Paul's true position on the subjects addressed and presents his position consistently with what the audience had previously been instructed.

Not only does 2 Thessalonians explicitly appeal to Paul and his associates' longstanding relationship with the church at Thessalonica, but also the rhetoric of the letter connects in distinctive ways to what Paul, Silvanus, and Timothy wrote in 1 Thessalonians. The format and style of the two letters closely resemble each other. Although the letters exhibit differences in some of their individual themes and language, especially in their respective outlooks on "the day of the Lord," still both books follow very similar forms and address similar subjects. Even a few specific sentences from one letter have near twins in the other: both letters offer thanksgivings for the Thessalonians' perseverance despite the persecution they suffer (1 Thess 1:2–10, 2 Thess 1:3–12), and both ask God to strengthen the Thessalonians' hearts (1 Thess 3:13; 2 Thess 2:16–17). The evidence indicates that one of the letters deliberately imitates the other's rhetoric. They appear to belong together.

Given all the striking similarities between the letters, the differences between them appear all the more stark and inexplicable. The theological content and pastoral concerns expressed in 2 Thessalonians diverge considerably from what appears in 1 Thessalonians. For example, the two letters offer differing perspectives on Jesus' *parousia*. Unlike 1 Thessalonians, 2 Thessalonians does not seem to support the idea that Christ's appearance, although it is imminent, is still unpredictable, bound to transpire without any prior indications, "like a thief in the night" (1 Thess 5:2). Second Thessalonians states, rather, that calamitous events must come before Jesus returns (2 Thess 2:3–12). Those events evidently make it easier to anticipate when Christ will arrive. It is unclear why the same authors would choose to promote two different perspectives about the *parousia* on two different occasions, especially when 2 Thessalonians claims to be congruent with Paul's earlier teaching (2 Thess 2:5).

A more dramatic difference between the letters resides in what they each assume about their audience's beliefs. It appears odd to many interpreters that 2 Thessalonians sets out to counter unrestrained enthusiasm among the letter's audience, a church whose *lack* of hope receives major attention in 1 Thessalonians. How the believers in Thessalonica might have suddenly developed their new understanding of living in expectant watchfulness for a "day of the Lord" that "is already here" (2 Thess 2:2)—as opposed to coming at an unknown time in the future "like a thief in the night"—remains difficult to determine. The ambiguity of the letter's language about the day of the Lord having already arrived only complicates the question for interpreters.

The sharp differences in some of the two letters' basic assumptions therefore cause interpreters to question whether both documents originally could have been written to the same audience by the same authors within a short span of years. Some have proposed, then, that 2 Thessalonians originated at a much later time in history and perhaps was written by someone or a group of people other than the authors of 1 Thessalonians—namely, Paul, Silvanus, and Timothy.

Debates about the origins of 2 Thessalonians cannot avoid extensive speculation because the letter itself allows interpreters to see so little of its history. It offers only a very general sketch of its audience's circumstances, mostly calling attention to a heightened sense of eschatological expectation among the church in Thessalonica. It makes no references to historical-temporal markers, such as specific journeys

Paul or others might have taken to various cities in the past or might have planned for the future. It is nearly impossible to orient the letter, then, within a larger timeline or a plausible series of events in Paul's life. If Paul, Silvanus, and Timothy originally sent this document to Thessalonica as a follow-up to 1 Thessalonians, they offer no indication of how much time elapsed between the two communications, no explanation for why the theological mood in the city underwent such an intense change, and no accounting for why they seem to have altered their own views about Christ's return and what to teach others about the *parousia*'s timing.

When all of the evidence from the book has been collected and weighed, no letter among the thirteen that bear Paul's name proves more difficult to set within a historical context than 2 Thessalonians. The difficulty does not make it impossible to understand what 2 Thessalonians says, but it does create formidable challenges for unraveling the letter's nuances and for making sense of why the book might have been written, and to whom, in the first place. At a basic level, the wider setting in which 2 Thessalonians originally spoke may be indiscernible, although the message the book speaks is not. An overview of various ways in which one might understand the origins and authorship of 2 Thessalonians will provide a closer look at some of this letter's particularities.

The Question of Authorship

Persistent debates about the authorship and historical setting of 2 Thessalonians may be impossible to resolve to everyone's satisfaction, but the debates are hardly frivolous pursuits. The content of 2 Thessalonians provokes questions about how it should be read, especially given all of its commonality with 1 Thessalonians. Because both letters purport to come from the same authors and address the same church, interpreters need to consider what the audience's circumstances were like when 2 Thessalonians was written and why the conditions of the church in Thessalonica might have changed so profoundly between the two letters. If, however, 2 Thessalonians is a pseudepigraphic letter, then separate questions arise. For example, the conspicuous similarities between the two letters lead interpreters to wonder why an author might have created a pseudepigraphic letter that so closely imitates another piece of correspondence.

To oversimplify the matter in advance, the debates about the authorship of 2 Thessalonians are not overly important for understanding *what* the letter says, although they are rather important for understand *why* the letter says what it does. Interpreters do not need to settle all the questions about the letter and its original audience's context. That is fortunate, because scholars can hardly agree on this particular issue, and only a brief review of the debates is possible here. The review creates an opportunity to move deeper into the letter itself, to consider how it might have spoken to ancient Christ-followers.

One possibility is that Paul or one of his close associates, including Silvanus or Timothy, authored 2 Thessalonians to address changes that occurred within the Christian community in Thessalonica sometime after 1 Thessalonians was sent. Perhaps influential members of the Thessalonian church misunderstood or deliberately misrepresented the teachings Paul and his friends had formerly sent in 1 Thessalonians. Or perhaps other, unknown teachers came to the city and propagated false information about Paul's ideas. Those kinds of developments might have triggered significant and rapid changes in the church's ethos. Or perhaps social ostracism and economic sanctions against the Christ-followers in Thessalonica intensified, causing a panic among them that expressed itself with a kind of dire eschatological enthusiasm. A number of causes could have compelled Paul and his associates to write again to the same audience in hopes of addressing new and very different circumstances.

Another set of hypotheses holds that someone other than Paul wrote 2 Thessalonians. Perhaps that author was a person within the Thessalonian church who deviously aimed in the early 50s CE to distort the teachings conveyed in 1 Thessalonians by creating a letter meant to deceive its intended audience. More likely, however, the author wrote at a much later time in the first century, and perhaps to an entirely different church somewhere in the Roman Empire, as a means of offering support to a congregation suffering some kind of sustained and corrosive persecution. The author of the pseudepigraphic letter, according to one plausible hypothesis, crafted the document to resemble 1 Thessalonians as a means of summoning Paul's authority and reputation to speak words of comfort, correction, and warning into a new, developing situation in a congregation's life. In other words, 2 Thessalonians might imitate 1 Thessalonians as an additional way of celebrating Paul and the ongoing importance of his teachings and example.

The proposals that 2 Thessalonians is a pseudepigraphic letter have their own ways of making sense of all the pronounced differences between 2 Thessalonians and 1 Thessalonians. To take one glaring issue, the two letters' teachings about the day of the Lord may diverge to such a degree because they come from different eras, and therefore they indicate two different audiences and perhaps two different understandings of what believers should expect concerning the *parousia*. Moreover, the letter's references to "traditions" received from Paul and others may indicate a period in a church's history, after Paul's death, when the apostle's influence and legacy were in dispute, perhaps in part because different people were claiming to speak as his legitimate interpreters (cf. 2 Thess 2:2–3, 15). To provide a platform for Pauline ideas or Paul's legacy in such a setting, an author may have written 2 Thessalonians as a pseudepigraphic letter of his own, mimicking the style of the earlier letter to the Thessalonians for added effect. Moreover, he might have enhanced the pseudepigraphic letter's appearance and fictionalized rhetoric in order to make it resemble actual correspondence by including curious references to spurious letters (2 Thess 2:2) and to Paul's distinctive mark or handwriting (2 Thess 3:17).

Interpreters cannot settle the question of whether an author created 2 Thessalonians as a pseudepigraphic document specially designed to deceive audiences unaware of the letter's true origins or whether he wrote it to honor Paul's legacy with overly effusive—but nevertheless candidly made-up—attempts to give the document the feel of authenticity. Uncertainty about an unknown author's motives need not necessarily prejudice how one should interpret 2 Thessalonians or even appraise its ongoing value as Scripture. The more pressing question remains what the letter communicates and how its teachings compare and contrast with other writings in the New Testament.

With this letter there is no end to generating hypotheses. Other possibilities exist. Interpreters have proposed that Paul and his coauthors were indeed responsible for both letters, but 2 Thessalonians was sent first. Yet another proposal holds that Paul and his associates wrote both letters at approximately the same time but sent them to two different groups residing in or near Thessalonica. The sheer amount of hypotheses underscores the mysteries surrounding this curious letter, yet the creativity behind those hypotheses gives voice to the important fact that interpreters have to consider the wide variety of circumstances, pressures, opportunities, and worries that confronted Christian communities in the church's earliest decades. The wide range of experiences among the earliest Christ-followers may mean that rarely did two different teachers or documents seek to be influential in exactly the same way. The diversity of the church in its various settings required a diversity of teaching. Some people wrote letters. Some wrote pseudepigraphic letters. Some thought the *parousia* was imminent. Some thought the church still had a degree of breathing space until that day would come. Some looked forward in time with effusive hope. Some expressed their hope with an accent on divine vengeance.

Finally, theories about the authorship and occasion of 2 Thessalonians influence estimates about when it was written. If it came directly from Paul, Silvanus, Timothy, or their secretary and was sent to Thessalonica, then it probably originated within a year or two after 1 Thessalonians, in the early 50s CE. But if, as the following overview of the letter assumes, a later Pauline disciple or advocate wrote it in the name of Paul and his associates, then it could have been written at almost any point in the latter half of the first century, but most likely between 80 and 95 CE. Because some Christian authors from the early second century refer to material from 2 Thessalonians, one can assume that the document began to circulate with other Pauline letters no later than around 100 CE.

Overview

Even though the specific circumstances behind 2 Thessalonians remain beyond modern interpreters' range of vision, the letter's messages to its audience present themselves with much greater clarity. Its author, whoever he was, wrote to protect and strengthen an audience so they could withstand the threats they faced. The general direction the letter points is toward reinforcement and endurance. It instructs the Thessalonian believers to close ranks and remain faithful to the gospel. Much like 1 Thessalonians, it roots its confidence in God and God's character, contending that the church can persevere because God makes it possible. The grace and call of God deserve the credit for providing believers with the strength to endure.

Salutation and Thanksgiving (2 Thess 1:1–4)

The letter's opening sentence nearly duplicates 1 Thess 1:1. Paul, Silvanus, and Timothy greet the Thessalonians with words of divine grace and peace. They thank God for the faith and love the Thessalonians demonstrate, praising God but also indirectly praising the audience themselves for manifesting those qualities of the gospel in increasing measure. As in 1 Thessalonians, the letter describes the audience's endurance in the midst of persecution as exemplary and an encouragement to other churches. Right away, therefore, 2 Thessalonians commends vitality and durability as characteristics a church should pursue and guard.

Judgment, Vengeance, and the Coming of the Lord
(2 Thess 1:5–2:12)

The letter looks at the Thessalonians' faithful steadfastness as they endure suffering and considers it an indicator of both God's just character and the audience's worthiness for God's "kingdom." The mention of God's justice leads to a glance into the future toward God's coming judgment, at which time God will give relief to the faithful who suffer now and will "repay" persecutors with afflictions of their own. The letter promises angels will unleash "vengeance on those who do not know God and on those who do not obey the gospel" and finally those people will suffer "the punishment of eternal destruction, separated from the presence of the Lord and the glory of his might." On the other side of that judgment, Christ will "be glorified by his saints" (2 Thess 1:7–10). In the meantime, the letter says that its authors pray for the Thessalonians, asking that they and Jesus would be glorified.

The latter half of 2 Thessalonians 1 has influenced Christian doctrines about judgment and hell, as is plainly visible in the book's references to flames, punishment, and separation from God. These verses do not sound like Paul's other letters, however. While judgment and the glorification of believers are themes in several of Paul's undisputed letters, nowhere in those writings does Paul associate judgment so closely with vengeance. More telling, those other letters never speak of a future, "eternal" punishment as an expression of divine retribution. When 2 Thessalonians offers those images specifically to reassure and encourage an audience of beleaguered Christ-followers, the letter promotes a mind-set of deriving comfort from the prospect of divine retaliation someday overtaking one's oppressors. While some theological positions and other New Testament writings might support such an understanding of judgment qua vengeance as a legitimate view of God's just character or as an accurate expression of the future God intends, Paul does not explicitly endorse it in the seven writings that certainly come from him.

Similar to 1 Thessalonians, this letter devotes substantial effort to teaching about Christ's future coming, or *parousia*, as the arrival of the long-anticipated "day of the Lord." The letter appears designed to correct certain views that were circulating about that expected event. The letter singles out those who mistakenly claim "the day of the Lord is already here" (2 Thess 2:2). Presumably that claim means that some believers thought the *parousia* was immediately imminent, surely coming any day now, or it was already in the process of occurring as an extended or somehow spiritually realized event. In any case, the belief evidently "alarmed" some of the Thessalonians.

Perhaps the authors of 1 Thessalonians would have corrected that belief by calling speculation about the *parousia*'s timing a futile effort, since the day will come without warning (1 Thess 5:2–4). By contrast, however, 2 Thessalonians insists that the day of the Lord cannot be already here, since two things must occur before it arrives: a period of "apostasy" (a better rendering of the word the NRSV translates as "rebellion" in 2 Thess 2:3) and the manifestation of a figure called "the lawless one." Something (2 Thess 2:6) or someone (2 Thess 2:7) currently restrains that figure; nevertheless, signs of his future appearance can be detected now in the lies and deceptions that keep people from realizing the truth of God's salvation. Those deceitful forces manifest "the working of Satan." Only after the lawless one is revealed will Christ return, and at that time the Lord Jesus will annihilate him with hardly any effort.

Second Thessalonians says very little about the lawless one. It introduces him mostly to steer the audience away from assuming that Christ can return right away, before additional distress afflicts the church and its efforts to make the gospel known. By discussing the lawless one and the apostasy that will come with him, the letter aims to accomplish at least two objectives. First, it counters inaccurate beliefs and misleading teachers in their focus on the *parousia* as something near on the horizon. Second, it braces the audience to expect more difficulty to come. Possibly the letter's author has concerns that the audience might start to relax in their resolve to endure opposition if they think the day of the Lord is already waiting at the door. Instead, the church needs to ready itself for more, extended travails. Circumstances in the world will get worse before they get better, which is a refrain heard also in other New Testament writings produced near the end of the first century (e.g., Luke 21:7–17; 2 Tim 3:1; 1 Pet 4:12–19; Revelation; cf. 2 Pet 3:3–4).

Additional Thanksgivings and Appeals (2 Thess 2:13–3:5)

In case the preceding comments about rebellion, lawlessness, deception, and even a delusion sent by God might cause excessive consternation or worry among the audience, the letter quickly turns to console them. The book reassures believers that God has elected them for salvation, holiness (or "sanctification"), knowledge of the truth, and eventual glorification. The letter appeals to God with a prayer or benediction requesting comfort and strength for the Thessalonians. As 2 Thessalonians 2 ends, the letter thus continues to posit a sharp difference between those who perish in falsehood and those who enjoy the promise and benefits of God's salvation.

As 2 Thessalonians 3 begins, the letter redirects attention away from descriptions of ultimate events and toward Christian life and ministry in the present tense. It asks the Thessalonians to pray for Paul, Silvanus, and Timothy. Even though God sends delusion to some and chooses others as "the first fruits for salvation" (2 Thess 2:13), still the letter believes that "the word of the Lord may spread rapidly and be glorified everywhere" (2 Thess 3:1). Reasons still exist for spreading the gospel message, even when the church's or the world's conditions appear inalterable or degenerative. The life of faith and Christian witness still matter. The letter speaks very confidently about the Thessalonians' faithfulness even as it implores them to continue on the right track by remaining obedient to all that Paul and his coworkers have commanded.

Stern Exhortations against Idleness and Rebelliousness (2 Thess 3:6–15)

As the letter turns to offer concluding exhortations, it keeps its eyes on the internal dynamics of the audience as a Christian community. The letter levels strong criticism toward those in the community who have ceased working or otherwise neglected their basic responsibilities. Nothing explicitly connects the "people living in idleness" with those in the letter's previous chapter who believe "the day of the Lord is already here," but the implication may be that some overly enthusiastic members of this already imperiled church have ceased to work or earn money. Their withdrawal from ordinary responsibilities could have created burdens for others in the community who had to support them or endure increased mockery from outsiders as a result. Their misdirected enthusiasm makes them generally guilty of letting their lives proclaim both faulty hopes about Jesus' *parousia* and misguided notions of the church's purpose and witness as it awaits God's consummating act. As in 1 Thessalonians, so also in 2 Thessalonians: God has not called the church to sectarian isolationism.

The language in this section indicates that laziness or stupidity is not the core problem for those who do not conduct their lives properly. Rather, the behavior is criticized because it manifests an attitude of disruptiveness and disobedience. "Idleness" stands counter to the memory of Paul, Silvanus, and Timothy's hard work in their initial interactions among the Thessalonians, which 1 Thessalonians also notes (1 Thess 2:3–10).

The letter instructs readers to shun the troublemakers and let some of them suffer hunger as a consequence for their refusal to contribute to the community's well-being and public witness by working and promoting a harmonious fellowship. Nothing indicates whether the people in question were wealthy people whose bad choices harmed the community's overall livelihood, vulnerable or impoverished people who exploited others' charity, dejected people who hoped that avoiding work would lessen the harassment and persecution they regularly suffered outside their homes, or something else entirely. Whatever it was that motivated certain believers to bring disruption to the community—a community already suffering from the strain caused by persecutions of some kind—the letter characterizes their actions as rebellion against traditions and commands linked to Paul and his associates. To shun those troublesome believers does not mean ultimate banishment, however, for the letter stipulates they should be warned and not expelled or treated as enemies.

Conclusion and Benedictions (2 Thess 3:16–18)

The letter concludes quickly with two benedictions about peace and grace, respectively, separated by a final greeting that supposedly authenticates the letter as coming from Paul himself. Other Pauline letters conclude with a few words originally written in the apostle's own hand, although nowhere do they claim to be Paul's standard "mark" or signature (e.g., 1 Cor 16:21; Gal 6:11; Phlm 19; cf. Col 4:18). The letter's final greeting can neither prove nor disprove Pauline authorship of 2 Thessalonians, but it does call attention to the letter's repeated attempts to speak for Paul within a setting in which different parties were contesting his opinions and the enduring "traditions" about his teachings. The letter expresses its final benediction with a sentence nearly identical to the concluding sentence in 1 Thessalonians (1 Thess 5:28).

The Letter's Themes and Theological Emphases

Second Thessalonians is hardly the only book in the New Testament that concerns itself with equipping a struggling community to endure hardship and strengthen its communal bonds. As noted, 1 Thessalonians operates in a similar way. In addition, other New Testament writings identify Christian communities as sharply distinguished from the wider culture. Several of those writings were, like 2 Thessalonians, evidently written to support churches beset by false teachings and dissensions. Most of those other books, such as Acts, 1 Timothy, 1 Peter, the Johannine Letters, and Revelation, come from late in the first century, which appears to be a time when Christ-followers were forced to make sense of their extended existence as communities still awaiting a *parousia* that many believers had expected to occur by then. Some churches during that period also deemed it necessary to enforce greater uniformity of belief and practice among their members, perhaps in attempts to prevent people from leaving Christian congregations. Those similarities among various New Testament writings and their themes do not require a late first-century date for 2 Thessalonians; they do, however, sketch a picture of an evolving cultural and ecclesial landscape that may resonate with some of the concerns expressed in this enigmatic letter.

Second Thessalonians has a solemn and unyielding character about it since the issues it addresses pertain to a community in crisis and possibly also an author's attempt to counter specific beliefs he considered false and disruptive. There is more to this letter's theological vision, however. Underlying the document's claims about future events is a vision of God who remains unquestionably powerful over the forces of evil and destruction. The letter encourages believers to refuse to accept suffering and oppression as the final word, for glory and relief will one day, in the end, replace those hardships. Second Thessalonians also insists that church communities must tend to the actions and beliefs that make them strong and able to bear authentic witness to the gospel, even when simple but resolute faithfulness is all that believers can muster in climates flush with peril, opposition, division, and trauma.

Persecution and Retribution

In some of the seven letters Paul undoubtedly wrote, he discusses how Christ's return will bring benefits to the faithful. Second Thessalonians says similar things but also goes out of its way to describe a coming judgment that will mean the destruction of enemies, whether they be those who persecute the church or simply those who do not know God or heed the gospel. The rhetoric of retribution and exclusion, a highly unusual sight in a letter associated with the apostle Paul, comes as part of the document's overriding interest in encouraging a harassed church to trust in God's judgment, in spite of what seems like runaway hostility and lawlessness in the world.

It can be tempting to isolate the letter's description of future vengeance and then to criticize the moral validity of appealing to divine judgment as a basis for comfort and encouragement in the present. In other words, revenge fantasies are not always the most helpful encouragements one can give to those who suffer hardships brought on by other people. Such fantasies often prove to excuse, perpetuate, or even multiply oppression. But the letter's references to a wider context of oppression and suffering nevertheless have to inform how interpreters understand the letter's distinctive views on future punishment. The kind of judgment yearned for by people who suffer unjustly can understandably differ from the kind of judgment that those living more comfortable lives would prefer to see. It is also important to evaluate the letter's references to judgment, and perhaps also to temper them, in light of other parts of 2 Thessalonians, such as the insistence that God's character and the blessings God bestows include "grace" and "peace" (2 Thess 1:2; 3:16, 18).

It remains enticing to decide that 2 Thessalonians offers an overly stringent and thus irredeemably distorted picture of divine judgment. Those verdicts are understandable and maybe justified in some instances, yet they need to be made with care, especially when the interpreter who issues them resides very far away—in terms of time, place, material conditions, and recourse to political and legal power—from the historical situation of oppression and struggle that 2 Thessalonians assumes its original audience was enduring. For this is a letter that speaks particularly to people who belong to embattled and vulnerable communities. If the letter were focused *solely* on reveling in the idea of some people receiving their just deserts, that could be reasonable grounds for criticizing the letter's theological perspective and moral vision. But it is also true that 2 Thessalonians draws its energy from a conviction that the Christian gospel can reassure and dignify people who truly suffer because of their identification with Jesus Christ.

The Coming (Parousia) of the Lord and the Revealing (Apokalupsis) of "the Lawless One"

Second Thessalonians includes no mention of Jesus' death and resurrection. Much of the letter sets its sights instead on a future moment when he will be "revealed from heaven" (2 Thess 1:7) to vindicate the faithful, punish others, and destroy "the lawless one." No other biblical writing refers to a figure with that name (cf. Isa 57:3–4 in the Septuagint, which speaks of "lawless sons" and "lawless offspring"), making it difficult to say much about what or who the letter has in mind. The treatment of the lawless one assumes the letter's original audience would have had particular insights into the references to various forces and developments mentioned in 2 Thess 2:3–12; presumably original readers had received an orientation to those matters that permitted them to recognize more than modern interpreters can.

At the same time, 2 Thess 2:3–12 has spawned confusion and various proposals since ancient times. Some interpreters have equated the lawless one with the beast that figures in Rev 13:11–18 and with comments about "antichrist(s)" in the Johannine Letters (1 John 2:18, 22; 4:3; 2 John 7), but none of those texts provides a clear warrant for making such a simple, direct association. Others have heard in 2 Thess 2:4 faint echoes of the Old Testament's references to the king of Tyre in Ezek 28:1–10 and to Antiochus IV (Epiphanes) in Dan 11:21–45. If there are connections among those passages, they owe themselves to common rhetoric used for describing idolatrous rebellion against God. It is doubtful that 2 Thessalonians makes an attempt to identify a specific historical individual as a new manifestation of others, as if the lawless one indicates a particular tyrant from the past brought back to life or reproduced in a new ruler.

The letter draws attention to the lawless one not because it intends to offer instruction about him but because it aims to demonstrate that Christ's return cannot be imminent, at least not until the revealing—literally, "the apocalypse"—of that lawless figure has occurred. If 2 Thessalonians was in fact written near the end of the first century, then its comment about the lawless one sitting in the temple (2 Thess 2:4) might be a vague reference to the general Titus, representing the Roman Empire, who entered the Jerusalem temple just before the building's destruction in 70 CE. If so, then the letter could be a post-70 attempt to claim that Jesus' *parousia* was indeed near or nearer precisely at that point in time, since the ruinous Great Revolt had recently concluded. If that is the case, then 2 Thessalonians might represent an unknown ancient author's attempt to assert that Paul and his coworkers had stipulated the necessity for such a catastrophic event years previously, when Paul was still alive.

In the end, then, not much can be said with confidence about what exactly this letter expects concerning "the lawless one," "the mystery of lawlessness," and the means by which they are "revealed" in the ongoing drama of a world caught up in a cosmic struggle. Although the relevant verses are brief and relatively incoherent, on their surface they resonate with rhetoric from Jewish apocalyptic writings (e.g., 1 Enoch and 4 Ezra; cf. Jubilees) that describes rampaging evil coming before God's final victory at the initiation of the new age. The warnings in 2 Thessalonians about apostasy and lawlessness express a dualistic perspective on a world divided into the obedient and the disobedient, those guided by truth and those beset by lies. Those associations are relatively common fare in apocalyptic theology. While the rhetoric shows the influence of various streams from ancient Jewish traditions and theology, the main value for noting it is to see that its overarching testimony focuses on God's power and activity. Second Thessalonians may remain difficult to locate in a specific historical context, and its comments on specific future events and figures may remain obscure, but the book's resonances with apocalyptic themes remind interpreters to notice the overriding theological emphasis in the book and its future-oriented perspective. The letter's most enduring and obvious message lies in its assertions about God's just character and Christ's supremacy over the forces of evil and idolatry.

13

The Pastoral Letters
(1 Timothy, 2 Timothy, and Titus)

The Pastoral Letters—1 Timothy, 2 Timothy, and Titus—instruct Christian communities to nurture faithfulness among their leaders, urging those leaders to prize correct doctrine and resist rival teachings. To help churches maintain a culture of loyal devotion and good order that manifests the salvation Jesus provides, the letters offer their audiences a healthy dose of moral exhortation. They praise believers who imitate Paul's pattern of faithful living and perseverance and who remain committed to the truth that Paul taught. Repeatedly they tell their audiences about the inherent connections between sound doctrine and virtuous lifestyles; therefore, church leaders should guard the former and cultivate the latter.

As the Pastoral Letters make their case to their audiences, they frequently hold up Paul as the chief representative of a reliable and enduring tradition. The letters devote themselves to the importance of maintaining that tradition in the face of other options while teaching their audiences to arrange congregations' common life to meet the new and ongoing challenges they face. The letters therefore provide insights into how some ancient Christ-followers reacted to the prospect of changes in their midst—changes in leadership, changes in ways of understanding the nature of the gospel, and changes in views about how best to articulate the gospel through churches' organizational structures and shared values. In their attempts to guide ancient Christian communities through some of those changes brought on by the passing of time, one the Pastoral Letters' enduring contributions is their ability to prompt serious reflection on how churches understand their identity and calling in light of their existence within a wider cultural matrix. The letters especially raise the question of how a society's conventional mores might rightly or wrongly influence a Christian vision of what the church is and how Christian communities should conduct themselves.

Even though their messages are not identical, 1 Timothy, 2 Timothy, and Titus possess striking family resemblances. Even a cursory reading of the letters reveals that the documents belong together in some way. In fact, together the three books share more in common with each other than any single one of them does with the ten other letters that bear Paul's name. The striking correspondences among their style, vocabulary, and theological rhetoric infer that they share similar origins and purposes. Most indications suggest the letters were written by the same person at around the same time to speak to comparable circumstances in the life of one or more Christian congregations. All three Pastoral Letters articulate an author's attempts to draw from traditions and speak theologically to other Christ-followers during a discrete and apparently challenging period in the church's history.

For nearly three centuries, the name *Pastoral Letters* or *Pastoral Epistles* has been used to identify these letters as a distinct collection. The designation *pastoral* means to acknowledge that the three documents' primary stated purpose concerns the exercise of proper pastoral leadership. It does not imply that other letters associated with Paul do not speak in a pastoral voice or also pursue pastoral goals. Considering the three letters as a group has disadvantages, since of course each document has its own integrity and focus. For example, 2 Timothy, which presents Paul speaking to an audience as a man who believes he is about to die, reads differently and pursues different emphases, almost as if it aligns itself with a slightly different literary genre than 1 Timothy and Titus. But exploring the Pastoral Letters together as a trio has more than enough advantages to outweigh the cautions, especially when conducting an introductory analysis of the books.

The Letters' Origins and Ancient Audience

The letters directly address themselves to individual church leaders, Timothy and Titus, and not churches at large. Each document names its audience in fond terms, identifying Timothy or Titus as Paul's "loyal" or "beloved" "child." Those two men were eminent figures among Paul's trusted associates in ministry, according to the undisputed letters (Timothy in Rom 16:21; 1 Cor 4:17; 16:10; 2 Cor 1:1, 19; Phil 1:1; 2:19, 22; 1 Thess 3:2, 6; Phlm 1; Titus in 2 Cor 2:13; 7:6, 13–15; 8:6, 16–24; 12:18; Gal 2:1, 3). The Pastoral Letters speak to Paul's friends as they attempt to lead churches effectively and faithfully and to counter anyone who teaches contrary things to believers.

Even as they speak explicitly to two individual church leaders, the letters are not strictly personal in scope. In other words, they keep whole church communities in view. Several examples illustrate the letters' wider scope: Suffering, or the prospect of some undefined kind of suffering, appears to have been a consequence of living as a Christ-follower in the communities the letters have in mind; or, at least, believers in those settings feared suffering. The broader Christian fellowships that the letters have their eye on included a variety of members, men and women, young and old. Comments about proper attitudes toward wealth, about wealth's power to corrupt, and about generosity that promotes good works (e.g., 1 Tim 6:17–19) indicate that some in the audiences possessed considerable resources and maybe social capital. The presence of a few instructions concerning slaves' conduct suggests that a portion of the audiences was slaves, although the letters appear more interested in addressing and reassuring those Christ-followers who were the owners of the slaves.

Almost everything about these letters signals that their author expected them to influence larger communities and not just a pair or an otherwise small number of individual church leaders. The letters empower some groups within those communities and denigrate others. Each of the three writings ends with the same final word, a "you" that completes a concluding benediction. As a departure from the letters' consistent pattern of syntax and rhetoric directed toward a singular reader, each of those concluding occurrences of "you" is plural in its Greek form. That final syllable may offer a kind of concluding acknowledgment that the Pastoral Letters were meant for larger groups, as if at the end the author indicates that all along each letter was designed to instruct a wider community or communities. The letters address individuals, but they count on whole congregations to listen.

As mentioned, the communities that were the letters' original audiences appear to have been undergoing changes and were attempting to navigate their way through those changes' potential to affect churches' beliefs, values, and leadership structures. To say more about those audiences requires interpreters to consider what the letters reveal about their own origins, including their possible author and date of composition.

Based solely on what the documents state about their addressees, the letters were composed for Timothy, as he performed ministry in Ephesus (1 Tim 1:3), and Titus, in Crete (Titus 1:5). If so, then that would place the letters sometime late in Paul's lifetime and support assumptions that they were written by Paul or by a trusted associate with Paul's direct blessing. If the letters were in fact sent to Timothy and Titus, then the letters themselves are essentially the only sources for knowledge about those men's leadership of specific congregations in Ephesus and Crete.

The probability that these letters came from Paul or even from someone else who wrote before Paul died is extremely slim, however. If the letters were composed after Paul's death by someone writing in Paul's name—which, as will be discussed soon, is the much more likely scenario—then it remains difficult to determine exactly who the letters' intended audiences were. As pseudepigraphic writings, honoring or otherwise piggybacking on Paul's authority and reputation for faithful endurance and theological insight, each letter actually may have been directed to multiple audiences, and thus only ostensibly meant for Timothy and Titus. Given that the Pastoral Letters encourage readers to cling tightly to the traditions and teachings they have received while resisting new and different theological claims, the books' author might have distributed them to communities embroiled in divisive debates about doctrine and practices. Given that the letters' moral exhortations promote an idea that Christian communities should organize and order themselves in ways that resemble an upstanding and trustworthy Greco-Roman household, their author might have directed them to Christian groups in any number of areas throughout the Roman Empire, but probably outside of Palestine. The documents could have gone to churches where people had once known Timothy or Titus, or they could have been directed elsewhere. Many aspects of the Pastoral Letters' contents support the conclusion that they were written around 100 CE, long after Paul's death. A brief overview of the question of the books' authorship introduces the relevant evidence, even as the discussion also provides additional details about what the letters have to say.

The Question of Authorship

Because the Pastoral Letters share so many characteristics in common, debates about their authorship almost always consider them as a group. If one was written by Paul, surely all three were. If one is pseudepigraphic, then so were the other two.

The teachings expressed in the letters themselves raise the questions about their authorship and audiences, for these books express a theology that does not easily cohere with what the undisputed Pauline letters say. Although the differences are subtle and not patently contradictory, they are pervasive and noteworthy. For one thing, Paul's undisputed letters speak about the gospel and his ongoing preaching of the good news as providing people a means of participating with Christ in his death, resurrection, and glorification. "Faith" for Paul indicates not only a deep trust and reliance but also a means of connecting existentially with God's actions of defeating sin and bringing new life from death through Christ. When Paul's undisputed letters instruct Christian communities about how to live, those books' arguments proceed from theological convictions about what it means to embody the gospel and the sufferings of Jesus. By contrast, the Pastoral Letters often speak of "faith" without the same existential accent. Instead, faith comes across as an inheritance to preserve (e.g., 2 Tim 4:7; Titus 1:13; cf. 1 Tim 1:13–14; 6:20). These letters employ the expression *the faith* as an institutional identifier or a summary of correct doctrine, a heritage that a person should "keep" (e.g., 1 Tim 1:2, 19; 3:9; 4:1, 6; 5:8; 6:10, 12, 21; 2 Tim 4:7; Titus 1:4; cf. Col 1:23, 2:7; 2 Pet 1:1; Jude 3). For another example of differences, when the Pastoral Letters offer instructions about church order and practice, they do not construct theological rationales based on the work of God in Jesus Christ as much as they caution in general terms against corrupting influences and people.

In addition, some of the virtues commended and the vocabulary employed in the Pastoral Letters share affinities with Greco-Roman moral writings that address good behavior and the proper ordering of households and civil society. That phenomenon alone does not rule out Paul as the three letters' author, but it catches attention when an unusually high percentage of the vocabulary used in these books does not appear in the seven undisputed letters, which themselves manifest remarkable consistency in their vocabulary. Moreover, many of the virtues that the Pastoral Letters endorse, as well as the rationale behind those endorsements, are not discussed or are hardly discussed in the same way in the undisputed letters. Overall, the ethical rhetoric of the Pastoral Letters appears more at home in a moral thought world quite different from Paul's.

To cite another point of difference, 1 Timothy and Titus devote considerable attention to how a church should organize itself and choose its leaders. Those books prescribe moral qualifications for people who would serve in certain positions of leadership, including bishops, elders, and deacons. With the exception of one verse in a letter from relatively late in his life (Phil 1:1), Paul's undisputed letters never clearly use any of those terms to designate formal offices. Given the importance and presumed familiarity of those offices in the Pastoral Letters' discussions of church organization, these letters appear to come from a time significantly later than Paul's undisputed writings—a time in which church leadership had taken on a more systematized structure, at least in some settings.

Finally, the Pastoral Letters make references to Paul's travels (e.g., 1 Tim 1:3; 2 Tim 1:16–18; Titus 1:5), but the locations and attending circumstances mentioned do not fit into hypotheses about the overall itinerary and timeline of Paul's public ministry, whether those reconstructions of Paul's career draw from Acts, the undisputed letters, or both. For Paul to have visited the places named in the Pastoral Letters at certain points in his ministry, he would have had to have made voyages not mentioned elsewhere in the New Testament and even in contradiction to Acts, whose narrative strongly implies that Paul's arrival in Rome was his last stop in life before his martyrdom. The Pastoral Letters therefore apparently include various details about Paul's travels and relationships with other people (e.g., 2 Tim 4:9–15, Titus 3:12–13) that are fictional or the results of memories altered to construct a new and embellished narrative of Paul's ministry. Such creative embellishments were not unusual for pseudepigraphic letters, which express realistic but ultimately fictional or dramatized communications from start to finish. For those writings to be effective—whether in perpetuating a deception or in honoring a revered individual by inserting him and his voice into new circumstances—they needed to possess verisimilitude. By staging an imagined literary exchange between Paul and an audience whom an author thinks stands to benefit from Paul's example, legacy, and presumed insights, these letters introduce Paul's memory into new settings; they imagine an old Paul as if he is still present and active, speaking and shaping Christian ministry for a new day.

All of those observations about the books, cumulatively considered, contribute to a rather persuasive argument for reading the Pastoral Letters as pseudepigraphic writings. Their views on ecclesiastical offices, their efforts to combat certain currents of false teachings, and their use of vocabulary that resonates with material found in certain strains of Greco-Roman moralistic literature all support the hypothesis that these letters were written sometime near 100 CE.

The author of the Pastoral Letters, whose identity remains unknown, clearly held Paul in high regard, especially Paul's reputation for faithful endurance. Various claims about women and their inherent weaknesses (e.g., 1 Tim 2:8–15, 5:11–13; 2 Tim 3:6) give good reason to suppose the letters' actual author was a man. By citing material from Christian liturgies or hymns (e.g., 1 Tim 2:5–6a; 3:16; 2 Tim 2:11b–13), he indicates his familiarity with at least some streams of tradition in the church. The letters give more attention to those traditional materials than to Jewish Scriptures; nevertheless, a few references to Old Testament characters appear in the Pastoral Letters. The author's emphasis on perseverance, on the imperative to hold fast to received doctrine, and on the need for the church to uphold a moral reputation indicates his concern for how churches should position themselves to meet the challenges of surviving into new generations. Moral instructions in the letters betray a desire for communities of believers to embrace certain social norms and thus avoid offending outsiders, especially those in genteel circles of Greco-Roman society. Instead of dwelling much on the character of God and the new possibilities God creates through the gospel, the author's manner of articulating theology aimed to equip Christian communities with an understanding of who they were and how best to situate themselves within their cultural milieu without attracting disrepute or seeing their beliefs corrupted.

The Pastoral Letters serve as reminders that expressions of Christian faith unavoidably operate within a cultural context and an institutional history. To be meaningful and understandable, those expressions always draw from familiar traditions and interact with the social norms they encounter, embracing some, rejecting some, and reconfiguring others. The author of the Pastoral Letters attempted to guide those expressions of Christian faith so they would speak and embody a message about salvation in ways that certain people in the ancient world would have experienced as relevant and attractive. The letters therefore offer perpetual reminders that churches never exist separate from wider cultural values and means of expression. A question for interpreters to ponder is how and why the letters advocate certain priorities and forms of churches' existence over others.

Overview of 1 Timothy

First Timothy begins with a clear salutation (1 Tim 1:1–2), addressing the correspondence to Timothy, and ends with a couple of broad, final commands (1 Tim 6:20–21a) and a simple benediction (1 Tim 6:21b). In between, an exhortative vein runs throughout the letter's main body (1 Tim 1:3–6:19). There is no discrete, concluding section containing exhortations, as one finds in other Pauline letters. In addition, 1 Timothy, like Titus, departs from the familiar epistolary form in that it includes no thanksgiving, yet that omission appears not to reflect anger or frustration, as the absence of thanksgiving does in Galatians. By presenting itself as communication to probably the best-known of Paul's coworkers according to Acts and the undisputed letters, 1 Timothy implicitly claims itself to be an expression of Paul's legacy, a legacy that persists in those Christ-followers who, like Timothy, closely pattern their lives and ideas after Paul's example.

Right away, the letter's opening chapter commends ministry that consists of "instruction," and the author warns against "different doctrine." Correct teachings promote the vitality of what the letter calls "God's household management" in 1 Tim 1:4, which is a better translation than "divine training" (as in the NRSV). The image implies the church is a "household" (see 1 Tim 3:15; cf. 1 Pet 4:17) that, like ordinary households in Greco-Roman society, needs to order itself in a particular way to function well and carry out its God-ordained purposes. "The sound teaching that conforms to the glorious gospel" (1 Tim 1:10–11) resists disorderly and profane activities, insinuating that other, rival teachings encourage or permit those things.

The second chapter offers instructions concerning worship. It commends prayers on behalf of the governing authorities, which will contribute to Christ-followers' ability to "lead a quiet and peaceable life," promoting a friendly stance toward the Roman Empire and fostering the social respectability that this letter highly values. First Timothy values respectability not because the letter's author seeks the church's comfortable survival but because God desires the salvation of the world. The implied premise in this part of the letter's theological reasoning asserts that churches are best able to lead other people to know the truth about God when those churches present themselves to the societies they inhabit and the empire that governs them without giving cause for offense.

This letter's most notorious paragraph, 1 Tim 2:8–3:1a, turns from instructions about prayer to instructions about what women wear and how they should act. Most of the comments included in this paragraph reflect traditional values that were widespread, at least among the men who prized and disseminated them, in Greco-Roman culture. That culture expected virtuous women to exhibit modesty and submit to their husbands; for women to speak openly and publically would be to reveal too much of themselves. Upstanding Greco-Roman women were instead supposed to stay covered up in every way, concealing their flesh as well as their opinions. Those social mores corresponded to the domestic ordering or the underlying notion of "household management" that supposedly maintained society's ability to function well. The letter also endorses a foundational assumption that informed many of those social values: the belief that women easily fall victim to deceptions and false teachings. First Timothy offers a theological basis for that assumption with its peculiar summary of the Adam and Eve story from Genesis 2–3, a summary that essentially blames Eve for sin while exonerating Adam (cf. Rom 5:12–21).

When the letter turns to provide instructions about the church's overseers ("bishops") and helpers ("deacons"), its moral vision continues to align with values popular among many Greco-Roman moralistic thinkers. The virtues and behaviors that qualify men for those positions of church leadership correspond to what moralists commended among military leaders and heads of households. The Pastoral Letters give hardly any information about the practical duties and powers associated with churches' overseers and helpers, but a comment about a bishop's responsibility to "manage his own household" as he manages the church, itself "the household of God" (1 Tim 3:4–5, 15), suggests those men held significant authority over a congregation's life, just as the head of a household held primary, if not absolute, authority over his family's life and functions.

As the fourth chapter emphasizes Timothy's leadership in combating other teachings, it reveals that one of those deviant teachings involves an asceticism that denies the goodness of what God has created. Possibly the author was attempting to stem the influence of groups that equated God's salvation with an escape from the material world or the renunciation of its value. Such ideas neglect the reality of a Jesus who was "revealed in flesh" (1 Tim 3:16); they also could have made the church appear misanthropic and subversive in outsiders' eyes. In response to those aberrant beliefs, Timothy—and thus, by extension, all church leaders—should teach the foundations of "the faith" that he has followed to this point in his ministry. Furthermore, Timothy's manner of living should exhibit "godliness," love, faith, and purity to confirm the rightness of his teachings about God, "who is the Savior of all people" (1 Tim 4:10).

As the letter goes on to instruct Timothy about how to teach and superintend various groups in the church, the material resembles the household codes seen elsewhere in the New Testament (Eph 5:21–6:9, Col 3:18–4:1, 1 Pet 2:13–3:7). The references to widows indicate churches supported some who no longer had husbands or families to care for them. At the same time, the letter's classifications among different kinds of widows make distinctions about which women actually qualify for special treatment. First Timothy expresses concerns, then, about some women. Further remarks about the women who are idle and gossipers betray a general suspicion, common in Greco-Roman culture, about women's lack of self-control. In addition, instructions about "elders" who lead, preach, and teach, as well as directives meant to promote respectful submission among slaves, also align with standard Greco-Roman visions of an organized and respectable social microcosm. The author contends that churches' good works and conventional morality will prevent dishonor from falling upon God's name. The letter's outlook seems to indicate that churches should be caring communities, but people in those communities need to know what is expected of them.

Popular Greco-Roman moral discourse often associated correct teachings with upstanding behavior and characterized teachers who held differing views as people of flawed character. First Timothy likewise contrasts Timothy's conduct with the depravity and greed that the letter associates with contrary doctrines. As it moves toward its conclusion, the letter enjoins Timothy to persist, pursuing righteous behavior and remembering the "commandment" of his calling. Timothy's chief role, as a teacher and manager of the church's household, is to "guard what has been entrusted" to him (1 Tim 6:20; cf. 2 Tim 1:14).

Overview of 2 Timothy

Second Timothy follows the general form of letters from the Greco-Roman era, with a salutation (2 Tim 1:1–2) and a statement of thanksgiving (2 Tim 1:3–7) followed by the letter's main body (2 Tim 1:8–4:8), then brought to a close with final exhortations (2 Tim 4:9–15) and a conclusion with greetings and a benediction (2 Tim 4:16–22). With resemblance to 1 Timothy and Titus, 2 Timothy extols "godliness" (2 Tim 3:5, 12), "sound" doctrine (2 Tim 1:13, 4:3), and "good work" (2 Tim 2:21, 3:17). More pervasive, however, is this letter's focus on the pattern of faithfulness and trustworthiness Paul displayed in his ministry. The voice of Paul, contemplating the end of his life and ministry (2 Tim 4:6–8) while enduring incarceration (2 Tim 1:16, 2:9, 4:16), encourages Timothy to carry that ministry forward and resist those who teach other things. Only ostensibly speaking to Timothy, by extension the letter cautions whole communities against those who would lead them astray even as it commends faithfulness that exhibits itself in resolute endurance.

The letter begins with remembrance, looking back in time. Timothy's faith has deep roots in his grandmother's and mother's, and his gift for ministry stretches back to a commissioning he received from Paul. Timothy's faith and ministry therefore perpetuate things that are old and received; likewise, Timothy's endurance has the potential to uphold the faithful legacies of Paul and the influential women in Timothy's life, Lois and Eunice. Stretching back even further in time, Timothy's endurance reasserts "the faith and love that are in Christ Jesus" (2 Tim 1:13; cf. 1 Tim 1:14). What Timothy and the congregations he represents experienced is neither new nor unique; his own faith and ministry are rearticulations of his spiritual forebears' faith and ministry.

The early part of the letter exhorts Timothy to endure in multiple ways: through suffering without regard for the shame it brings, through persistence modeled by reliable people like Onesiphorus, and through entrusting Paul's teachings to others. The letter also asks Timothy to emulate the single-minded commitment and delayed gratification exemplified by soldiers, athletes, and farmers—three groups of stalwart contributors to Roman society's honor and well-being. Timothy's perseverance also takes its cue from Jesus, who always remains faithful to his people, according to what appears to be an early Christian hymn quoted in 2 Tim 2:11b–13.

When the letter turns to address specific aspects of Timothy's ministry, it commends instruction, exhortation, and steadfastness as central pieces of his duties. Timothy must explain "the word of truth" to others and avoid debates about false teachings (2 Tim 2:15). Second Timothy does not explain exactly which teachings qualify as false, but a quick mention of claims "that the resurrection has already taken place" identifies one (2 Tim 2:18). Probably some teachers who were poised to influence the letter's originally intended audiences downplayed or rejected the idea that believers would experience a future bodily resurrection. False teachers may assume a guise of godliness, the letter continues, but their veiled hypocrisy will shine through in the damage they inflict on those they deceive. Timothy should nevertheless engage the teachers with kindness, for he is a utensil meant to assist the work of God, a work that may cause even opponents to "repent and come to know the truth" (2 Tim 2:20–21, 25).

The letter reaches its rhetorical climax in 2 Tim 3:10–4:8, where it recalls Paul's experiences and example as one who endured persecution with poise and faithfulness. The rhetoric is motivational rather than instructional since it urges Timothy to persist with confidence in the things he has "learned and firmly believed" without explaining what those things are. Christ's future role as judge and the certainty of Paul's reward provide motivation for the charge that Paul conveys on Timothy: he should duplicate Paul's model by proclaiming, teaching, enduring hardship, and evangelizing. The letter punctuates that dramatic exhortation by referring to Paul's impending death. With the pathos supplied by words of a person expecting to die (2 Tim 4:6–8), the letter bears resemblance to Jewish testamentary literature, writings that depict a revered figure offering reflections on his life and instructions to family or friends who will succeed him (e.g., Gen 49:1–28, 1 Kgs 2:1–9, Acts 21:17–38, 2 Pet 1:12–15, and extrabiblical writings such as the Testaments of the Twelve Patriarchs).

The concluding commands and reports about those who deserted Paul add realism to the letter as a staged communication from Paul to Timothy. The commands reiterate the book's social perspective, for they speak about faith and ministry as shared things and not the possessions of individuals. The report of others' abandonment of Paul reiterates his legacy of one who remained faithful in all circumstances, as Timothy and other believers should.

Overview of Titus

The material and tone of Titus have much in common with 1 Timothy, especially when Titus warns against internal dissensions and commends both well-organized community and good works. The letter's basic form also resembles 1 Timothy in that both books devote so much attention to exhortation. There is no opening statement of thanksgiving. The salutation (Titus 1:1–4) immediately transitions into a series of instructions and exhortations (Titus 1:5–3:11). The book includes a few final commands (Titus 3:8b–11) followed by a conclusion with a benediction (Titus 3:12–15). Titus and 1 Timothy also have their differences, as some of the theological appeals in Titus proceed differently than what one finds in 1 Timothy.

Although Titus appears last of the three in the New Testament's ordering of the Pastoral Letters because it is shorter than 1 Timothy and 2 Timothy, it may have originally come first. There is no sure way of knowing when these letters were composed in relation to one another, but the first three verses of Titus, which introduce Paul with an extended description of his apostleship's theological purpose, may indicate that this letter once performed an introductory function. If the three letters originally circulated together, Titus could have set the stage for all of them. In any case, the salutation names several of the Pastoral Letters' most prominent theological themes: faith, knowledge, truth, godliness, revealing, and God's identity as Savior.

The opening chapter provides instructions about appointing older men ("elders," or presbyters) and overseers ("bishops"), noting that they contribute to silencing others who disseminate contrary teachings that disrupt households and that are tantamount to denying God. The letter assumes its audiences already know what exactly elders and bishops should do, for it gives attention instead to what virtues qualify a man to hold those positions (cf. 1 Tim 3:1b–7). Qualified men's stable family systems provide a contrast to other teachers who upend households (Titus 3:11). The letter also does not reveal the substance of the rival teachings the author had in mind, preferring instead to deprecate the character of those who teach them.

A series of exhortations appears in Titus 2:1–3:8a, telling Titus to encourage various groups—older men (or elders), older women, younger men, and slaves. The letter never names two additional groups mentioned in 1 Timothy: widows and helpers ("deacons"). The exhortations in Titus prize orderly living, in which each member of a Christian community performs appropriate roles, similar to how Greco-Roman moralists promoted a system in which each person in a household acted according to prescribed expectations. Some exhortations commend submission to civil authorities and warn against quarrels. The letter praises various behaviors as responses to God's salvation, not as the means of obtaining it. Honorable living provides "an ornament" (Titus 2:10); it is a way of life God makes possible, and it offers an appropriate illustration of God's grace. Moreover, Christian behavior manifests God's own "goodness and loving kindness," according to material in Titus 3:4–7, whose form suggests it was borrowed from an existing Christian liturgy or hymn.

As the letter moves toward its conclusion, exhortations become stronger, expressing a more unyielding attitude toward dissension that might erupt in Christian communities. Christ-followers should pursue good works and resist any people and teachings that create discord and disruptions. The image of leadership implied in the injunctions involves teaching and maintaining traditions, not entertaining theological debates. The letter makes no effort to explain or defend traditions associated with Paul's legacy; it merely assumes their value and correctness. The final reference to good works before the letter ends underscores the whole book's primary concern: to assert that believers' manner of living must manifest the virtues associated with the salvation God provides.

The Letters' Themes and Theological Emphases

A careful reading of the Pastoral Letters reveals evidence of church communities becoming more institutionalized than they were earlier in the first century. Having survived one or more generational transitions after original and older members died or left, those communities apparently developed internal organizational and doctrinal structures and a sense of their own identity that helped them maintain an understanding of their purpose. According to the Pastoral Letters, those communities' doctrinal foundations and organizational structures equipped them to persist as living representations of God's salvation as they awaited Jesus' return at a future and unknown time. It appears that, as such churches became more institutionalized, they confronted the question of whether or how their established traditions should inform responses to new circumstances and new ideas. In other words,

Christian communities had to determine whether and then how to adapt as they developed their institutional qualities. To speak of the gradual "institutionalization" of the church therefore also refers to how Christian communities developed ingrained cultures within themselves to regulate their understanding of their relationship to the wider society. Understanding that relationship, in any generation, involves considering what connects a Christian community to conventional social values and what differentiates a community from those values. No church can consider its identity and purpose in utter isolation from the setting in which it sits. Churches always assimilate, resist, change, and are changed. The Pastoral Letters provoke reflections on how and why churches do so in particular ways.

To oversimplify the matter, the Pastoral Letters show ways in which at least one stream of the ancient Christian movement, positioned at the junction between the first and second centuries, advocated more connection than differentiation in relation to dominant social values. On one hand, the letters embrace a commitment to extending Paul's influence and preserving memories associated with the apostle. On the other hand, they express that commitment with an effort to see churches exist in relative harmony with values promoted within their wider cultural context, especially values about hierarchical organization and respectable behavior. Exploring how and why these letters commend certain virtues provides a valuable case study in considering the challenges that any Christian community faces when it determines how to express the gospel in an understandable and compelling fashion within a specific context. Insofar as these letters insist that churches should view their values and their common life as ways of expressing God's salvation, the letters represent a form of thinking theologically. The issue remains, however, how to determine when certain values or structures actually end up distorting that salvation instead of promoting it.

Households, Godliness, and Order

The expressions *God's household management* (employing *oikonomia* in Greek, rendered "divine training" in the NRSV) and *household of God* (employing *oikos* in Greek, a word the NRSV sometimes translates as "family"; see also 1 Tim 3:4, 12; 5:4; Titus 1:11) offer important clues to the Pastoral Letters' strong focus on family structures and the church's orderly organization, particularly as seen in 1 Timothy and Titus. The two expressions appear only in 1 Tim 1:4 and 3:15, respectively, which is hardly frequently. Nevertheless, they give insight into concepts that guide the letters as they speak about Christian communities and households. In the Greco-Roman world, households were key social building blocks. Usually controlled by a male head of household and comprising extended family members, slaves, and even clients, households were primary economic units. Some ancient writers argued that households mirrored Roman society as a whole as microsocieties governed by a hierarchical structure in which all members had roles assigned to them appropriate to their status with respect to the head of the household. A well-organized household hierarchy encapsulated virtues that Romans, especially those with privilege, widely praised.

First Timothy and Titus view a church community as such a household, one constructed with God at the pinnacle of its identity. Mirroring values common in the dominant culture, these letters imply the church should function as a society regulated by God, a society made possible through God's salvation. The two letters do not offer much of a theological argument for that position. They do not root it specifically in, for example, reflections on Jesus' nature, his obedience, or aspects of his life, death, and resurrection. Rather, the letters mostly equate certain conventional values and concerns for orderliness with the idea of the reliable and durable existence of a household under God's leadership. The statements these letters therefore offer concerning women, bishops, slaves, and others would have surprised few ancient audiences. The ethical assumptions on which the instructions stand were rather common. The hierarchy the letters commend largely endorses ancient notions of propriety. Likewise, a good deal of the letters' legacy throughout the church's history has been to sustain and reinforce hierarchical systems and the advantages those systems afford to the people nearest the top of a social pyramid.

The hierarchical leadership these letters prescribe is not without any theological basis, however. All three Pastoral Letters speak of "godliness" (sometimes rendered as "duty" or "religion" in published translations) that manifests itself in the teachings and pattern of life that Paul bequeaths to his successors. The "godliness" that the church's organization promotes is not synonymous with the notion of holiness or sanctification seen in other biblical writings. The term, which also appears in a variety of Greek philosophical writings, connotes a sense of devotion and loyalty to God. When the letters instruct Timothy and

Titus to pursue and promote godliness, they charge church leaders not merely to pursue an ethical vision but to shape churches to make them align with the kind of living the author believes will express a key point of the Christian message: God intends to bring salvation to all (e.g., Titus 2:11–13).

The author of these letters expresses concern about the church's reputation and issues warnings about God's name and work suffering dishonor if his audiences do not heed his instructions (e.g., 1 Tim 5:7, 14; 6:1; Titus 2:5). Interpreters can only speculate about the motives behind the author's advocacy for Christian communities whose structure and conduct will earn outsiders' respect. Likely the social values and hierarchies he commends were merely those that seemed most self-evident to him, given how his culture had formed him. Perhaps he sought to make the Christian movement more attractive to wealthy or high-status Romans who would not be eager to join a movement that asked them to surrender the privileges they already enjoyed in a hierarchical social milieu. It is conceivable that he knew of Christian communities that were suffering or had recently suffered castigation or exclusion from the dominant society, maybe because others perceived them as not supportive enough toward Roman values and rituals. In that case, the author might have used the letters to encourage churches to conform more closely to conventional social expectations as an attempt to ensure the church's long-term survival. Perhaps, in particular, the author was concerned that other forms of Christian teaching and practice were certain to offend those outside the church and thus precipitate trouble. A church cannot communicate the good news if it has ceased to exist, or if all of its neighbors have ceased watching and listening. That reality might have especially worried the author if he feared the other teachings that would fill the void left by a church that had been unable to perpetuate Paul's teachings for future generations. In other words, perhaps aligning churches with conventional Roman social values seemed to him like the safest option. No one knows for sure.

The Threat of False Teachings

There may have been a number of teachings that the letters' author considered false, pernicious, and also potentially offensive to those outside the church. It is difficult to identify the specific doctrines he had in mind, for he warns against them without describing them. Some appear to involve debates over circumcision (Titus 1:10) and what the author calls "Jewish myths" (Titus 1:14). A warning about people who claim that the general resurrection "has already taken place" (2 Tim 2:18) may be similar to the teaching that 2 Thessalonians attempts to refute, or it may indicate a movement that rejects the possibility or the relevance of any future bodily resurrection. If the latter, then 2 Tim 2:18 would be one of multiple voices in the New Testament that criticize beliefs and practices associated with currents that came to influence gnostic thought, specifically currents that associated salvation with a freedom from the constraints of material existence. For example, the author cautions that some deviant teachers advocate abstaining from marriage and certain foods, which could also indicate gnostic tenets (1 Tim 4:1–5). Warnings against debates over myths and genealogies (1 Tim 1:4; Titus 3:9) could refer to gnostic narratives about cosmology and specially enlightened individuals. Perhaps most telling, 1 Timothy warns, "Avoid the profane chatter and contradictions of what is falsely called knowledge [Greek, *gnōsis*]; by professing it some have missed the mark as regards the faith" (1 Tim 6:20b–21a). These letters thus provide evidence of opposition growing in some Christian circles against patterns of thinking that would blossom into the more recognizable and widely influential gnostic movements of the mid-second century.

Ascetic practices (1 Tim 4:1–5), whether rooted in gnostic claims or not, might have potentially caused offense to people who witnessed them from outside of a Christian community. The letters include an implicit theological rationale to discredit those practices, seen in the appeals to the incarnation of Jesus (1 Tim 3:16; cf. 2 Tim 1:9) and the goodness of God's creation (1 Tim 4:4–5). The author also accuses false teachers of bad morals (e.g., 2 Tim 3:1–9). As did others in the early Christian movement, he employs both doctrinal and ethical arguments in the struggle against teachings he considered mendacious. The Pastoral Letters warn that unsound teachers' moral depravity will be infectious and deeply disruptive, for those people have the potential to infiltrate and corrupt households (2 Tim 3:6; Titus 1:11; cf. 2 Tim 2:18). In response, and to defend against future threats, the letters' audiences should not be drawn into debates or offer their own fresh ways of articulating the teachings on which they have always relied. Rather, they must preserve the doctrinal, ethical, and pastoral inheritance they originally received from Paul, as symbolized by Paul's trusted successors, Timothy and Titus.

Perspectives on Women and Leadership

The Pastoral Letters describe church leadership—at least the offices of bishop, elder, and deacon—as the exclusive province of men. There is one possible exception: the ambiguous comments about "women" and "older women" who are discussed in conjunction with deacons and said to teach and encourage other women (1 Tim 3:11; Titus 2:3–5). The letters' embrace of what looks like an entirely male leadership structure appears to be a departure from the apostle Paul's own practices and values, for in some of the undisputed letters he names and commends specific women engaged in public leadership within Christian communities. The departure reflected in the Pastoral Letters eventually became the norm, for in the second century, churches' leadership structures increasingly reserved formal leadership positions for men. The letters give evidence of that development even as they bear responsibility for promoting it. While a male-dominated organizational structure remained the standard for most streams of Christianity throughout the church's history, recent generations have seen significant changes in some quarters of the church, where women now occupy leadership positions and perform roles that were formerly denied them. For many modern Christians, that development requires a hard look at the Pastoral Letters and the books' history of interpretation to try to understand these writings' assumptions about women and leadership in light of the ancient setting.

Many factors contributed to the relegation of women to less visible roles in the ancient church. The desire to replicate household hierarchies in church communities, as expressed in 1 Timothy and Titus, was one of the causes. At the same time, that desire alone does not explain the Pastoral Letters' partiality against women as visible leaders. Not every Greco-Roman household was led by a man, and so a household structure did not have to entail a patriarchal structure. Furthermore, women exercised public leadership in the worship and cultic life of other religious groups. Although it was relatively uncommon in most cultural settings, there would have been nothing *necessarily* or *universally* scandalous about Christian communities allowing women to hold recognizable authority. Ancient churches therefore had opportunity to adopt other traditions, values, and structures concerning their leadership, had they wished to do so. The rationale behind the Pastoral Letters' perspective on leadership probably was complex and rooted in more than just an inalterable reflex to extend an inherited patriarchy. Several assumptions in the Pastoral Letters reveal additional reasons why some in the early church might have thought it wise to organize church leadership in such an exclusionary manner.

By restricting women's roles in public worship and leadership structures to conform with particular household norms, the letters' author appears to be attempting to stem the influence of certain women who had been swayed by other teachers (e.g., 2 Tim 3:6–7). Perhaps the author even knew of women who were active leaders among those rival groups. Those women might have provided convenient fuel for rumors or for smear campaigns within churches aligned with the Pastoral Letters' perspective. Such female leaders might also have contributed to situations that the author associates with behaviors that he considers inappropriate or liable to invite disgrace (e.g., 1 Tim 2:8–3:1a; 5:13–15; Titus 2:3–5), although there is no good way to test that proposal.

Untangling the author's motives or prejudices is finally impossible. He may have written these letters out of a deep desire to help embattled congregations or out of an attempt to hoard power for some people—men—at the expense of others. Also impossible to determine are the specific circumstances the author was addressing. Whether he was intending to protect women he considered vulnerable to the deceptive allure of false teachings or he was reacting against women who were disseminating those teachings, he nevertheless makes his case by insinuating that women are naturally disposed to be overrun by their passions or led astray by manipulators and charlatans (2 Tim 3:6–7; cf. 1 Tim 5:13–15).

As strange or misogynistic as those claims justifiably sound to most modern ears, the author was not alone in his beliefs about women. Other ancient writers held that women were naturally vulnerable to falsehoods; they claimed a woman's anatomy mirrored or contributed to her impressionable mind. Construing a woman's sexuality as a passively penetrable partner, many argued that a female body could not resist the infiltration of others' ideas. As one first-century author put it, "Because of [a woman's physical] softness she easily gives way and is taken in by plausible falsehoods which resemble the truth" (Philo, *Questions and Answers on Genesis* 1.33). That general belief provides context for understanding, although not for justifying, the blame assigned to Eve in 1 Timothy's odd summary of Genesis 2–3 (1 Tim 2:13–14). Of course, the author of 1 Timothy might instead have drawn explicit theological inspiration from Gen 1:27 and its statement about men and women together bearing God's image or from the Pauline assertion that in Christ "there is no longer male and female" (Gal 3:28). But he apparently did not. Ancient assumptions about women help explain 1 Timothy's assumptions, but they do not excuse the author from discounting other ways in which ancient theological traditions available to him viewed women, their value, and their abilities in a more positive or egalitarian light.

Understanding the cultural soils that fed the Pastoral Letters' perspectives on women's vulnerability, conduct, and roles illuminates how ordinary and acceptable those teachings might have appeared—at least to some people—in the ancient setting. When modern church leaders appeal to these books as a timeless warrant for excluding women from public ministry and for characterizing women as intellectually inferior to men, they do more than simply recite a biblical text. They also tacitly reaffirm the same kinds of ancient sociological and physiological assumptions that informed the letters' author. Those interpretations essentially assert that the Pastoral Letters communicate permanent, transhistorical realities about the nature of men and women and about how the two groups relate to one another. The problematic nature of such an interpretive move is clear to many.

Conversely, interpreters who recognize how the author relied on ancient cultural values to inform the books' statements about the ways in which Christian faith should be articulated and practiced can and should justifiably criticize those ancient perspectives on women. It takes little effort to see those perspectives as outdated, insidious, and thus hardly warranting the label *normative*. Because the letters depend so much on those moribund assumptions, the letters' perspectives on women can be considered either a forgettable chapter in the church's history, a gross mistake to grieve and from which to learn, or an ancient Christian author's naïve willingness to endorse systems of patriarchal power, among other possibilities.

The issues for modern interpreters to confront extend beyond trying to discern the mind-set of the letters' author. Interpreters must also explore the effects of these documents, or the books' ongoing capacity to contribute to or detract from people's understanding of what finally gives definitive shape to expressions of Christian faith. Interpreters also do well to explore how *any* interpretation involves presuppositions and prejudices. They are wise to recognize that all interpretations of texts, just like all expressions of Christian faith, involve interactions with contemporary values—values that change from time to time and place to place. Honest interpreters need to demonstrate that other biblical texts, interpreters' cultural presuppositions, and interpreters' convictions about the nature of human beings provide a reasonable and just basis for criticizing, reshaping, or discarding any of the Pastoral Letters' assertions about leadership, women, and men. Those who only ignore or mock these books and their antiquated vision of "household management" short-circuit the opportunity to learn from how the Pastoral Letters arrive at their theological and ethical conclusions. Interpreters need to consider how the letters' perspectives on women and their leadership have made a significant—and mostly regrettable—impact on Christianity's development and reputation.

Jesus Christ's Epiphanies and God's Salvation

References to Jesus Christ's previous and future appearances contribute to a key theme in the Pastoral Letters' distinctive theological vocabulary. When these letters describe Jesus' "appearing," they use forms of the Greek word *epiphaneia*, the root of the English word *epiphany* (1 Tim 6:14; 2 Tim 1:10; 4:1, 8; Titus 2:11–13; 3:4; cf. 1 Tim 3:16; Titus 1:3). Ancient Greek speakers understood that familiar word as indicating a manifestation of a deity through a physical appearance, divine activity, or oracles offered by a god or goddess' representative. Since an epiphany implied the transit of a deity into the sphere of human experience, it meant a special event. An epiphany offered clarity of vision—the ability to perceive the divine in the midst of normal circumstances that usually permit no such thing. In several places the Pastoral Letters suggest that the salvation wrought by Jesus' original epiphany in the past belongs to the whole world (e.g., 1 Tim 4:10; Titus 2:11; cf. 2 Tim 1:10, 2:10). As a result, even if people have not yet seen the manifestations of God's salvation, this salvation will nevertheless benefit them.

Jesus' original appearance was an epiphany, as will be his future return. With that language the Pastoral Letters express an incarnational theology, treating Jesus' entire life as God's appearance. That life, as Titus presents it by citing a liturgical formula in Titus 3:4–7, expressed "the goodness and loving kindness of God our Savior." The terms *goodness* and *loving kindness* were a familiar couplet in Greek literature, in writings from both Jewish and gentile circles, which employed such language to describe divine actions toward humanity and virtuous conduct among human beings. The Pastoral Letters imply that as believers live in the interim between Jesus' two epiphanies, fulfilling their charge to produce "good works," they express those same generous qualities among themselves and toward outsiders (Titus 3:8). Like many other New Testament writings, the Pastoral Letters urge audiences to make God's salvation visible in how they conduct themselves and arrange their common life. For those writings, being a Christ-follower involves, in part, how a Christian community presents itself to the wider world. According to the Pastoral Letters, God set a precedent for doing precisely that by having become manifest to the world in person, in Jesus Christ.

14

The Letter of Paul to Philemon

Philemon, by far the shortest and most personal of Paul's surviving letters, offers a compelling look at certain challenges that arise when people's identity as Christ-followers obligates them to act in ways that conflict with established and seemingly inalterable social norms. The letter speaks to a deliberation taking place concerning how God's work through Jesus Christ has real effects on how believers should view and relate to one another. Paul writes to convince his friend and coworker, Philemon, that the gospel demands transformations in how he must treat another believer, specifically a man named Onesimus, who evidently was Philemon's slave. Because Philemon and his slave share a new identity as brothers in Christ, their relationship should no longer conform to typical expectations concerning masters and slaves. The letter shows that such a monumental change was perhaps easier said than done.

Given that slavery was such a constitutive and prominent part of Greco-Roman socioeconomic life, Paul's rhetoric and Philemon's decision involve more than a choice about whether a certain master should choose to show generosity toward an individual slave. Larger cultural assumptions and systemic realities also were in play when Philemon read and weighed Paul's letter. Swirling beneath the surface of this document are questions about whether believers' faith in Jesus sometimes provokes them to resist or reshape core cultural and economic institutions. Paul does not state the matter so bluntly, but anyone in his ancient social context would have recognized instantly how complicated and volatile it could be to talk about altering the conventional relationship between a master and a slave.

Paul appears to recognize that his letter walks into potentially explosive territory, for he proceeds very cautiously. Instead of directly commanding Philemon, he gives occasionally equivocal instructions. Paul also speaks with two slightly different voices. On one hand, the letter notes his position of honor and authority, for he claims he has the standing, probably by virtue of his identity as an apostle, to command Philemon if he chooses (Phlm 8). Paul also mentions that Philemon owes Paul his "own self" (Phlm 19), maybe a reference to Paul's having introduced Philemon to the good news about Jesus Christ. On the other hand, Paul forthrightly notes that he writes while held in custody as a prisoner, a status that could confer shame on him and on those who claimed too close an association with him. Depending on the conditions of his incarceration, his vulnerability as a prisoner might have allowed others to discount his opinions, should they be inclined to do so. Paul nevertheless makes his case without expecting that either authority, pathos, or even a strong ethical argument will carry the day. More than anything else, Paul's theological rhetoric aims to persuade Philemon, for the apostle's letter deftly appeals to the kind of new communal realities into which Christ brings believers. Although the letter is brief and its specific goals difficult to decipher, Paul nevertheless makes it clear that he seeks to see Philemon set Onesimus' life on a whole new course, as would be appropriate to who those two men truly are as Christ-followers—brothers.

The Letter's Origins and Ancient Audience

The letter proceeds as if it is essentially a piece of correspondence from one individual to another, even though Paul formally indicates multiple authors and addressees. The document itself claims to have two authors, Paul and Timothy, yet it speaks to its audience almost entirely in a first-person singular voice. That syntax, along with the letter's general stylistic resemblances to other undisputed letters, indicates Paul wrote or dictated Philemon. In addition, even though the letter's traditional title implies Paul wrote to only one person, a man named Philemon, the salutation directs Paul's words to others as well: Apphia, Archippus, and the church affiliated with Philemon's "house." At the same time, with the exception of only a few phrases (Phlm 3, 22b, 25), the letter's Greek syntax consistently addresses a singular "you"—Paul's friend Philemon.

Paul, who refers to himself in this letter as an elder or an aged man, probably sent this correspondence to Philemon sometime in the mid- or late 50s CE, around the same time he wrote Romans and Philippians. The salutation suggests that Philemon was the head of a household with enough prosperity to host or sponsor a house church and, as becomes clearer as the letter progresses, a household wealthy and large enough to own slaves. Apphia, who is addressed immediately after Philemon, may have been his wife, mother, or sister. Archippus may have been his son or brother. Because the final chapter of Colossians includes a command to an Archippus and mentions other names that also appear in Philemon—Onesimus, Epaphras, Mark, Aristarchus, Demas, and Luke—it is possible that this man named Philemon resided in or was reputed to have connections to Colossae, a city in the southwestern part of Asia Minor. Beyond those minor details and additional information that this letter from Paul reveals, nothing else is known about Philemon and his family.

Philemon was no stranger to Paul, for the apostle expresses great affection for Philemon, referring to him as beloved (or "a friend"), a coworker, a brother, and a partner. Paul praises Philemon's faith and his reputation for loving and encouraging fellow "saints" in the church. He also writes to Philemon concerning Onesimus, a man Paul met during his incarceration. Paul notes that Onesimus had been "separated from" Philemon for a time, and the letter expresses Paul's hope that Philemon will welcome Onesimus back "no longer as a slave" but as "a beloved brother" (Phlm 15–16). The letter was meant to allow Paul to speak on Onesimus' behalf when he returned, appealing to Philemon to receive Onesimus graciously, according to the new relationships God creates through Christ—to treat him as a member of the family and not as a household slave.

Reading between the letter's lines allows interpreters to tease out what might have been the specific circumstances that prompted Paul to write to Philemon. The letter suggests this basic scenario: an incarcerated Paul sent a slave who had recently become a Christ-follower back to his owner, who also was a believer. Exactly how and why Onesimus might have left his master in the first place remains a more contested question. Some interpreters suspect that Philemon sent Onesimus to Paul to care for him during his incarceration. The letter's rhetoric, however, gives stronger support to a view that Onesimus had not been authorized to leave his owner's household. He might have fled and been seeking a slim chance at freedom when he fortuitously encountered Paul, or he might left Philemon's household specifically to search for Paul, his master's friend, so he could complain to a trustworthy figure about Philemon's severity.

Whether Onesimus originally intended to escape Philemon for good or only temporarily until he could enlist Paul's advocacy, he could have expected serious consequences for departing from his master. For Paul, therefore, it would have been a delicate and controversial thing to ask a man to receive back his wayward slave—his property—with anything other than punishment, scorn, violence, and perhaps death. Against those prevailing currents, however, Paul slickly contends for other options, for God has created new identities and new possibilities for Onesimus and Philemon alike. In Christ, the men have become brothers. They should therefore live like it. Significant changes would therefore have to occur.

Overview

Salutation and Thanksgiving (Phlm 1–7)

The terms Paul uses in his salutation to name his audience are so familiar from his rhetoric that some interpreters might easily fail to notice them. Nevertheless, his identifiers set the tone for what will follow in this letter about families and partnerships: Timothy the brother, Philemon the beloved and coworker, Apphia the sister, Archippus the cosoldier, God the Father, and Jesus Christ the Lord. Paul's terms evoke images of a theological household composed of people related to one another, with God as the Father. The family has work to carry out, requiring workers and soldiers. It does this work not for its own sake or simply to promote its own survival, for Jesus is its Lord and master.

The rest of the letter directs its communication to Philemon nearly exclusively, but nevertheless, the mention at the outset of Apphia, Archippus, and their local church provides a subtle reminder that Philemon does not exist as a lone individual but as part of a community, one that might be figuratively looking over his shoulder as he reads this letter and weighs how he will respond to what Paul asks him to do. For his part, Philemon enjoys renown in the community. His home provides a setting for believers to gather. He is not only the church's patron but also one of its leaders insofar as he invigorates others in the church, showing love to "all the saints."

As for Paul, he writes as a prisoner, a fact he hardly tries to hide (see also Phlm 9, 10, 13, 23). Not every city in the Roman Empire had prisons, understood as dedicated buildings with cells and guards. Those that did often did not employ them for long-term punishment of sentenced criminals but for holding prisoners awaiting trial, judgment, or execution. Most likely Paul was held somewhere in a government or a military building or was confined to house arrest as he waited for a case against him to go forward or for local officials' anger and apprehensiveness to subside. He does not reveal how long his current term of incarceration has lasted or where he is. Although he expects to secure his freedom (Phlm 22), it is not known if or when that happened.

Appeal on Behalf of Onesimus (Phlm 8–16)

When Paul speaks explicitly about making an "appeal," he reveals the main purpose for writing the letter. Clearly his appeal is on Onesimus' behalf, but Paul never states exactly what he wants Philemon to do, preferring to leave that unstated. It is up to each reader to judge whether the elliptical nature of Paul's appeal stems from timidity, diplomacy, neglect, subtle encouragement, or a savvy intention to allow Philemon to receive full credit for his actions with regard to Onesimus. Some interpreters fault Paul for not speaking frankly to Philemon, a man who holds complete power over Onesimus. At the same time, if Paul trusts Philemon and knows his character well, as the letter suggests, then it is more likely that Paul wants and counts on Philemon to make what Paul believes to be the appropriate decision—or a voluntary "good deed" (Phlm 14)—regarding Onesimus. The rest of the letter offers inklings about what Paul considers the appropriate response for Philemon to make.

The name *Onesimus* means "useful" or "beneficial," so Paul employs a pun when he says Onesimus was formerly useless to Philemon but now both Paul and Philemon see him as a benefit. Although Paul does not identify him as a slave until Phlm 16, Onesimus' name on its own may be telling. The name was appropriate for a slave, for most slaves in the Roman Empire had no legal identities or families of their own but were essentially valued only for the services they could provide.

A slave's body was a master's asset, a resource. The sheer fact of Onesimus' name implies others determined his value based on his functions and not his fundamental humanity. Paul, however, declares Onesimus' value as his son and as Philemon's brother.

Paul expresses great fondness for the man, calling him "my own heart," identifying Onesimus as an expression of Paul's deepest capacity for compassion. Paul wonders aloud about the advantages of letting Onesimus remain with him to support him in his advanced age as he remains in his "imprisonment for the gospel." When Paul refers to himself as "father" to his "child" Onesimus, he indicates that he has introduced Onesimus to the gospel of Jesus Christ (cf. 1 Cor 4:15, Gal 4:19) or has done much to guide Onesimus further in his discipleship as a Christ-follower (cf. 1 Thess 2:11–12). Whether Onesimus himself was incarcerated concurrently with Paul, perhaps due to his being apprehended as a runaway slave or for some other infraction, Paul does not say. In any case, the letter is more concerned with what will happen to Onesimus in the future, when he returns to his owner.

Paul wants Philemon to receive Onesimus "no longer as a slave" but as something more: "a beloved brother." Paul's minimal language about how to receive Onesimus could entail a variety of possibilities for Philemon, including relinquishing his prerogative to punish or kill his slave if Onesimus had indeed fled, keeping Onesimus as a slave but treating him uncommonly well, releasing him from slavery, and considering Onesimus as now a full member of Philemon's family whether he persists as a slave or not. Some of Paul's subsequent exhortations suggest that Paul expects Philemon to display incredible generosity, much more than one could ordinarily expect a freeperson in that culture to show to a slave.

Exhortations about Receiving Onesimus (Phlm 17–22)

Paul exhorts Philemon to welcome Onesimus as if the returning slave was Paul himself—a very tall request. Paul offers to settle any outstanding debts Onesimus may have incurred; perhaps he had stolen from Philemon or found himself in slavery in the first place because of money he or his relatives owed. Paul frames Philemon's opportunity as a chance for him to serve and encourage Paul, allowing Philemon to do for Paul the same thing Philemon has done for other saints (cf. Phlm 7, 20). Expressing confidence in Philemon, Paul exhorts him to "do even more" than Paul requests. Finally, Paul announces that he expects to visit Philemon and his household soon, once he gains his release. The announcement communicates more than a casual statement about travel plans, for Paul implies that Philemon will have to reckon with him in person if his written appeal concerning Onesimus has not been properly heeded.

Conclusion and Benediction (Phlm 23–25)

When Paul includes greetings from other "fellow workers," he again acknowledges the wider communal or familial character of those who are in Christ. Both Paul and Philemon represent larger communities. Therefore, the question of how Philemon should treat Onesimus, who has become his brother in Christ, matters not only for those two men but also for the wider Christian spiritual family of which they are a part, as people with a shared identity rooted in their shared participation in Christ.

The Letter's Themes and Theological Emphases

Paul, Slavery, and Living in Response to the Gospel

Because Paul does not offer clear, unmistakable instructions about his expectations for Philemon's reception of Onesimus, about whether welcoming Onesimus as "a beloved brother" should bring an end to his status as a slave, interpretations of the letter over the centuries have hardly agreed about how it speaks to the practice of slavery in the Roman world and beyond. The disagreements have not prevented many from turning to Philemon to ask how it should inform Christians' views on slavery, however. For much of the church's history, interpreters tended to refer to the letter to extol the benefits of a supposedly compassionate model of slavery dressed in Christian garb, as if Christian slave owners somehow rendered slavery beneficial to slaves. In nineteenth-century America, both abolitionists and proslavery advocates alike appealed to Philemon to claim biblical support for their respective causes. All of those interpretations of the letter may reveal more about the interpreters and their opinions of slavery and the worth of enslaved peoples than they reveal about Paul's conviction about what the gospel demanded from Philemon at a moment in time two thousand years ago.

The complicating factor in the discussion resides in an important consideration: it is difficult to say that this letter to Philemon communicates anything approaching a comprehensive account of Paul's views on slavery in a general sense. The specific, unique conditions concerning Paul, Onesimus, and Philemon; the relationships those men shared with one another; and the very personal nature of this correspondence make it difficult to contend that Paul used his letter to make known either an endorsement or a repudiation of slavery as it was practiced in the Greco-Roman world. Even if Paul cared deeply about Onesimus and wanted him to enjoy his God-given dignity, that does not necessarily translate into Paul having concern for other slaves, whether those in Philemon's household or anywhere else in the empire.

The relative absence of comments about slavery in Paul's undisputed letters, letters written to Christian communities that surely included slave owners and slaves, seems to indicate that Paul gave little thought to issuing value judgments on slavery as it existed in the Roman world. In one instance, for example, he shows scant interest in considering any other option for slaves beyond their need to endure their condition (1 Cor 7:21–24; cf. Eph 6:5–9; Col 3:22–4:1; 1 Pet 2:18–25). Since slavery was so deeply ingrained as a given or necessary aspect of his culture, perhaps Paul never even thought about the prospect of targeting it for explicit criticism or approval; from Paul's perspective, slavery simply *was*. At the same time, the letter to Philemon does reveal something about how Paul regarded Christian community and the transformative implications of the gospel he preached. His perspectives on those theological issues might be said to apply to slavery in a general sense, just as they can inform Christian deliberations about many other types of interpersonal relationships and the challenges of negotiating constellations of power.

In Philemon Paul does the same basic thing he does in his other letters: he offers theological rationales to guide Christ-followers in their efforts to live in ways that are commensurate with the gospel of Jesus Christ. He helps others comprehend what God has done and then urges his audience to live in ways that respond appropriately and express the good news of God's gracious work. In this particular letter, Paul obviously attempts to dissuade Philemon from inflicting the harsh treatment that Roman law and social customs would allow or even encourage if Onesimus had indeed fled or been otherwise disobedient. Paul's primary theological point contends that since Onesimus is

Philemon's brother in Christ, that new spiritual reality requires Philemon to express their filial relationship also as a new social, lived reality.

But living out that new relationship may have been more difficult to accomplish than it sounds. What Paul may have desired about seeing Onesimus treated well had the potential to disrupt a variety of expectations. Paul undoubtedly knew that if Philemon were to free Onesimus, the act could make both the former master and the former slave very vulnerable. At some times and in some places in the Roman Empire, adopting slaves into one's own family was not legal. Other influential slave-owning families would certainly not appreciate Philemon's deed or consider it charitable. There could be serious economic or social repercussions. Onesimus would himself be at risk and perhaps not able to find employment or to support himself. Accepting one's slave into one's life and social sphere as "a beloved brother" might even prove more shocking and complicated than setting him free. For Philemon to receive Onesimus in such a generous way could imply changes in more than just Onesimus' legal status. The relationship Paul desired for Onesimus and Philemon might have appeared both delicately complicated but also practically impossible in a society in which slavery, status, and honor were so deeply ingrained in people's socioeconomic interactions.

Yet Paul still argues that something new must emerge, even if he cannot or does not describe all the contours of what he has in mind. He expresses his desire for the two men to move into an altogether different and perhaps unimaginable kind of relationship, conferring on Onesimus—just as God already had—dignity, privilege, honor, and belonging that he never before enjoyed and probably never thought he could possess. The slave's purpose was to be useful to others. Paul persuades Philemon to give Onesimus the standing and personal liberty that a common slave probably could never have previously dreamed of having, given the disposable nature and contingent identities of most slaves in that setting. By welcoming Onesimus into the household as a brother, Philemon would give him an identity, actually confirming the identity Christ had already conferred on him. By receiving Onesimus in such a way, Philemon would be violating and thus expressing contempt for countless social norms. It would be a bold and potentially dangerous act. But Paul thinks it would be an act consistent with the new realities created by God through Jesus Christ.

In Gal 3:28, Paul insists that the identities of slaves and freepersons undergo seismic changes because of Christ; neither group can claim true superiority or advantage over the other, for both become one in Christ Jesus (cf. 1 Cor 12:13). Yet Paul's potentially far-reaching theological conviction seems never to have prompted the apostle to criticize slavery as a cultural foundation or to declare slavery in all its forms as finally incommensurate with the new creation God accomplishes. Whether Paul's silence on slavery stemmed from willful or passive neglect or from the apparent impossibility of imagining a society without slavery is difficult to say. If Paul had been a slave or a slave owner and not a privileged free male who was skilled in a trade, perhaps his perspective would have been different. If Paul had anticipated that the church would continue for millennia and that Christians would become deeply complicit in the evils of new forms of chattel slavery, perhaps his perspective would have been different. The scope of Paul's vision, like everyone's, was unable or unwilling to see things his cultural context prevented him from seeing.

Although the letters Paul wrote do not address questions of the rightness or wrongness of slavery in general terms, they essentially assume slavery exists as an axiomatic piece of the collective human condition. No other biblical author appears to have seen the situation differently, either. At least in Philemon, Paul comes close to raising the question of whether ancient Christ-followers should own slaves and how they should treat slaves who are also members of the church. Yet raising the question and pointing his friend Philemon down a benevolent path are not the same as solving the problem or advocating for systemic change. The letter does lay theological foundations on which interpreters might build—and indeed have built—more detailed and sweeping arguments about what it means for modern Christians to promote human dignity in various settings. The Letter of Paul to Philemon has spoken in new ways and had various effects throughout the history of its interpretation. The task for interpreters is to analyze what Paul communicates in Philemon, but interpreters can do that while also advancing the discussion beyond the ambiguous and particular appeals that appear in the letter. The interpretive discussions that result will prove to have little value if they opt for overstating the clarity of Paul's instructions to Philemon—in an attempt to defend Paul as a resolute enemy of slavery—or if they opt for disregarding the complexity of Paul's cultural context and thus simplistically accuse Paul of an utter lack of compassion or courage. Both of those generalizations neglect the brittle and complicated quality of Paul's somewhat restrained appeals to Philemon. Interpreters do better instead to keep this letter and its underlying theological convictions in conversation with other biblical passages and learn from the ways in which various interpretations of Philemon have in the past compounded—and occasionally relieved—human experiences of suffering and oppression.

Incarceration, Its Burdens, and the Work of God

In Philemon, references to Paul's incarceration acknowledge the burdens that custody might have placed on him, just as similar references do in Philippians, which is the other letter that Paul wrote as a prisoner, and in the disputed letters that depict Paul in custody (Ephesians, Colossians, and 2 Timothy). A primary burden for nearly all prisoners in the Roman Empire involved the challenges of staying alive. Officials had no obligation to feed, clothe, or provide care to the people they detained. Prisoners of little means needed a social or familial network to supply them with necessities until they could be freed from custody. Even individuals designated for house arrest, such as Paul probably was, in many cases still required concrete assistance from associates to ensure their livelihood.

In Philemon Paul mentions coworkers and a fellow detainee named Epaphras, suggesting he had access to the material resources he needed. If Onesimus, however, was a prisoner himself when he encountered Paul, he would almost certainly have lacked sustenance. Whether Paul and others showed charity to Onesimus in such circumstances remains unknown, but if Onesimus required such support, charity from Paul or other believers might have been part of the process by which Paul introduced him to the gospel.

Another burden for Paul was custody's potential for limiting his influence as a leader in the church. Roman culture generally viewed incarceration as a severe detriment to a person's public honor. Paul construes the nature of his circumstances differently, however. In this letter Paul recognizes that his current confinement and isolation could be an impediment to his ability to convince Philemon to receive Onesimus as a brother, yet he exploits his circumstances for his advantage as one who labors on behalf of the gospel. Paul discounts the ways that being a detained prisoner might shame him or minimize his influence in others' eyes. He inverts incarceration's potential for shame, construing it instead as a sign of honor. He is a "prisoner of Christ Jesus" (Phlm 1, 9) and endures custody specifically "for the gospel" (Phlm 13). He thereby refers to his incarceration as a confirmation of his faithfulness to his calling. Those rhetorical moves represent one of the many ways in which Paul's letters speak about God's power to generate strength in conditions of weakness, to wrest honor out of apparent shame, and to bring life from death (e.g., 1 Cor 1:18–31; 15:43; 2 Cor 11:23–12:10; Phil 1:12–14, 20). In the experiences where Greco-Roman cultural assumptions might see failure and humiliation, Paul sees opportunities for God's new realities to show themselves. Likewise, Paul hopes the liberative power of the gospel will be mirrored in Onesimus' own life, if he can move from servitude and contempt to belonging and dignity. Paul's friend Philemon, the letter implies, has an opportunity to declare good news about transformation and new life, depending on how he acts toward his brother Onesimus.

Recommended Resources for Ongoing Exploration of the New Testament

Since there is always more to see in the New Testament, interpreters return to it again and again. Rereading the New Testament itself is only part of the work. Learning from other interpreters along the way is essential for acquiring knowledge, sharpening insight, and joining the lively conversations that biblical interpretations provoke. The following materials provide more detail about the New Testament and its ancient contexts than this companion can. They will help readers conduct deeper investigations of each New Testament writing and related subject matter. For convenience's sake, the list is compact and limited to books, especially those that are well suited for students and others who are relatively new to in-depth study of the New Testament. Only a few of these books are expressly technical analyses. Although the bibliography extends across the entire New Testament—and not just the writings covered in this volume—it is hardly exhaustive or able to represent the full range of opinions concerning interpretive methods and specific debates.

The New Testament's History and Cultural Setting

Adams, Samuel L. *Social and Economic Life in Second Temple Judea*. Louisville, Ky.: Westminster John Knox, 2014.

Carey, Greg. *Apocalyptic Literature in the New Testament*. Core Biblical Studies. Nashville: Abingdon, 2016.

Carter, Warren. *The Roman Empire and the New Testament: An Essential Guide*. Nashville: Abingdon, 2006.

Cohen, Shaye J. D. *From the Maccabees to the Mishnah*. 3rd ed. Louisville, Ky.: Westminster John Knox, 2014.

Collins, John J., and Daniel C. Harlow, eds. *The Eerdmans Dictionary of Early Judaism*. Grand Rapids: Eerdmans, 2010.

Conway, Colleen M. *Behold the Man: Jesus and Greco-Roman Masculinity*. New York: Oxford University Press, 2008.

D'Ambra, Eve. *Roman Women*. Cambridge Introduction to Roman Civilization. New York: Cambridge University Press, 2007.

Freyne, Seán. *The Jesus Movement and Its Expansion: Meaning and Mission*. Grand Rapids: Eerdmans, 2014.

Gamble, Harry Y. *The New Testament Canon: Its Making and Meaning*. Guides to Biblical Scholarship. Philadelphia: Fortress, 1985.

Garnsey, Peter, and Richard Saller. *The Roman Empire: Economy, Society and Culture*. Berkeley: University of California Press, 1987.

Glancy, Jennifer A. *Slavery in Early Christianity*. New York: Oxford University Press, 2002.

Goodman, Martin. *The Ruling Class of Judaea: The Origins of the Jewish Revolt against Rome, A.D. 66–70*. Cambridge: Cambridge University Press, 1987.

Hezser, Catherine, ed. *The Oxford Handbook of Jewish Daily Life in Roman Palestine*. New York: Oxford University Press, 2010.

Hurtado, Larry W. *Destroyer of the gods: Early Christian Distinctiveness in the Roman World*. Waco, Tex.: Baylor University Press, 2016.

Kraemer, Ross Shepard. *Maenads, Martyrs, Matrons, Monastics: A Sourcebook on Women's Religions in the Greco-Roman World*. Philadelphia: Fortress, 1988.

Kraemer, Ross Shepard, and Mary Rose D'Angelo, eds. *Women and Christian Origins*. New York: Oxford University Press, 1999.

Kugel, James L., and Rowan A. Greer. *Early Biblical Interpretation*. Library of Early Christianity 3. Philadelphia: Westminster, 1986.

Law, Timothy Michael. *When God Spoke Greek: The Septuagint and the Making of the Christian Bible*. New York: Oxford University Press, 2013.

MacDonald, Margaret Y. *The Power of Children: The Construction of Christian Families in the Greco-Roman World*. Waco, Tex.: Baylor University Press, 2014.

Magness, Jodi. *Stone and Dung, Oil and Spit: Jewish Daily Life in the Time of Jesus*. Grand Rapids: Eerdmans, 2011.

McDonald, Lee Martin, and James A. Sanders, eds. *The Canon Debate*. Peabody, Mass.: Hendrickson, 2002.

Meyers, Eric M., and Mark A. Chancey. *Alexander to Constantine: Archaeology of the Land of the Bible*. Anchor Yale Bible Reference Library. New Haven, Conn.: Yale University Press, 2012.

Moyise, Steve. *The Old Testament in the New: An Introduction.* 2nd ed. T&T Clark Approaches to Biblical Studies. New York: Bloomsbury T&T Clark, 2015.

Sanders, E. P. *Judaism: Practice and Belief, 63 BCE–66 CE.* Philadelphia: Trinity International, 1992.

VanderKam, James C. *The Dead Sea Scrolls Today.* 2nd ed. Grand Rapids: Eerdmans, 2010.

Vermes, Geza. *The True Herod.* New York: Bloomsbury T&T Clark, 2014.

Jesus, the Gospels, and the Acts of the Apostles

Allison, Dale C., Jr. *The Historical Christ and the Theological Jesus.* Grand Rapids: Eerdmans, 2009.

Brown, Raymond E. *The Birth of the Messiah: A Commentary on the Infancy Narratives in Matthew and Luke.* Anchor Bible Reference Library. New York: Doubleday, 1993.

———. *The Death of the Messiah: From Gethsemane to the Grave: A Commentary on the Passion Narratives in the Four Gospels.* 2 vols. Anchor Bible Reference Library. New York: Doubleday, 1994.

Burridge, Richard A. *What Are the Gospels? A Comparison with Graeco-Roman Biography.* 2nd ed. Grand Rapids: Eerdmans, 2004.

Ehrman, Bart D. *Did Jesus Exist? The Historical Argument for Jesus of Nazareth.* New York: HarperOne, 2012.

Fredriksen, Paula. *From Jesus to Christ: The Origins of the New Testament Images of Christ.* 2nd ed. New Haven, Conn.: Yale University Press, 1988.

Keck, Leander E. *Who Is Jesus? History in Perfect Tense.* Studies on Personalities of the New Testament. Columbia: University of South Carolina Press, 2000.

Keith, Chris, and Larry W. Hurtado, eds. *Jesus among Friends and Enemies: A Historical and Literary Introduction to Jesus in the Gospels.* Grand Rapids: Baker Academic, 2011.

Kloppenborg, John S. *Q, the Earliest Gospel: An Introduction to the Original Stories and Sayings of Jesus.* Louisville, Ky.: Westminster John Knox, 2008.

Le Donne, Anthony. *Historical Jesus: What Can We Know and How Can We Know It?* Grand Rapids: Eerdmans, 2011.

Levine, Amy-Jill. *The Misunderstood Jew: The Church and the Scandal of the Jewish Jesus.* San Francisco: HarperSanFrancisco, 2006.

———. *Short Stories by Jesus: The Enigmatic Parables of a Controversial Rabbi.* New York: HarperOne, 2014.

Perkins, Pheme. *Introduction to the Synoptic Gospels*. Grand Rapids: Eerdmans, 2007.

Sanders, E. P., and Margaret Davies. *Studying the Synoptic Gospels*. Philadelphia: Trinity International, 1989.

Matthew

Boring, M. Eugene. "The Gospel of Matthew: Introduction, Commentary, and Reflections." Pages 87–505 in vol. 8 of *The New Interpreter's Bible*. Edited by Leander E. Keck et al. Nashville: Abingdon, 1995.

Carter, Warren. *Matthew and the Margins: A Sociopolitical and Religious Reading*. Maryknoll, N.Y.: Orbis, 2000.

Overman, J. Andrew. *Church and Community in Crisis: The Gospel according to Matthew*. The New Testament in Context. Valley Forge, Penn.: Trinity International, 1996.

Saldarini, Anthony J. *Matthew's Christian-Jewish Community*. Chicago Studies in the History of Judaism. Chicago: University of Chicago Press, 1994.

Senior, Donald. *Matthew*. Abingdon New Testament Commentaries. Nashville: Abingdon, 1998.

Mark

Byrne, Brendan. *A Costly Freedom: A Theological Reading of Mark's Gospel*. Collegeville, Minn.: Liturgical, 2008.

Dowd, Sharyn. *Reading Mark: A Literary and Theological Commentary on the Second Gospel*. Reading the New Testament. Macon, Ga.: Smyth & Helwys, 2000.

Hooker, Morna D. *The Gospel according to Saint Mark*. Black's New Testament Commentaries. Peabody, Mass.: Hendrickson, 1991.

Malbon, Elizabeth Struthers. *In the Company of Jesus: Characters in Mark's Gospel*. Louisville, Ky.: Westminster John Knox, 2000.

Marcus, Joel. *Mark: A New Translation with Introduction and Commentary*. 2 vols. Anchor Yale Bible. New Haven, Conn.: Yale University Press, 2000–2009.

Myers, Ched. *Binding the Strong Man: A Political Reading of Mark's Story of Jesus*. Maryknoll, N.Y.: Orbis, 1988.

Luke

Carroll, John T. *Luke: A Commentary*. Louisville, Ky.: Westminster John Knox, 2012.

González, Justo L. *Luke*. Belief: A Theological Commentary on the Bible. Louisville, Ky.: Westminster John Knox, 2010.

Green, Joel B. *The Gospel of Luke*. New International Commentary on the New Testament. Grand Rapids: Eerdmans, 1997.

Parsons, Mikeal C. *Luke: Storyteller, Interpreter, Evangelist*. Peabody, Mass.: Hendrickson, 2007.

Ringe, Sharon H. *Luke*. Westminster Bible Companion. Louisville, Ky.: Westminster John Knox, 1995.

Seim, Turid Karlsen. *The Double Message: Patterns of Gender in Luke and Acts*. Nashville: Abingdon, 1994.

John

Bauckham, Richard. *Gospel of Glory: Major Themes in Johannine Theology*. Grand Rapids: Baker Academic, 2015.

Carter, Warren. *John: Storyteller, Interpreter, Evangelist*. Peabody, Mass.: Hendrickson, 2006.

Koester, Craig R. *The Word of Life: A Theology of John's Gospel*. Grand Rapids: Eerdmans, 2008.

Moloney, Francis J. *Love in the Gospel of John: An Exegetical, Theological, and Literary Study*. Grand Rapids: Baker Academic, 2013.

O'Day, Gail R. "The Gospel of John: Introduction, Commentary, and Reflections." Pages 491–865 in vol. 9 of *The New Interpreter's Bible*. Edited by Leander E. Keck et al. Nashville: Abingdon, 1995.

Schneiders, Sandra M. *Written That You May Believe: Encountering Jesus in the Fourth Gospel*. Rev. ed. New York: Herder & Herder, 2003.

Thompson, Marianne Meye. *John: A Commentary*. New Testament Library. Louisville, Ky.: Westminster John Knox, 2015.

Acts

Chance, J. Bradley. *Acts*. Smyth & Helwys Bible Commentary. Macon, Ga.: Smyth & Helwys, 2007.

Gaventa, Beverly Roberts. *Acts*. Abingdon New Testament Commentaries. Nashville: Abingdon, 2003.

Jennings, Willie James. *Acts.* Belief: A Theological Commentary on the Bible. Louisville, Ky.: Westminster John Knox, 2017.

Johnson, Luke Timothy. *The Acts of the Apostles.* Sacra pagina 5. Collegeville, Minn.: Liturgical, 1992.

Skinner, Matthew L. *Intrusive God, Disruptive Gospel: Encountering the Divine in the Book of Acts.* Grand Rapids: Brazos, 2015.

Spencer, F. Scott. *Journeying through Acts: A Literary-Cultural Reading.* Peabody, Mass.: Hendrickson, 2004.

Tannehill, Robert C. *The Narrative Unity of Luke-Acts: A Literary Interpretation.* Vol. 2, *The Acts of the Apostles.* Minneapolis: Fortress, 1990.

Paul and the Pauline Letters

Bassler, Jouette M. *Navigating Paul: An Introduction to Key Theological Concepts.* Louisville, Ky.: Westminster John Knox, 2007.

Beker, J. Christiaan. *Paul the Apostle: The Triumph of God in Life and Thought.* Philadelphia: Fortress, 1980.

Cousar, Charles B. *The Letters of Paul.* Interpreting Biblical Texts. Nashville: Abingdon, 1996.

Horrell, David G. *An Introduction to the Study of Paul.* 3rd ed. T&T Clark Approaches to Biblical Studies. New York: Bloomsbury T&T Clark, 2015.

Meeks, Wayne A. *The First Urban Christians: The Social World of the Apostle Paul.* 2nd ed. New Haven, Conn.: Yale University Press, 2003.

Polaski, Sandra Hack. *A Feminist Introduction to Paul.* St. Louis: Chalice, 2005.

Roetzel, Calvin J. *Paul: The Man and the Myth.* Personalities of the New Testament. Minneapolis: Fortress, 1997.

Ruden, Sarah. *Paul among the People: The Apostle Reinterpreted and Reimagined in His Own Time.* New York: Pantheon, 2010.

Stowers, Stanley K. *Letter Writing in Greco-Roman Antiquity.* Library of Early Christianity 5. Philadelphia: Westminster, 1986.

Romans

Byrne, Brendan. *Romans.* Sacra pagina 6. Collegeville, Minn.: Liturgical, 1996.

Gaventa, Beverly Roberts. *When in Romans: An Invitation to Linger with the Gospel according to Paul.* Grand Rapids: Baker Academic, 2016.

Grieb, A. Katherine. *The Story of Romans: A Narrative Defense of God's Righteousness.* Louisville, Ky.: Westminster John Knox, 2002.

Johnson, Luke Timothy. *Romans: A Literary and Theological Commentary.* New York: Crossroad, 1997.

Keck, Leander E. *Romans.* Abingdon New Testament Commentaries. Nashville: Abingdon, 2005.

Lampe, Peter. *From Paul to Valentinus: Christians at Rome in the First Two Centuries.* Edited by Marshall D. Johnson. Translated by Michael Steinhauser. Minneapolis: Fortress, 2003.

First Corinthians

Fee, Gordon D. *The First Epistle to the Corinthians.* New International Commentary on the New Testament. Grand Rapids: Eerdmans, 1987.

Hays, Richard B. *First Corinthians.* Interpretation. Louisville, Ky.: John Knox, 1997.

Keener, Craig S. *1–2 Corinthians.* New Cambridge Bible Commentary. New York: Cambridge University Press, 2005.

Sampley, J. Paul. "The First Letter to the Corinthians: Introduction, Commentary, and Reflections." Pages 771–1003 in vol. 10 of *The New Interpreter's Bible.* Edited by Leander E. Keck et al. Nashville: Abingdon, 2002.

Wire, Antoinette Clark. *The Corinthian Women Prophets: A Reconstruction through Paul's Rhetoric.* Minneapolis: Fortress, 1990.

Second Corinthians

Collins, Raymond F. *Second Corinthians.* Paideia. Grand Rapids: Baker Academic, 2013.

Matera, Frank J. *II Corinthians: A Commentary.* New Testament Library. Louisville, Ky.: Westminster John Knox, 2003.

Roetzel, Calvin J. *2 Corinthians.* Abingdon New Testament Commentaries. Nashville: Abingdon, 2007.

Sampley, J. Paul. "The Second Letter to the Corinthians: Introduction, Commentary, and Reflections." Pages 1–180 in vol. 11 of *The New Interpreter's Bible.* Edited by Leander E. Keck et al. Nashville: Abingdon, 2000.

Wan, Sze-kar. *Power in Weakness: The Second Letter of Paul to the Corinthians.* The New Testament in Context. Harrisburg, Penn.: Trinity International, 2000.

Galatians

Braxton, Brad Ronnell. *No Longer Slaves: Galatians and African American Experience.* Collegeville, Minn.: Liturgical, 2002.

De Boer, Martinus C. *Galatians: A Commentary.* New Testament Library. Louisville, Ky.: Westminster John Knox, 2011.

Eastman, Susan. *Recovering Paul's Mother Tongue: Language and Theology in Galatians.* Grand Rapids: Eerdmans, 2007.

Hays, Richard B. "The Letter to the Galatians: Introduction, Commentary, and Reflections." Pages 181–348 in vol. 11 of *The New Interpreter's Bible.* Edited by Leander E. Keck et al. Nashville: Abingdon, 2000.

Williams, Sam K. *Galatians.* Abingdon New Testament Commentaries. Nashville: Abingdon, 1997.

Ephesians

Best, Ernest. *Ephesians: A Shorter Commentary.* London: T&T Clark, 2003.

Fowl, Stephen E. *Ephesians: An Introduction and Study Guide: Being a Christian, at Home and in the Cosmos.* T&T Clark Study Guides to the New Testament. London: Bloomsbury T&T Clark, 2017.

MacDonald, Margaret Y. *Colossians and Ephesians.* Sacra pagina 17. Collegeville, Minn.: Liturgical, 2000.

Maier, Harry O. *Picturing Paul in Empire: Imperial Image, Text and Persuasion in Colossians, Ephesians and the Pastoral Epistles.* London: Bloomsbury T&T Clark, 2013.

Perkins, Pheme. "The Letter to the Ephesians: Introduction, Commentary, and Reflections." Pages 349–466 in vol. 11 of *The New Interpreter's Bible.* Edited by Leander E. Keck et al. Nashville: Abingdon, 2000.

Thurston, Bonnie. *Reading Colossians, Ephesians, and 2 Thessalonians: A Literary and Theological Commentary.* Reading the New Testament. New York: Crossroad, 1995.

Philippians

Craddock, Fred B. *Philippians.* Interpretation. Atlanta: John Knox, 1985.

Fee, Gordon D. *Paul's Letter to the Philippians.* New International Commentary on the New Testament. Grand Rapids: Eerdmans, 1995.

Hooker, Morna D. "The Letter to the Philippians: Introduction, Commentary, and Reflections." Pages 467–549 in vol. 11 of *The New Interpreter's Bible.* Edited by Leander E. Keck et al. Nashville: Abingdon, 2000.

Osiek, Carolyn. *Philippians, Philemon.* Abingdon Commentary on the New Testament. Nashville: Abingdon, 2000.

Colossians

Barclay, John M. G. *Colossians and Philemon*. New Testament Guides. Sheffield: Sheffield Academic, 1997.
Hay, David M. *Colossians*. Abingdon New Testament Commentaries. Nashville: Abingdon, 2000.
Lincoln, Andrew T. "The Letter to the Colossians: Introduction, Commentary, and Reflections." Pages 551–669 in vol. 11 of *The New Interpreter's Bible*. Edited by Leander E. Keck et al. Nashville: Abingdon, 2000.
MacDonald, Margaret Y. *Colossians and Ephesians*. Sacra pagina 17. Collegeville, Minn.: Liturgical, 2000.
Sumney, Jerry L. *Colossians: A Commentary*. New Testament Library. Louisville, Ky.: Westminster John Knox, 2008.

First and Second Thessalonians

Furnish, Victor Paul. *1 Thessalonians, 2 Thessalonians*. Abingdon New Testament Commentaries. Nashville: Abingdon, 2007.
Gaventa, Beverly Roberts. *First and Second Thessalonians*. Interpretation. Louisville, Ky.: John Knox, 1998.
Malherbe, Abraham J. *Paul and the Thessalonians: The Philosophic Tradition of Pastoral Care*. Philadelphia: Fortress, 1987.
Smith, Abraham. "The First Letter to the Thessalonians: Introduction, Commentary, and Reflections." Pages 671–737 in vol. 11 of *The New Interpreter's Bible*. Edited by Leander E. Keck et al. Nashville: Abingdon, 2000.
———. "The Second Letter to the Thessalonians: Introduction, Commentary, and Reflections." Pages 739–72 in vol. 11 of *The New Interpreter's Bible*. Edited by Leander E. Keck et al. Nashville: Abingdon, 2000.

The Pastoral Letters

Bassler, Jouette M. *1 Timothy, 2 Timothy, Titus*. Abingdon New Testament Commentaries. Nashville: Abingdon, 1996.
Collins, Raymond F. *I & II Timothy and Titus: A Commentary*. New Testament Library. Louisville, Ky.: Westminster John Knox, 2002.
Hultgren, Arland J. *1–2 Timothy, Titus*. Augsburg Commentary on the New Testament. Minneapolis: Augsburg, 1984.
Long, Thomas G. *1 & 2 Timothy and Titus*. Belief: A Theological Commentary on the Bible. Louisville, Ky.: Westminster John Knox, 2016.
Young, Frances. *The Theology of the Pastoral Epistles*. New Testament Theology. New York: Cambridge University Press, 1994.

Philemon

Barclay, John M. G. *Colossians and Philemon*. New Testament Guides. Sheffield: Sheffield Academic Press, 1997.

Callahan, Allen Dwight. *Embassy of Onesimus: The Letter of Paul to Philemon*. The New Testament in Context. Valley Forge, Penn.: Trinity International, 1997.

Felder, Cain Hope. "The Letter to Philemon: Introduction, Commentary, and Reflections." Pages 881–905 in vol. 11 of *The New Interpreter's Bible*. Edited by Leander E. Keck et al. Nashville: Abingdon, 2000.

Fitzmyer, Joseph A. *The Letter to Philemon: A New Translation with Introduction and Commentary*. Anchor Bible 34C. New York: Doubleday, 2000.

Osiek, Carolyn. *Philippians, Philemon*. Abingdon Commentary on the New Testament. Nashville: Abingdon, 2000.

Hebrews, the General Letters, and Revelation

Hebrews

Craddock, Fred B. "The Letter to the Hebrews: Introduction, Commentary, and Reflections." Pages 1–173 in vol. 12 of *The New Interpreter's Bible*. Edited by Leander E. Keck et al. Nashville: Abingdon, 1998.

deSilva, David A. *Perseverance in Gratitude: A Socio-Rhetorical Commentary on the Epistle "to the Hebrews."* Grand Rapids: Eerdmans, 2000.

Johnson, Luke Timothy. *Hebrews: A Commentary*. New Testament Library. Louisville, Ky.: Westminster John Knox, 2006.

Koester, Craig R. *Hebrews: A New Translation with Introduction and Commentary*. Anchor Bible 36. New York: Doubleday, 2001.

Long, Thomas G. *Hebrews*. Interpretation. Louisville, Ky.: John Knox, 1997.

James

Aymer, Margaret P. *James: An Introduction and Study Guide: Diaspora Rhetoric of a Friend of God*. T&T Clark Study Guides to the New Testament. London: Bloomsbury T&T Clark, 2017.

Johnson, Luke Timothy. "The Letter of James: Introduction, Commentary, and Reflections." Pages 175–225 in vol. 12 of *The New Interpreter's Bible*. Edited by Leander E. Keck et al. Nashville: Abingdon, 1998.

McKnight, Scot. *The Letter of James*. The New International Commentary on the New Testament. Grand Rapids: Eerdmans, 2011.

Tamez, Elsa. *The Scandalous Message of James: Faith without Works Is Dead*. New York: Crossroad, 1990.

First and Second Peter and Jude

Bartlett, David L. "The First Letter of Peter: Introduction, Commentary, and Reflections." Pages 227–319 in vol. 12 of *The New Interpreter's Bible*. Edited by Leander E. Keck et al. Nashville: Abingdon, 1998.

Bauckham, Richard. *Jude, 2 Peter*. Word Biblical Themes. Dallas: Word, 1990.

Boring, M. Eugene. *1 Peter*. Abingdon New Testament Commentaries. Nashville: Abingdon, 1999.

Donelson, Lewis R. *I & II Peter and Jude: A Commentary*. New Testament Library. Louisville, Ky.: Westminster John Knox, 2010.

Horrell, David G. *1 Peter*. New Testament Guides. New York: T&T Clark, 2008.

Kraftchick, Steven J. *Jude, 2 Peter*. Abingdon New Testament Commentaries. Nashville: Abingdon, 2002.

The Johannine Letters

Black, C. Clifton. "The First, Second, and Third Letters of John: Introduction, Commentary, and Reflections." Pages 363–469 in vol. 12 of *The New Interpreter's Bible*. Edited by Leander E. Keck et al. Nashville: Abingdon, 1998.

Edwards, Ruth B. *The Johannine Epistles*. New Testament Guides. Sheffield: Sheffield Academic Press, 1996.

Kysar, Robert. *I, II, III John*. Augsburg Commentary on the New Testament. Minneapolis: Augsburg, 1986.

Lieu, Judith M. *I, II, & III John: A Commentary*. New Testament Library. Louisville, Ky.: Westminster John Knox, 2008.

Rensberger, David K. *1 John, 2 John, 3 John*. Abingdon New Testament Commentaries. Nashville: Abingdon, 1997.

Revelation

Blount, Brian K. *Can I Get a Witness? Reading Revelation through African American Culture*. Louisville, Ky.: Westminster John Knox, 2005.

———. *Revelation: A Commentary*. New Testament Library. Louisville, Ky.: Westminster John Knox, 2009.

Gorman, Michael J. *Reading Revelation Responsibly: Uncivil Worship and Witness: Following the Lamb into the New Creation.* Eugene, Ore.: Cascade, 2011.

Koester, Craig R. *Revelation and the End of All Things.* Grand Rapids: Eerdmans, 2001.

Rossing, Barbara R. *The Rapture Exposed: The Message of Hope in the Book of Revelation.* Boulder, Colo.: Westview, 2004.

Schüssler Fiorenza, Elisabeth. *Revelation: Vision of a Just World.* Proclamation Commentaries. Minneapolis: Fortress, 1991.

General Studies of the New Testament Writings

Aymer, Margaret, Cynthia Briggs Kittredge, and David A. Sánchez, eds. *Fortress Commentary on the Bible: New Testament.* Minneapolis: Fortress, 2014.

Blount, Brian K., Cain Hope Felder, Clarice Jannette Martin, and Emerson B. Powery, eds. *True to Our Native Land: An African American New Testament Commentary.* Minneapolis: Fortress, 2007.

Freedman, David Noel, et al., eds. *Anchor Bible Dictionary.* 6 vols. New York: Doubleday, 1992.

Horsley, Richard A., ed. *In the Shadow of Empire: Reclaiming the Bible as a History of Faithful Resistance.* Louisville, Ky.: Westminster John Knox, 2008.

Levine, Amy-Jill, and Marc Zvi Brettler, eds. *The Jewish Annotated New Testament.* New York: Oxford University Press, 2011.

Newsom, Carol A., Sharon H. Ringe, and Jacqueline E. Lapsley, eds. *Women's Bible Commentary.* 3rd ed. Louisville, Ky.: Westminster John Knox, 2012.

O'Day, Gail R., and David L. Petersen, eds. *Theological Bible Commentary.* Louisville, Ky.: Westminster John Knox, 2009.

Patte, Daniel, Teresa Okure, and J. Severino Croatto, eds. *Global Bible Commentary.* Nashville: Abingdon, 2004.

Petersen, David L., and Beverly Roberts Gaventa, eds. *The New Interpreter's Bible One-Volume Commentary.* Nashville: Abingdon, 2010.

Sakenfeld, Katharine Doob, et al., eds. *The New Interpreter's Dictionary of the Bible.* 5 vols. Nashville: Abingdon, 2006–2009.

Subject Index

hairstyles, 92–93

hardships, 16, 30, 31, 109, 116, 117, 125, 130, 186, 206, 223, 224, 232, 233, 237, 238, 241, 248–49

hell, 244

hierarchy, 101, 105, 146, 152, 170, 174, 183–84, 215, 226, 267, 268–69, 271

holiness, 60, 101–2, 221, 227–28, 231, 232, 246, 268

holy kiss, 43

Holy Spirit, 22–23, 32–33, 60–61, 73–74, 94–95, 104, 119, 143, 144, 145, 149, 152–53, 179, 185, 224, 228

homogenization, 190, 191

honor: *see* shame

hope, 28, 33, 97, 117, 129, 224, 226, 229, 232, 235

household code, 183–84, 210, 214–15, 262

household management, 161, 170, 256, 260–62, 265–66, 267–69, 271

hymnic material, 199, 205–6, 212, 216, 259, 263, 266

Iconium, 136

idleness, 246–47, 262

idolatry, 91, 176

Ignatius of Antioch, 165

incarceration, 281, 287–88; *see also* Paul, incarceration

incarnation, 27, 205, 212, 216–17, 219, 270, 274–75

inheritance, 145, 179, 187, 188, 189

interpolations, 107–8, 121, 158

Isaac, 148

Ishmael, 147–48

Isis, 93

isolationism: *see* sectarianism

Isthmian Games, 81

James, 141, 151

Jesus: appearance (in the Pastoral Letters), 232, 274; authority, 177, 180, 186, 188, 201, 204, 205–6, 207–8, 209, 210, 212, 216, 217, 251; death, 21–22, 24, 27, 72, 85, 94, 101–2, 102–3, 112, 119, 122, 128–29, 131, 142, 144, 149–50, 152, 180, 205, 216, 217–18, 250; faithfulness, 56–57, 72–73, 142, 263; future, 23, 28,

161, 177, 178, 197, 198, 206, 210, 228–30, 232, 233–35, 237–39, 242, 245, 247, 248, 250–51, 266, 274; "in Christ," 26–28, 119, 145–46, 152, 180; obedience, 20, 57, 72, 142, 199, 206; resurrection, 21–22, 24, 27, 97, 98–99, 119, 128–29, 142, 187, 203, 217, 250; teachings, 230

Jews and Judaism, 62–64, 138, 153–54, 189, 208; *see also* gentiles, relationships with Jews

John, 141

joy, 193, 197, 203

judgment, 23, 28, 94, 161, 230, 237, 244, 249–50, 264; *see also* Jesus, future

Julia, 68

Junia, 68, 74–75

justice, 21, 153, 244

justification, 57–61, 69–73, 135–36, 142, 143–44, 147, 150, 155, 231; *see also* righteousness

Kerygma Petrou: *see* Preaching of Peter

knowledge, 91, 115, 125, 179, 197, 246, 265

Laodicea, 175, 208, 215

law, 10, 15, 55–56, 60, 63, 117, 135–36, 137–38, 142–43, 144–47, 148–49, 150–51, 152, 153–54, 155, 162, 180–81, 189, 200

lawless one (in 2 Thess 2), 245, 250–51

lawsuits, 88

liberation: *see* freedom

Lois, 263

Lord's Supper, 94, 100–101

love, 20, 25, 77, 95–96, 149, 182, 197, 224, 226, 227, 232

Luke, 279

Luther, Martin, 17

Lystra, 136

Macedonia, 13, 121, 222

Marcion, 175

Mark, 279

marriage, 89–90, 177

Mary, 68

masculinity, 21, 132, 226

ministers: *see* deacons

moral exhortation, 88, 149, 214, 228, 253, 257, 259, 265–66; *see also* respectability

retribution, 244, 249–50

righteousness, 69; God's, 20–21, 54, 56, 58, 70–71, 119, 128–29, 145, 154, 201; *see also* justification

Roman Empire: colonies, 194; as context for understanding the New Testament, 4, 31–33, 64–65, 76, 183–84, 190–91, 195, 198, 200, 202–3, 204–5, 217–18, 222–23, 230, 234–35, 251, 261, 263, 268–69, 272–73, 281, 285, 287–88; imperial cult, 30–31

Rome, 13, 49–52, 258

Rufus' mother, 68

saints, 83, 197, 202

salvation, 20, 22, 53, 54, 57, 70–71, 142–43, 150, 173, 180, 199, 201, 231, 235, 261, 265, 266, 267, 269, 274–75

sanctification: *see* holiness

Sarah, 147–48

Satan/devil, 26, 118, 146, 177, 185, 186, 245

secretary: *see* amanuensis

sectarianism, 86, 120–21, 232, 247

self-definition of early churches, 41, 87, 88, 99, 155, 171, 173–74, 204, 232, 254, 259, 266–67

Septuagint, 10

sexual immorality, 87–88, 105, 227–28

sexuality, 55, 89–90, 100, 105, 227–28

shame, 16, 21, 30, 131, 194, 263, 287–88

Silvanus/Silas, 115, 223, 238

sin, 22, 25–26, 27, 55–56, 59–61, 71, 132, 146, 177

slaves and slavery, 67, 82, 90, 146, 183–84, 215, 255, 262, 265, 268, 277–87; to God/Jesus, 60, 71, 197, 215; to elemental spirits/law/sin, 56, 59–60, 145, 146–48, 153, 175

Sosthenes, 81

spiritual gifts, 73, 94–96, 104

Stoicism, 29, 93, 98

Suetonius, 50–51

suffering, 16, 61, 115, 123, 130–31, 132, 195, 241, 244, 249–50, 255, 263; *see also* hardships

super-apostles, 112, 124–25, 133

supersessionism, 62, 63

Syntyche: *see* Euodia

Syria, 13

Tavium, 136

teachers (in Galatians), 135, 137–39, 146, 147, 148–49, 150–52, 154–55, 200

temple, 251

Tertius, 164

testamentary literature, 264

Thessalonica, 222

thorn in the flesh, 125, 132

Tiberius, 32

Timothy, 82, 87, 111, 115, 196, 199, 208, 211, 223, 238, 254–55, 256, 260, 278

Titus (Paul's associate), 254–55, 256

Titus (Roman general), 251

torah: *see* law

trials: *see* hardships

Trinity, 216–17

Truman, Harry S. and Margaret, 36–38

trust: *see* faith

truth, 246, 251, 264, 265

Tryphaena, 68

Tryphosa, 68

Tychicus, 175, 185, 215

Tyre, king of, 250

undisputed letters, 13, 157–64, 174, 245, 257–58

unity, 33, 65–66, 73, 76–77, 82, 83, 84, 95, 101–2, 104, 120, 122–23, 141, 145–46, 150–52, 173–74, 176, 182, 188–91, 198–99, 201, 211, 231; *see also* divisions

vengeance: *see* retribution

victimization, 16, 103, 130, 132

violence, 31, 195–96, 223

visionary experiences, 125, 129, 132–33

weakness, 85, 102–3, 112, 115, 123, 125, 131–32, 288; *see also* power, God's

wealth, 255

wet nurses, 225–26

widows, 262, 265

wisdom, 85–86, 102, 183, 213, 217

women and their roles, 4, 14–15, 74–75, 92–93, 105–8, 138–39, 146, 183–84, 202, 225–26, 259, 261, 262, 268, 271–74

worship, 64, 92–96, 107, 260

wrath, 54–55, 214, 235

Zeno of Athens, 29